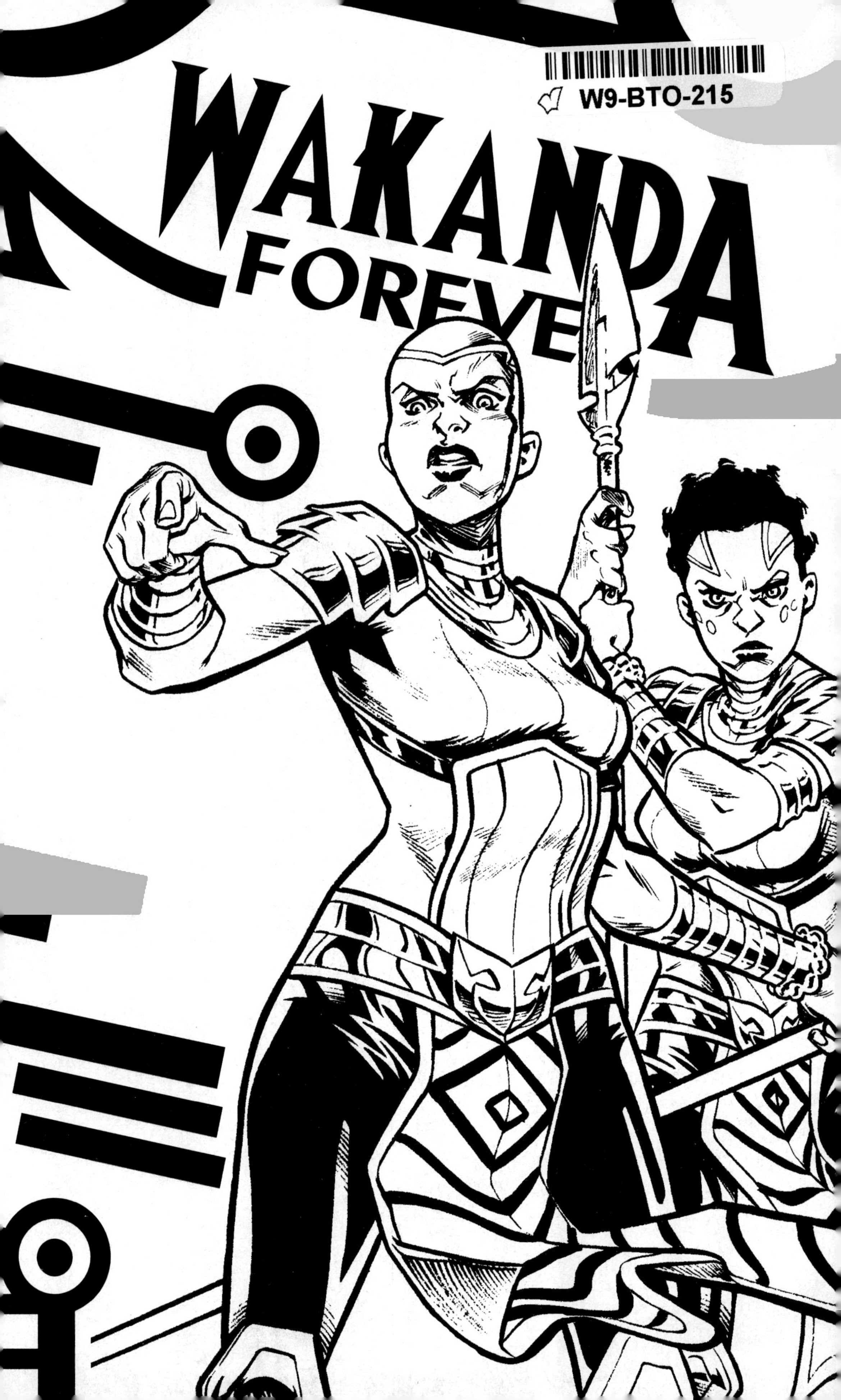
WAKANDA
FOREVE

WAKANDA FOREVER

Writer/**Nnedi Okorafor**

WAKANDA FOREVER: AMAZING SPIDER-MAN
Artist/**Alberto Alburquerque**

WAKANDA FOREVER: X-MEN
Pencilers/**Ray-Anthony Height &
Alberto Alburquerque**
Inkers/**Ray-Anthony Height,
Alberto Alburquerque,
Juan Vlasco &
Keith Champagne**

WAKANDA FOREVER: AVENGERS
Artist/**Oleg Okunev**

Color Artist/**Erick Arciniega**
Letterer/**VC's Joe Sabino**
Cover Art/**Terry Dodson &
Rachel Dodson**

BLACK PANTHER ANNUAL #1
Writers/**Priest,
Don McGregor &
Reginald Hudlin**
Artists/**Mike Perkins,
Daniel Acuña &
Ken Lashley**
Color Artists/**Andy Troy,
Daniel Acuña &
Matt Milla**
Letterer/**VC's Joe Sabino**
Cover Art/**Daniel Acuña**

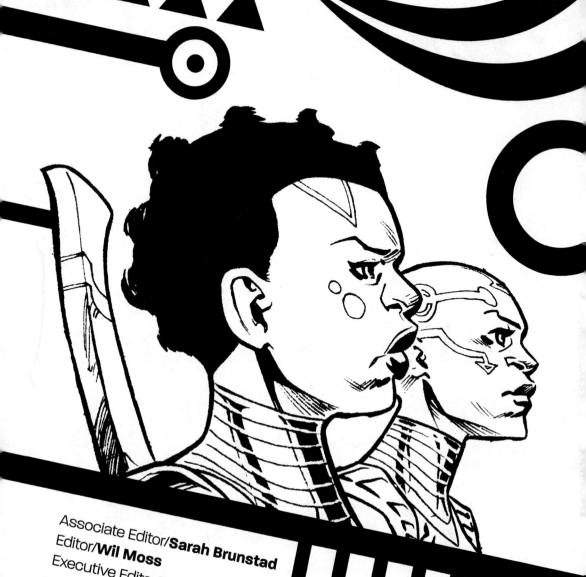

Associate Editor/**Sarah Brunstad**
Editor/**Wil Moss**
Executive Editor/**Tom Brevoort**

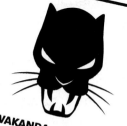

WAKANDA CREATED BY
STAN LEE & **JACK KIRBY**

COLLECTION EDITOR/**JENNIFER GRÜNWALD**
ASSISTANT EDITOR/**CAITLIN O'CONNELL**
ASSOCIATE MANAGING EDITOR/**KATERI WOODY**
EDITOR, SPECIAL PROJECTS/**MARK D. BEAZLEY**
VP PRODUCTION & SPECIAL PROJECTS/**JEFF YOUNGQUIST**
SVP PRINT, SALES & MARKETING/**DAVID GABRIEL**
BOOK DESIGNERS/**ADAM DEL RE** & **MANNY MEDEROS**

EDITOR IN CHIEF/**C.B. CEBULSKI**
CHIEF CREATIVE OFFICER/**JOE QUESADA**
PRESIDENT/**DAN BUCKLEY**
EXECUTIVE PRODUCER/**ALAN FINE**

WAKANDA FOREVER. Contains material originally published in magazine form as WAKANDA FOREVER: AMAZING SPIDER-MAN #1, WAKANDA FOREVER: AVENGERS #1, WAKANDA FOREVER: X-MEN #1 and BLACK PANTHER ANNUAL #1. First printing 2018. ISBN 978-1-302-91358-8. Published by MARVEL WORLDWIDE, INC., a subsidiary of MARVEL ENTERTAINMENT, LLC. OFFICE OF PUBLICATION: 135 West 50th Street, New York, NY 10020. Copyright © 2018 MARVEL No similarity between any of the names, characters, persons, and/or institutions in this magazine with those of any living or dead person or institution is intended, and any such similarity which may exist is purely coincidental. **Printed in the U.S.A.** DAN BUCKLEY, President, Marvel Entertainment; JOHN NEE, Publisher; JOE QUESADA, Chief Creative Officer; TOM BREVOORT, SVP of Publishing; DAVID BOGART, SVP of Business Affairs & Operations, Publishing & Partnership; DAVID GABRIEL, SVP of Sales & Marketing, Publishing; JEFF YOUNGQUIST, VP of Production & Special Projects; DAN CARR, Executive Director of Publishing Technology; ALEX MORALES, Director of Publishing Operations; DAN EDINGTON, Managing Editor; SUSAN CRESPI, Production Manager; STAN LEE, Chairman Emeritus. For information regarding advertising in Marvel Comics or on Marvel.com, please contact Vit DeBellis, Custom Solutions & Integrated Advertising Manager, at vdebellis@marvel.com. For Marvel subscription inquiries, please call 888-511-5480. **Manufactured between 8/31/2018 and 10/2/2018 by QUAD GRAPHICS SARATOGA, SARATOGA SPRINGS, NY, USA.**

10 9 8 7 6 5 4 3 2 1

WAKANDA
FOREVER

The **Dora Milaje** are the all-female warrior elite of Wakanda. Recruited from the country's various tribes, their original mission was to protect the **Black Panther** and the royal family, but they recently ended that arrangement and now protect the nation as a whole.

Before declaring their independence from the throne, one of their leaders, **Okoye**, was the personal bodyguard of King T'Challa, along with a fellow *Dora Milaje* named **Nakia**. Nakia grew dangerously obsessed with the king, and when she attacked his friends and family, T'Challa exiled her from the *Dora Milaje*. Embittered and cast out, Nakia developed an arsenal of weapons, including a drug named Jufeiro that gives her power over men. She has been a plague on Wakanda ever since...

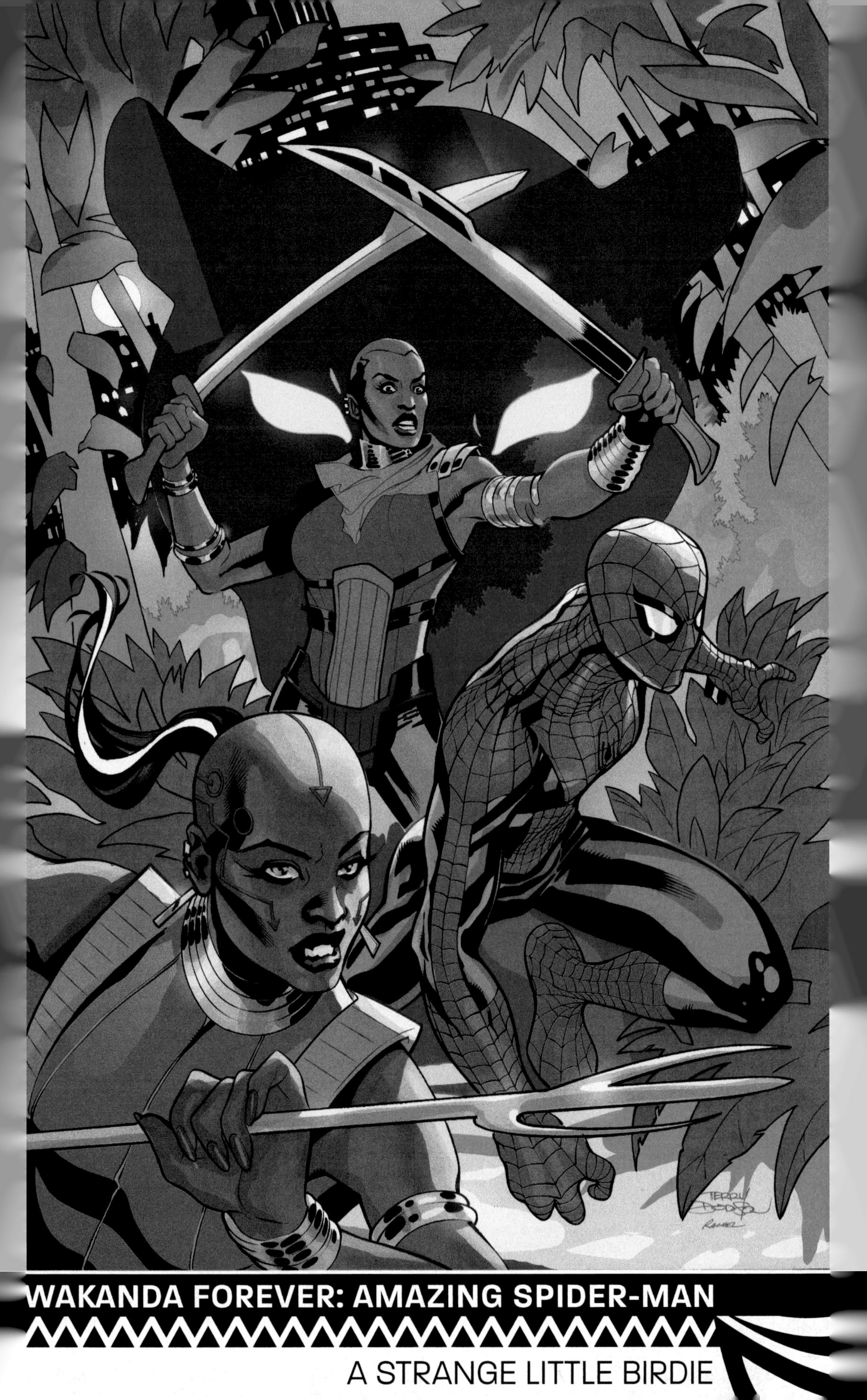

WAKANDA FOREVER: AMAZING SPIDER-MAN

A STRANGE LITTLE BIRDIE

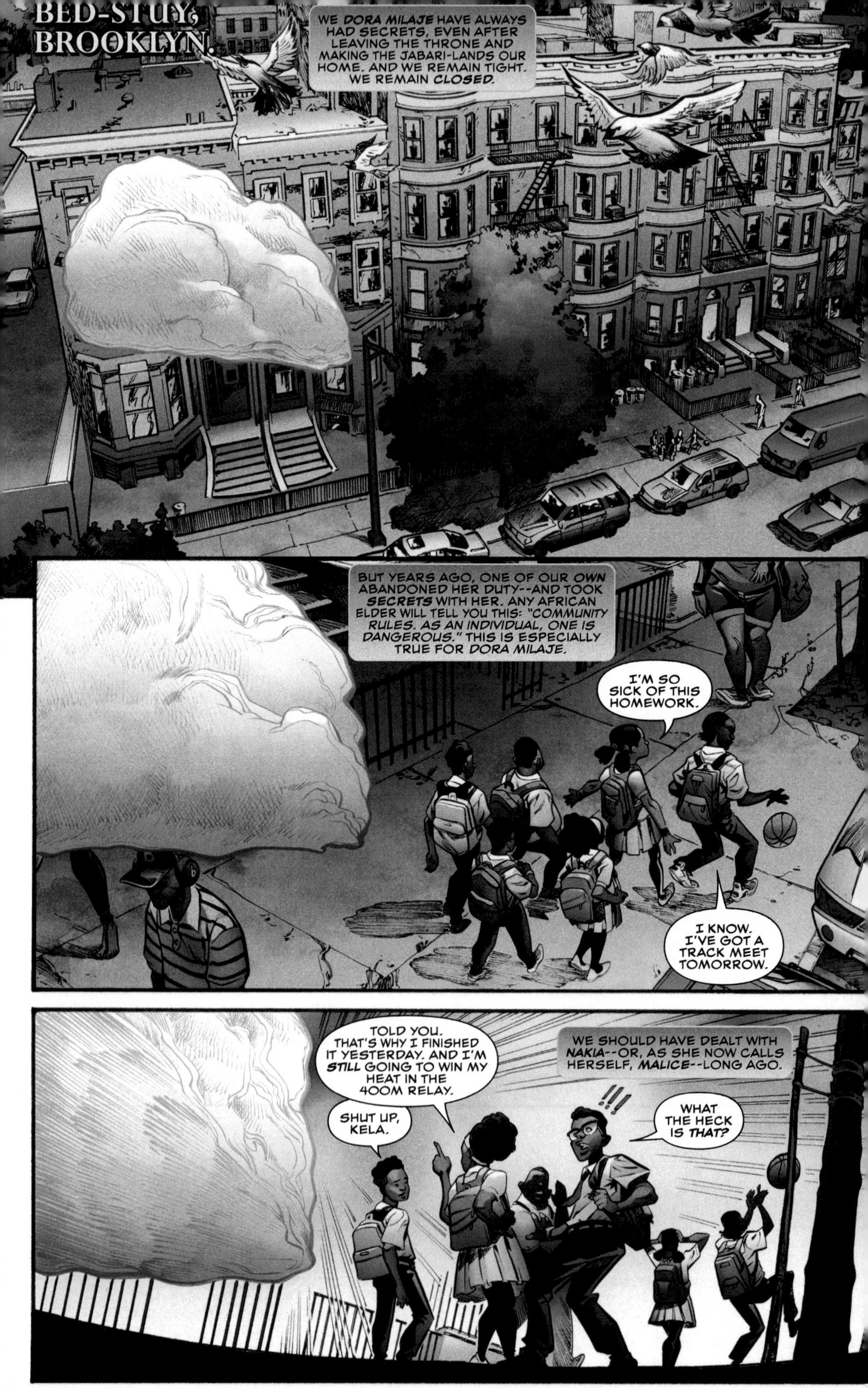
BED-STUY, BROOKLYN.
WE DORA MILAJE HAVE ALWAYS HAD SECRETS, EVEN AFTER LEAVING THE THRONE AND MAKING THE JABARI-LANDS OUR HOME. AND WE REMAIN TIGHT. WE REMAIN CLOSED.
BUT YEARS AGO, ONE OF OUR OWN ABANDONED HER DUTY--AND TOOK SECRETS WITH HER. ANY AFRICAN ELDER WILL TELL YOU THIS: "COMMUNITY RULES. AS AN INDIVIDUAL, ONE IS DANGEROUS." THIS IS ESPECIALLY TRUE FOR DORA MILAJE.
I'M SO SICK OF THIS HOMEWORK.
I KNOW. I'VE GOT A TRACK MEET TOMORROW.
TOLD YOU. THAT'S WHY I FINISHED IT YESTERDAY. AND I'M STILL GOING TO WIN MY HEAT IN THE 400M RELAY.
SHUT UP, KELA.
WE SHOULD HAVE DEALT WITH NAKIA--OR, AS SHE NOW CALLS HERSELF, MALICE--LONG AGO.
!!!
WHAT THE HECK IS THAT?

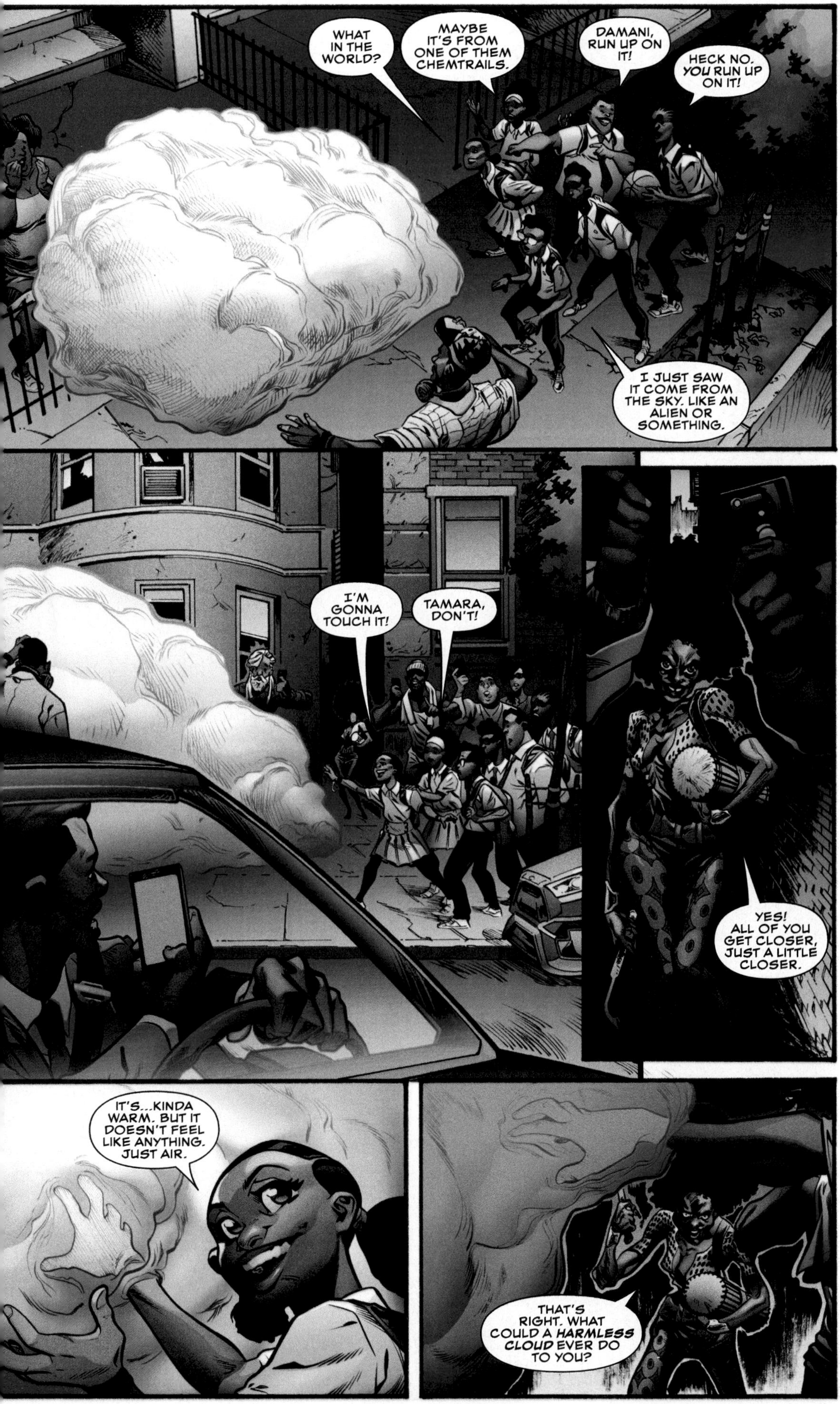
WHAT IN THE WORLD?
MAYBE IT'S FROM ONE OF THEM CHEMTRAILS.
DAMANI, RUN UP ON IT!
HECK NO. *YOU* RUN UP ON IT!
I JUST SAW IT COME FROM THE SKY. LIKE AN ALIEN OR SOMETHING.
I'M GONNA TOUCH IT!
TAMARA, DON'T!
YES! ALL OF YOU GET CLOSER, JUST A LITTLE CLOSER.
IT'S...KINDA WARM. BUT IT DOESN'T FEEL LIKE ANYTHING. JUST AIR.
THAT'S RIGHT. WHAT COULD A *HARMLESS CLOUD* EVER DO TO YOU?

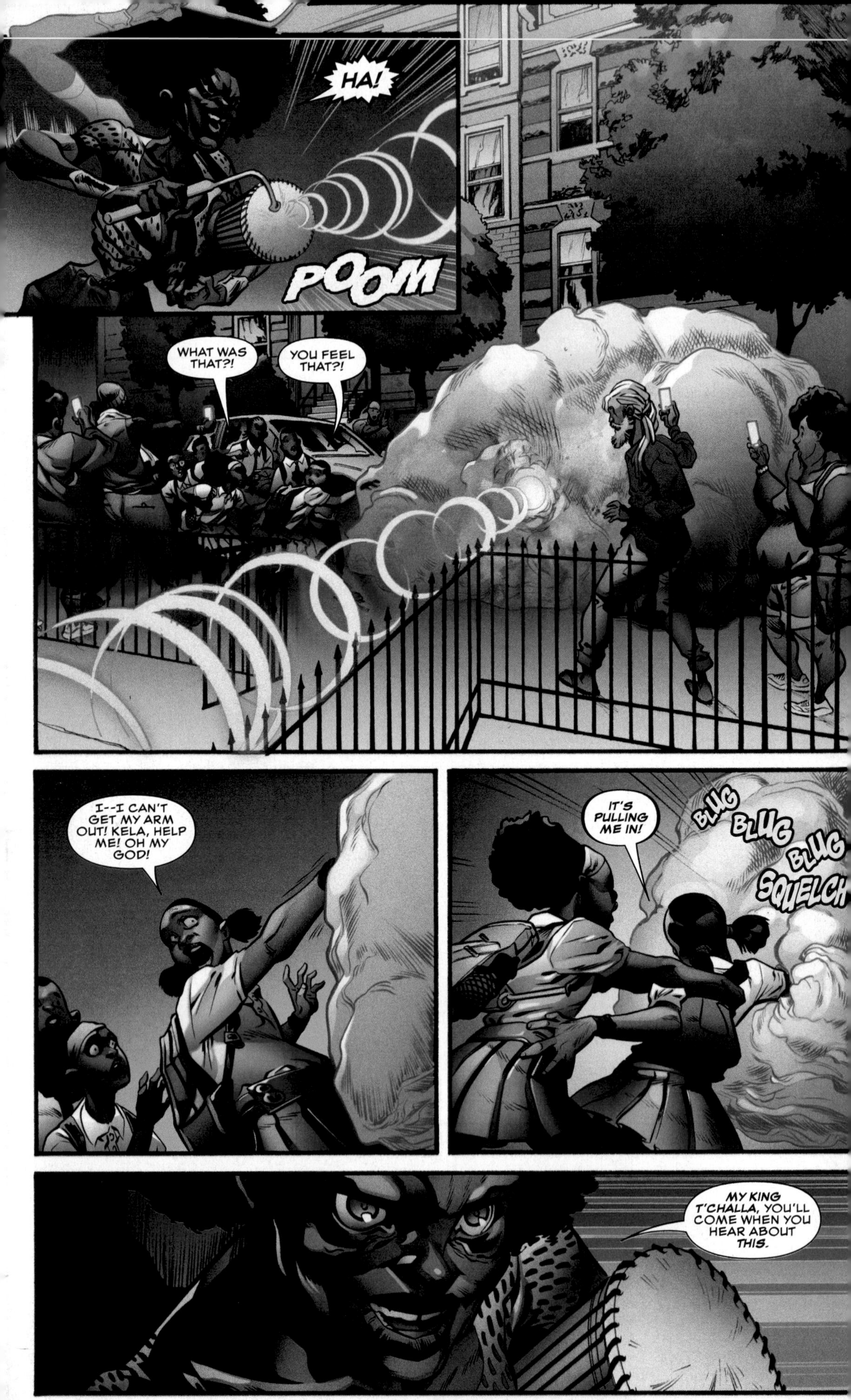

HA!
POOOM
WHAT WAS THAT?!
YOU FEEL THAT?!
I--I CAN'T GET MY ARM OUT! KELA, HELP ME! OH MY GOD!
IT'S PULLING ME IN!
BLUG
BLUG
BLUG
SQUELCH
MY KING T'CHALLA, YOU'LL COME WHEN YOU HEAR ABOUT THIS.

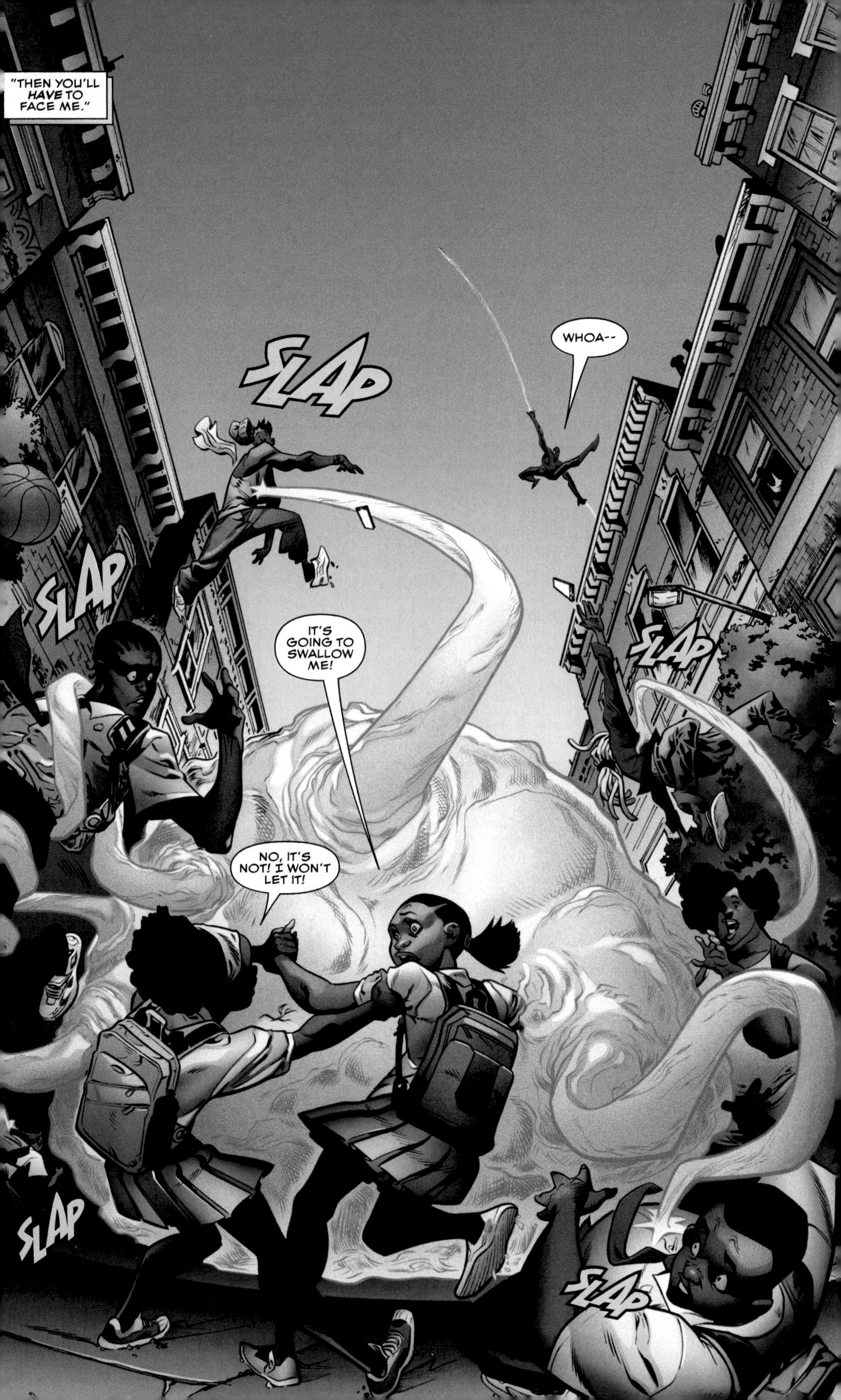

"THEN YOU'LL HAVE TO FACE ME."
SLAP
WHOA--
SLAP
SLAP
IT'S GOING TO SWALLOW ME!
NO, IT'S NOT! I WON'T LET IT!
SLAP
SLAP

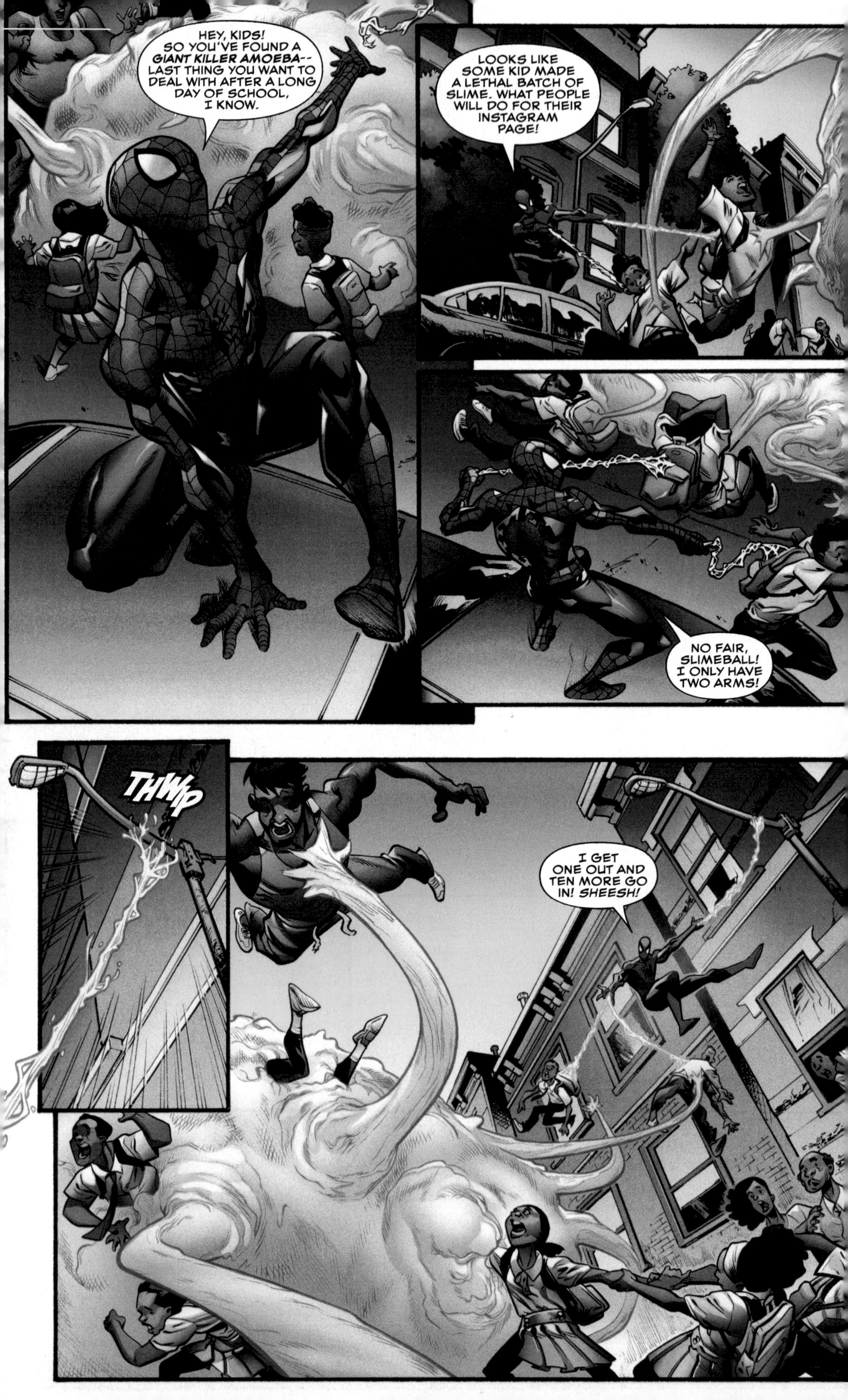
HEY, KIDS! SO YOU'VE FOUND A *GIANT KILLER AMOEBA*-- LAST THING YOU WANT TO DEAL WITH AFTER A LONG DAY OF SCHOOL, I KNOW.
LOOKS LIKE SOME KID MADE A LETHAL BATCH OF SLIME. WHAT PEOPLE WILL DO FOR THEIR INSTAGRAM PAGE!
NO FAIR, SLIMEBALL! I ONLY HAVE TWO ARMS!
THWIP
I GET ONE OUT AND TEN MORE GO IN! *SHEESH!*

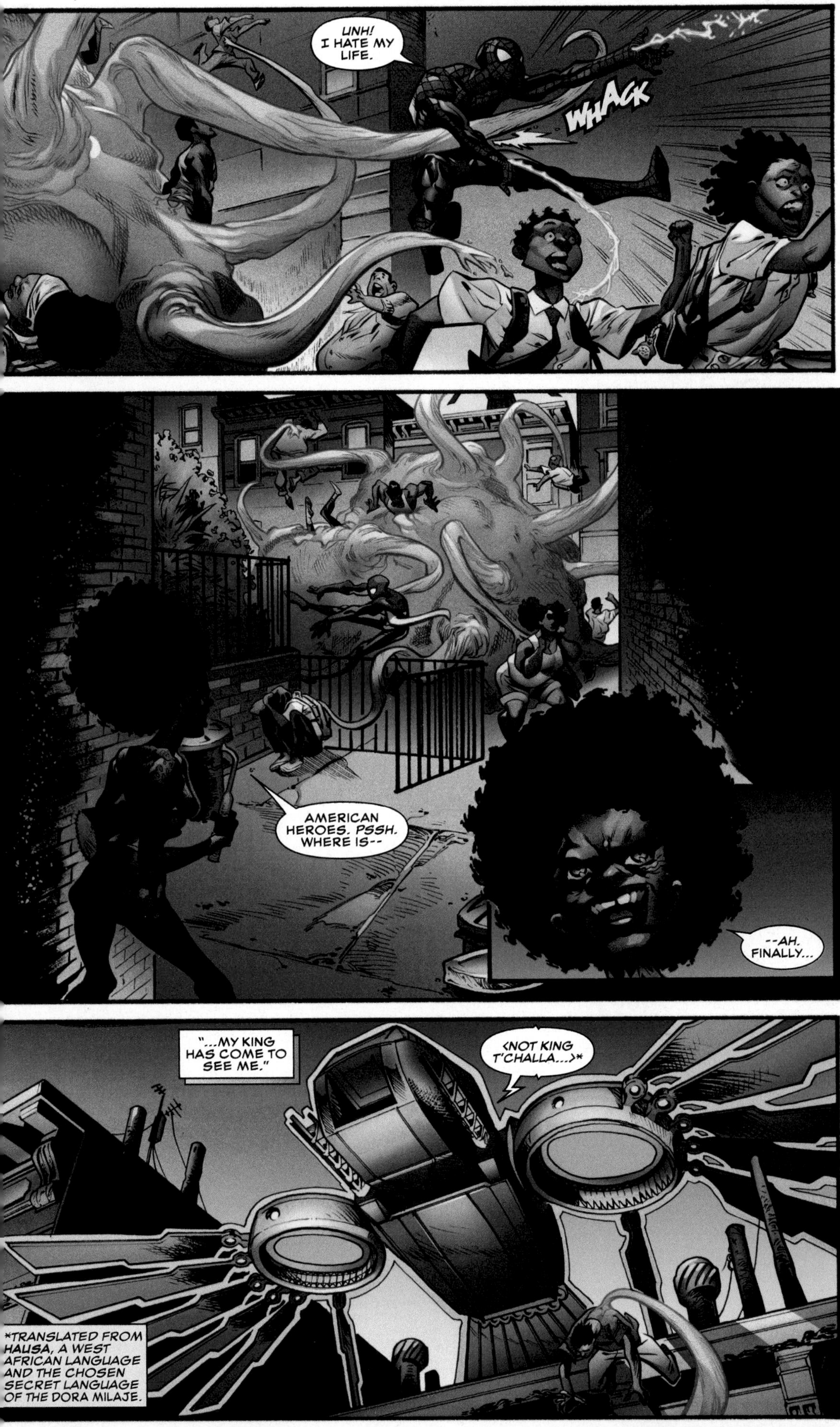
UNH! I HATE MY LIFE.
WHACK
AMERICAN HEROES. PSSH. WHERE IS--
--AH. FINALLY...
"...MY KING HAS COME TO SEE ME."
<NOT KING T'CHALLA...>*
*TRANSLATED FROM HAUSA, A WEST AFRICAN LANGUAGE AND THE CHOSEN SECRET LANGUAGE OF THE DORA MILAJE.

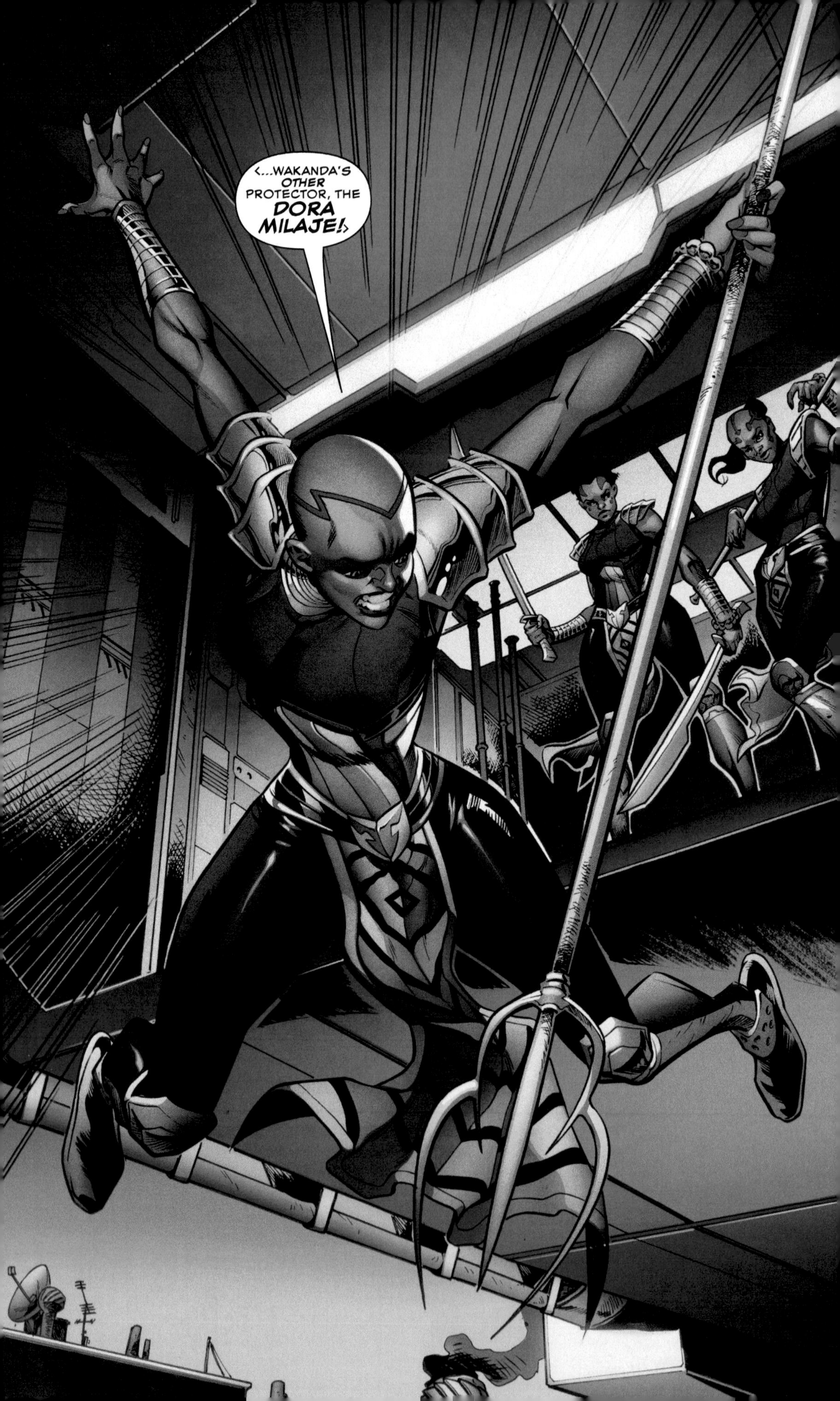

<...WAKANDA'S OTHER PROTECTOR, THE DORA MILAJE!>

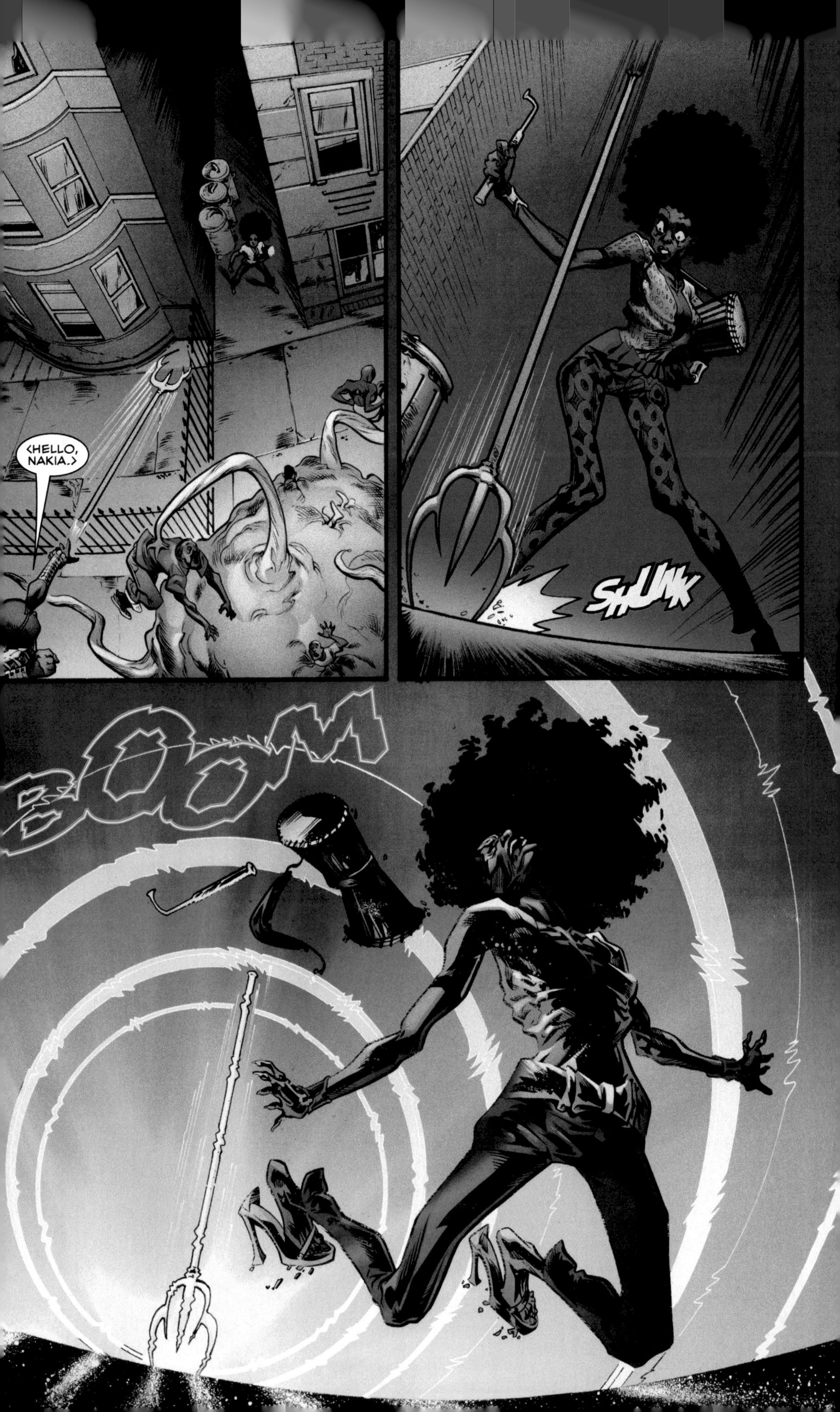
<HELLO, NAKIA.>
SHUNK
BOOM

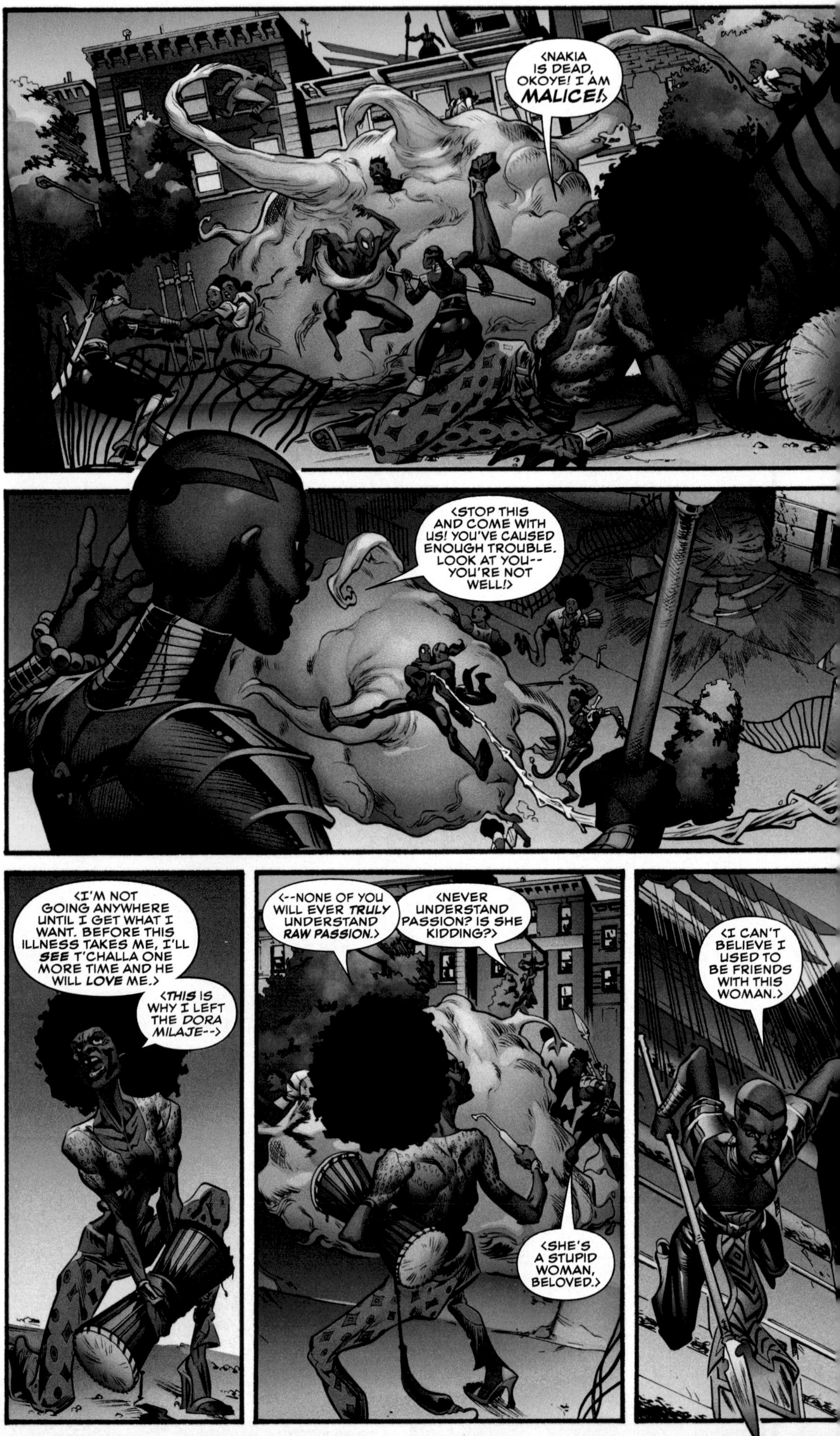

<NAKIA IS DEAD, OKOYE! I AM MALICE!>
<STOP THIS AND COME WITH US! YOU'VE CAUSED ENOUGH TROUBLE. LOOK AT YOU--YOU'RE NOT WELL!>
<I'M NOT GOING ANYWHERE UNTIL I GET WHAT I WANT. BEFORE THIS ILLNESS TAKES ME, I'LL SEE T'CHALLA ONE MORE TIME AND HE WILL LOVE ME.>
<THIS IS WHY I LEFT THE DORA MILAJE-->
<--NONE OF YOU WILL EVER TRULY UNDERSTAND RAW PASSION.>
<NEVER UNDERSTAND PASSION? IS SHE KIDDING?>
<SHE'S A STUPID WOMAN, BELOVED.>
<I CAN'T BELIEVE I USED TO BE FRIENDS WITH THIS WOMAN.>

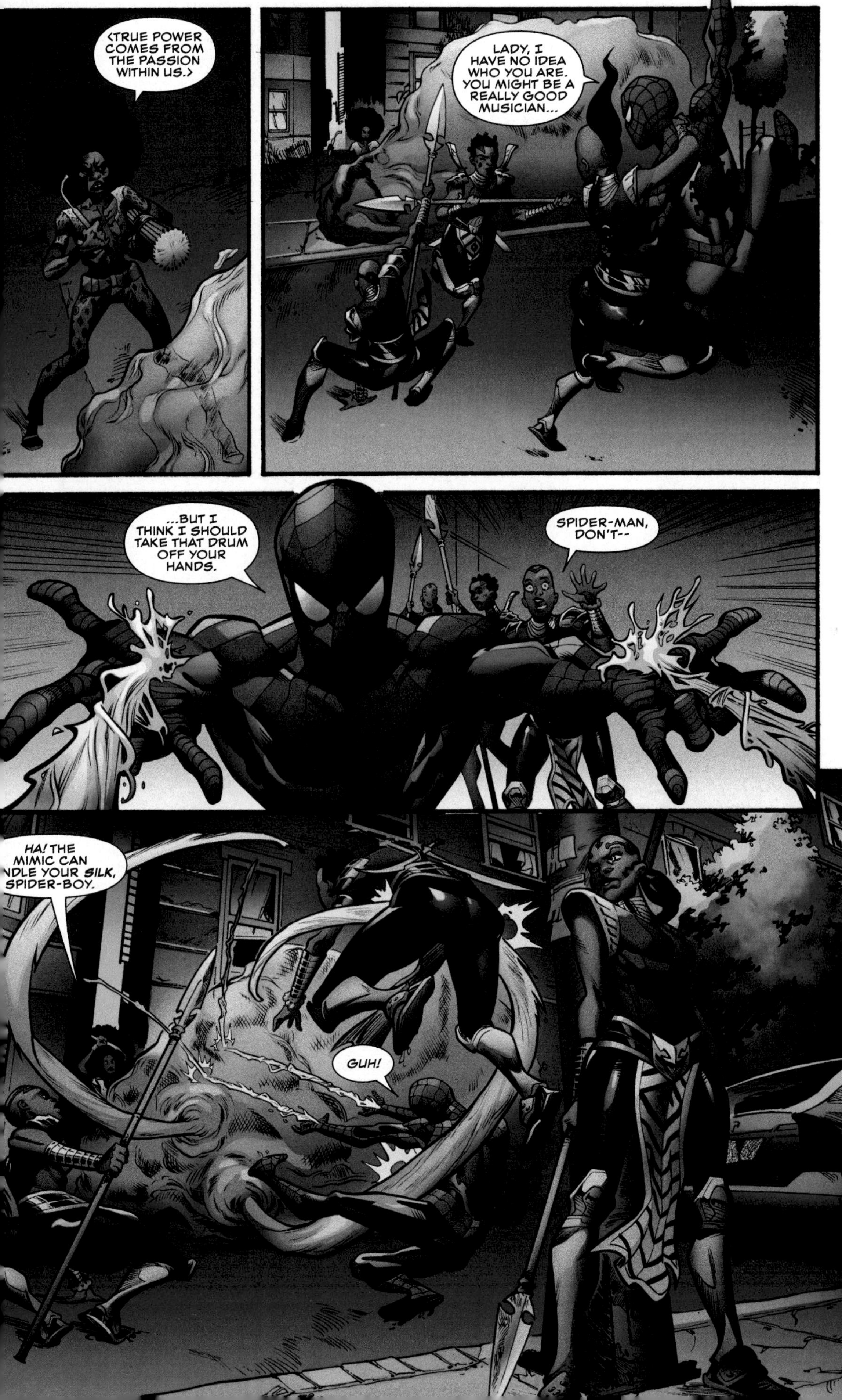
<TRUE POWER COMES FROM THE PASSION WITHIN US.>
LADY, I HAVE NO IDEA WHO YOU ARE. YOU MIGHT BE A REALLY GOOD MUSICIAN...
...BUT I THINK I SHOULD TAKE THAT DRUM OFF YOUR HANDS.
SPIDER-MAN, DON'T--
HA! THE MIMIC CAN NDLE YOUR SILK, SPIDER-BOY.
GUH!

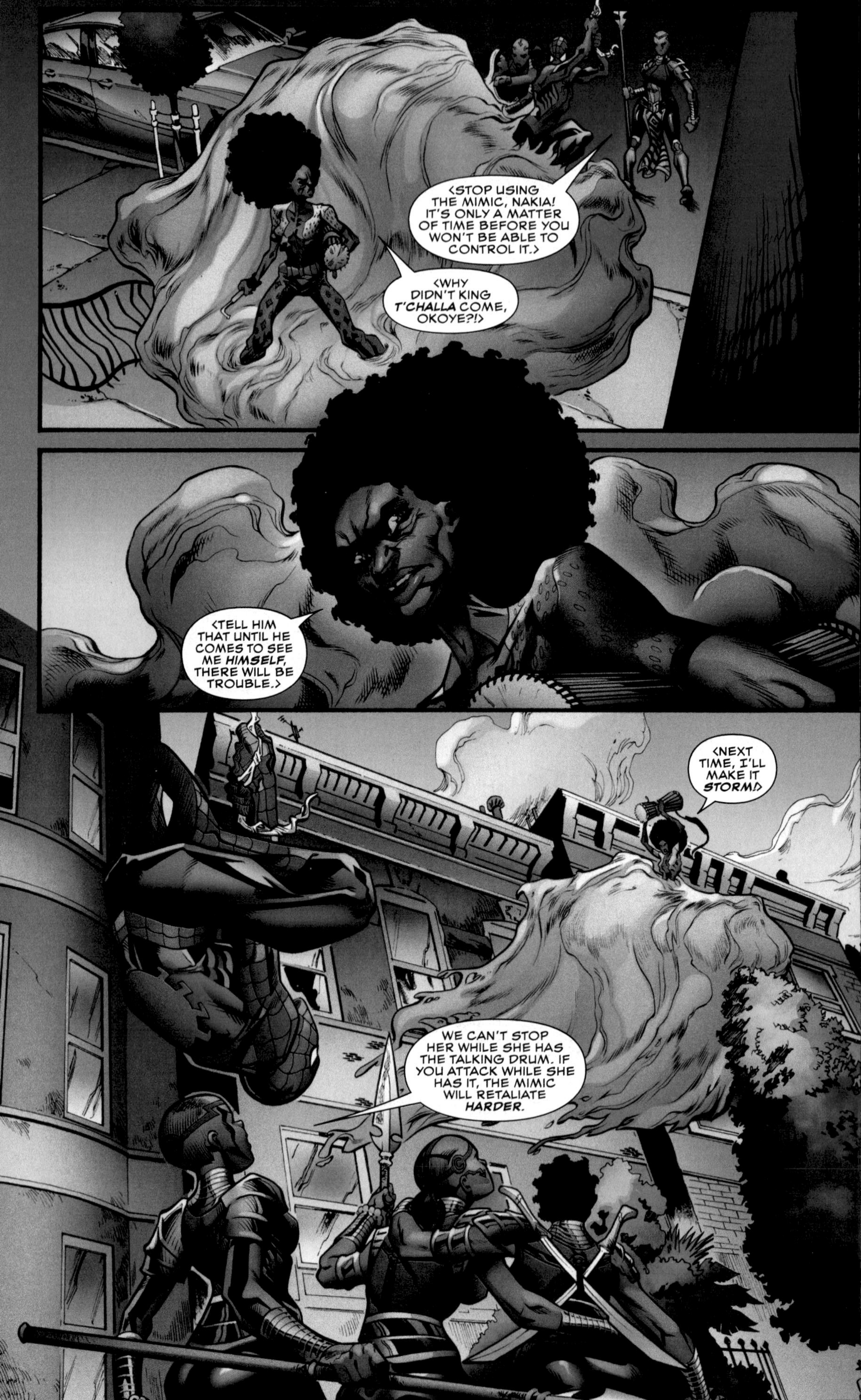

<STOP USING THE MIMIC, NAKIA! IT'S ONLY A MATTER OF TIME BEFORE YOU WON'T BE ABLE TO CONTROL IT.>
<WHY DIDN'T KING T'CHALLA COME, OKOYE?!>
<TELL HIM THAT UNTIL HE COMES TO SEE ME HIMSELF, THERE WILL BE TROUBLE.>
<NEXT TIME, I'LL MAKE IT STORM!>
WE CAN'T STOP HER WHILE SHE HAS THE TALKING DRUM. IF YOU ATTACK WHILE SHE HAS IT, THE MIMIC WILL RETALIATE HARDER.

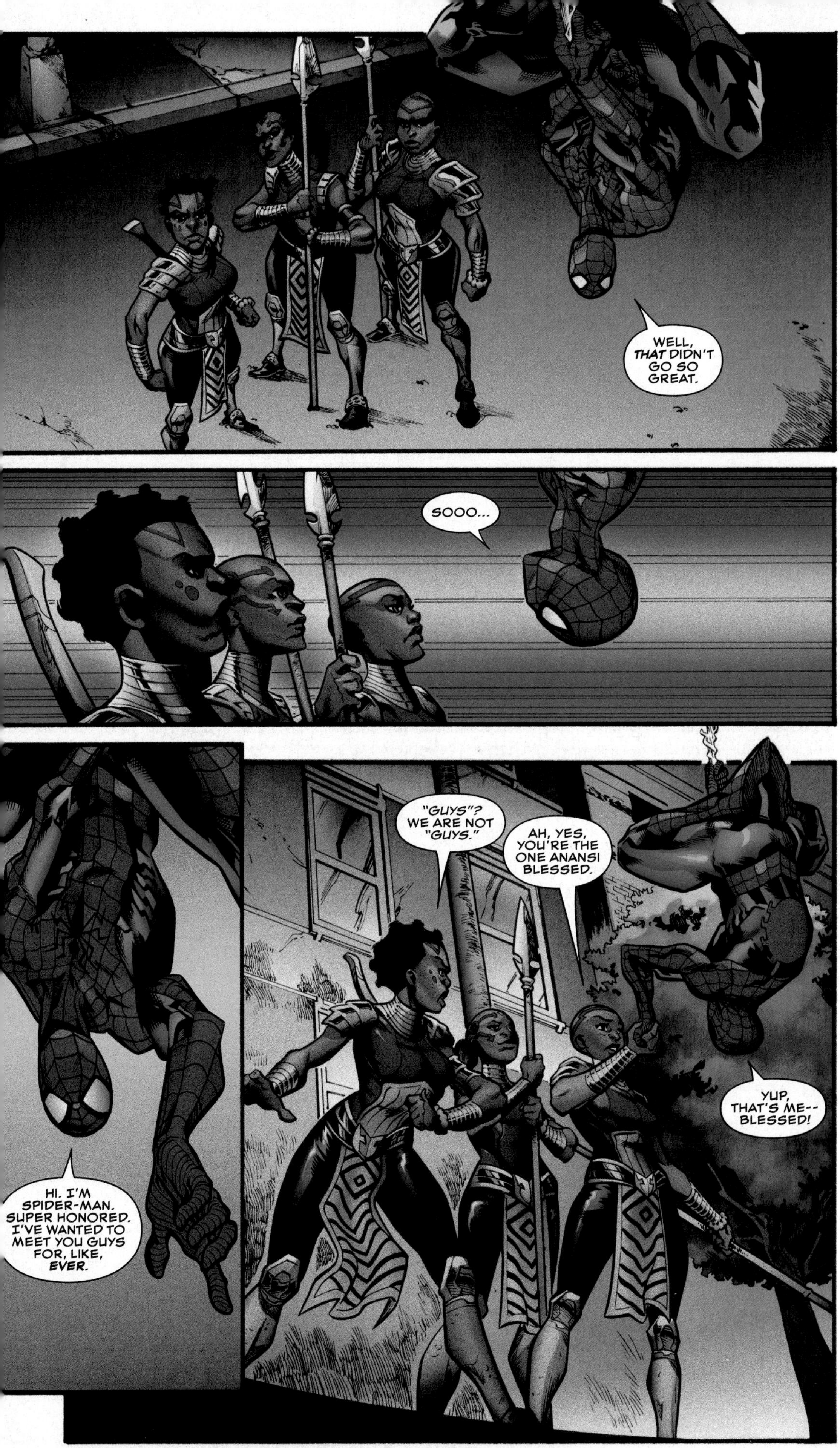
WELL, THAT DIDN'T GO SO GREAT.
SOOO...
HI. I'M SPIDER-MAN. SUPER HONORED. I'VE WANTED TO MEET YOU GUYS FOR, LIKE, EVER.
"GUYS"? WE ARE NOT "GUYS."
AH, YES, YOU'RE THE ONE ANANSI BLESSED.
YUP, THAT'S ME-- BLESSED!

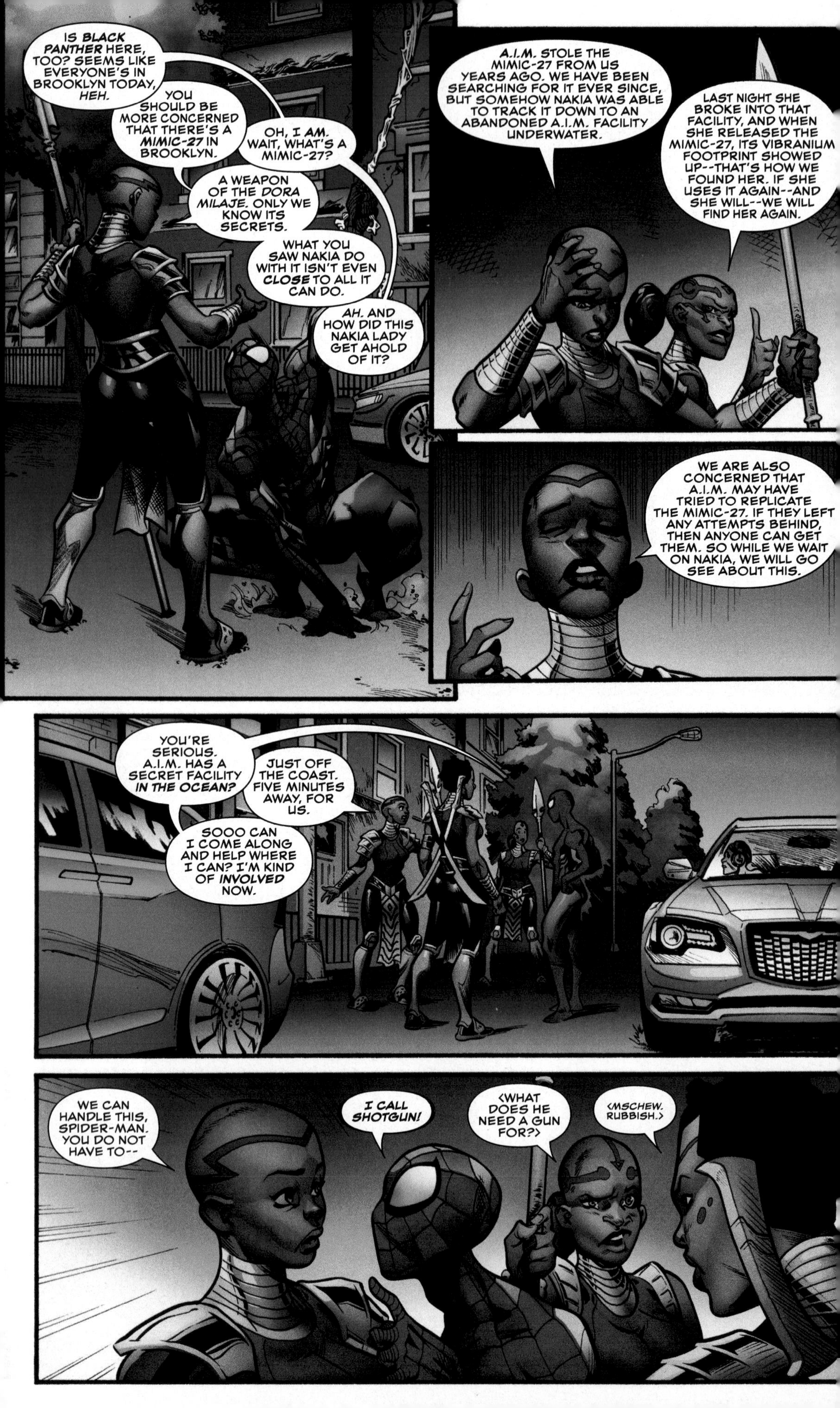

IS BLACK PANTHER HERE, TOO? SEEMS LIKE EVERYONE'S IN BROOKLYN TODAY, HEH.
YOU SHOULD BE MORE CONCERNED THAT THERE'S A MIMIC-27 IN BROOKLYN.
OH, I AM. WAIT, WHAT'S A MIMIC-27?
A WEAPON OF THE DORA MILAJE. ONLY WE KNOW ITS SECRETS.
WHAT YOU SAW NAKIA DO WITH IT ISN'T EVEN CLOSE TO ALL IT CAN DO.
AH. AND HOW DID THIS NAKIA LADY GET AHOLD OF IT?
A.I.M. STOLE THE MIMIC-27 FROM US YEARS AGO. WE HAVE BEEN SEARCHING FOR IT EVER SINCE, BUT SOMEHOW NAKIA WAS ABLE TO TRACK IT DOWN TO AN ABANDONED A.I.M. FACILITY UNDERWATER.
LAST NIGHT SHE BROKE INTO THAT FACILITY, AND WHEN SHE RELEASED THE MIMIC-27, ITS VIBRANIUM FOOTPRINT SHOWED UP--THAT'S HOW WE FOUND HER. IF SHE USES IT AGAIN--AND SHE WILL--WE WILL FIND HER AGAIN.
WE ARE ALSO CONCERNED THAT A.I.M. MAY HAVE TRIED TO REPLICATE THE MIMIC-27. IF THEY LEFT ANY ATTEMPTS BEHIND, THEN ANYONE CAN GET THEM. SO WHILE WE WAIT ON NAKIA, WE WILL GO SEE ABOUT THIS.
YOU'RE SERIOUS. A.I.M. HAS A SECRET FACILITY IN THE OCEAN?
JUST OFF THE COAST. FIVE MINUTES AWAY, FOR US.
SOOO CAN I COME ALONG AND HELP WHERE I CAN? I'M KIND OF INVOLVED NOW.
WE CAN HANDLE THIS, SPIDER-MAN. YOU DO NOT HAVE TO--
I CALL SHOTGUN!
<WHAT DOES HE NEED A GUN FOR?>
<MSCHEW. RUBBISH.>

SO LET ME GET THIS STRAIGHT: THIS MIMIC-27 IS A SORT OF SHAPE-SHIFTING SYMBIOTIC SUPER-SOLDIER THING? BASICALLY AN ORGANIC DOOMSDAY DEVICE?

THAT INFORMATION IS ABOVE YOUR PAY GRADE.

AS I SAID, IT'S A WEAPON.

NOW, WE MUST DO THIS QUICKLY, SO WE CAN GET BACK TO FINDING NAKIA.

PRESSURIZING.

SO YOUR FRIEND--NO DISRESPECT--SHE WAS LOOKING KINDA...ROUGH.

NAKIA IS NOT A FRIEND. SHE WAS ONE OF US, A DORA MILAJE, UNTIL SHE NO LONGER WAS. FOR MANY YEARS, SHE'S USED A TOXIC HERB TO MANIPULATE MINDS.

NOW IT SEEMS THE DRUG IS MAKING HER ILL. DEATHLY SO, BY THE LOOKS OF IT.

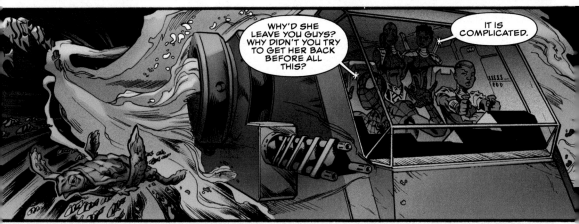

WHY'D SHE LEAVE YOU GUYS? WHY DIDN'T YOU TRY TO GET HER BACK BEFORE ALL THIS?

IT IS COMPLICATED.

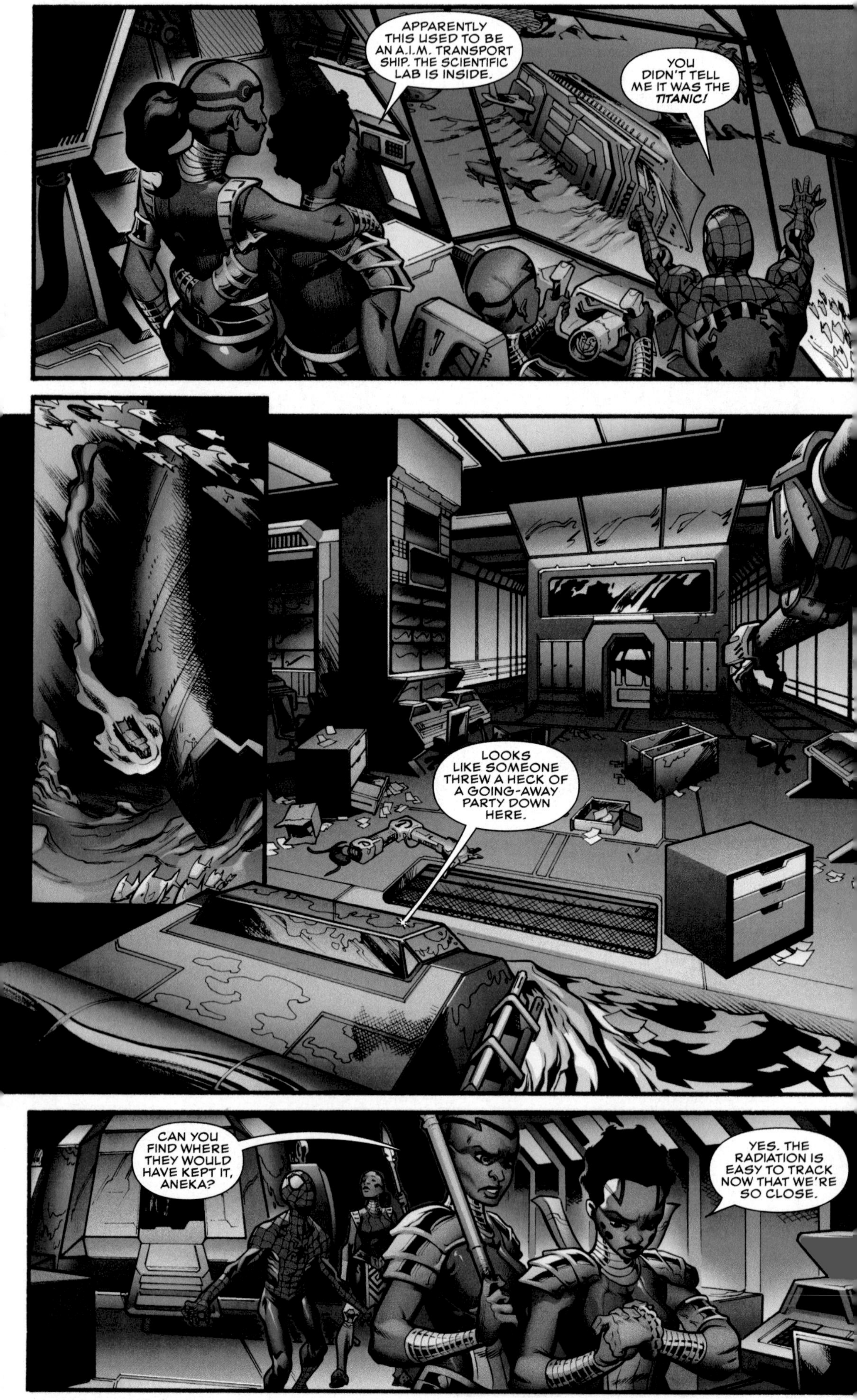
APPARENTLY THIS USED TO BE AN A.I.M. TRANSPORT SHIP. THE SCIENTIFIC LAB IS INSIDE.
YOU DIDN'T TELL ME IT WAS THE *TITANIC!*
LOOKS LIKE SOMEONE THREW A HECK OF A GOING-AWAY PARTY DOWN HERE.
CAN YOU FIND WHERE THEY WOULD HAVE KEPT IT, ANEKA?
YES. THE RADIATION IS EASY TO TRACK NOW THAT WE'RE SO CLOSE.

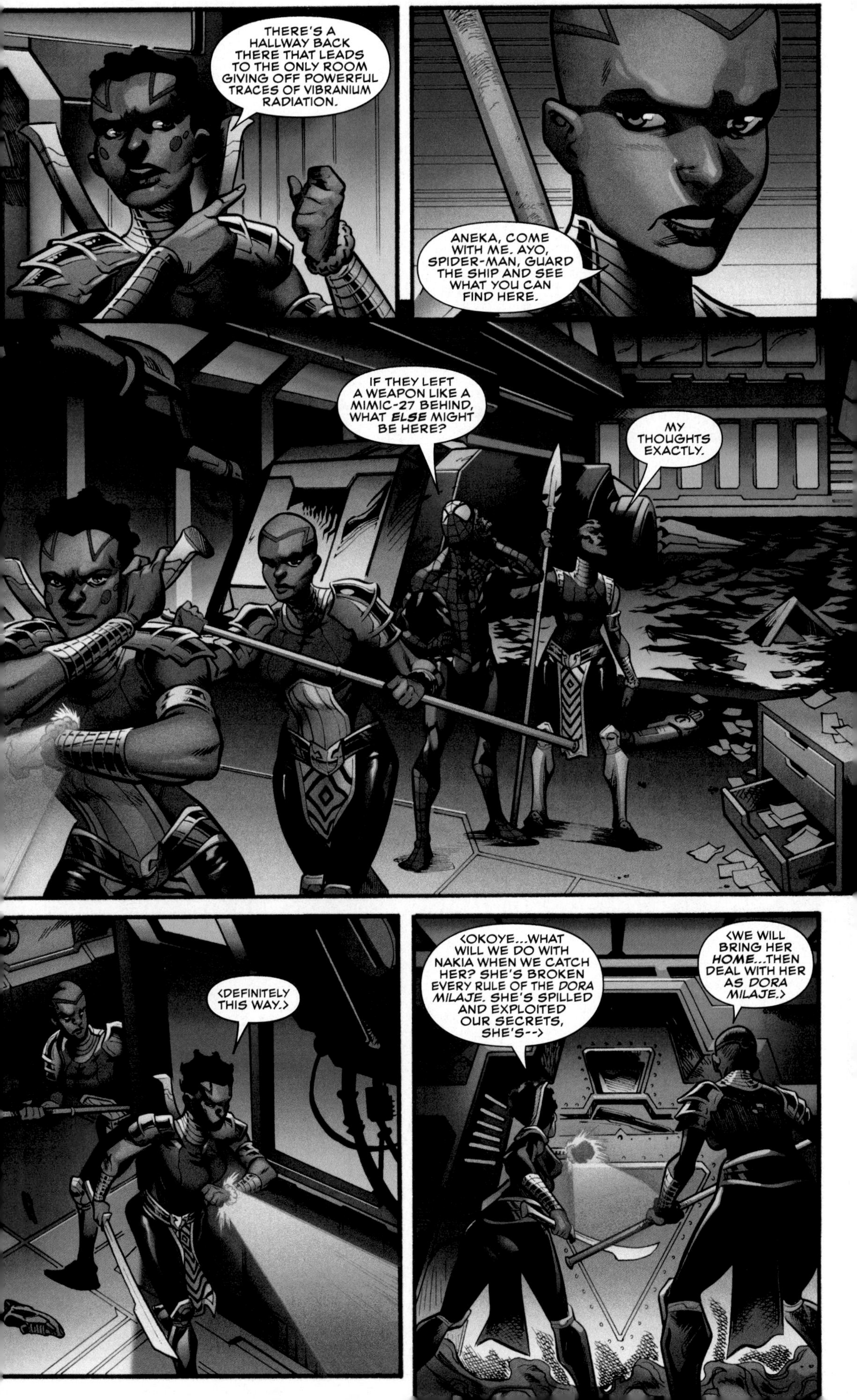
THERE'S A HALLWAY BACK THERE THAT LEADS TO THE ONLY ROOM GIVING OFF POWERFUL TRACES OF VIBRANIUM RADIATION.
ANEKA, COME WITH ME. AYO, SPIDER-MAN, GUARD THE SHIP AND SEE WHAT YOU CAN FIND HERE.
IF THEY LEFT A WEAPON LIKE A MIMIC-27 BEHIND, WHAT ELSE MIGHT BE HERE?
MY THOUGHTS EXACTLY.
<DEFINITELY THIS WAY.>
<OKOYE...WHAT WILL WE DO WITH NAKIA WHEN WE CATCH HER? SHE'S BROKEN EVERY RULE OF THE DORA MILAJE. SHE'S SPILLED AND EXPLOITED OUR SECRETS, SHE'S-->
<WE WILL BRING HER HOME...THEN DEAL WITH HER AS DORA MILAJE.>

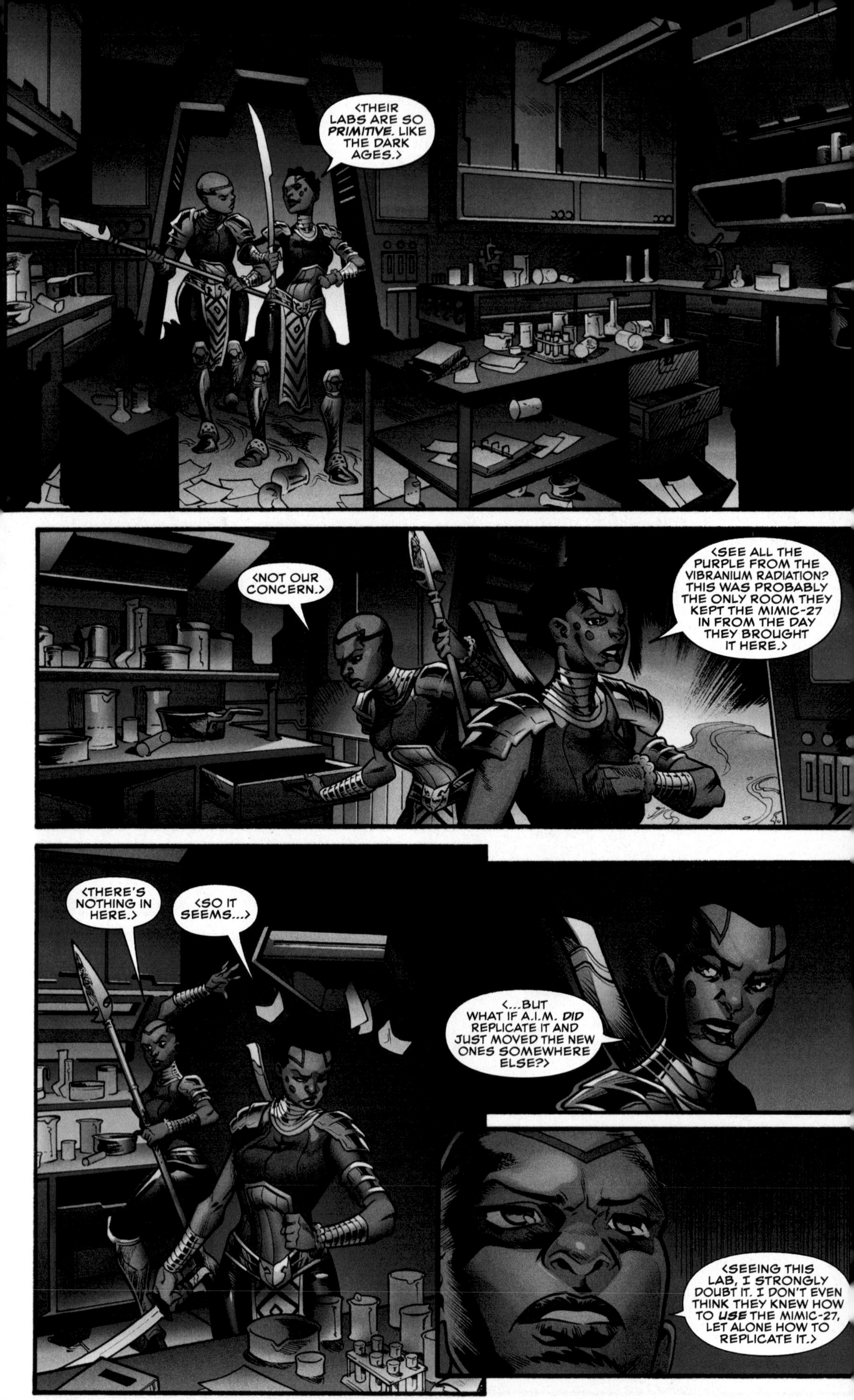

<THEIR LABS ARE SO PRIMITIVE. LIKE THE DARK AGES.>
<NOT OUR CONCERN.>
<SEE ALL THE PURPLE FROM THE VIBRANIUM RADIATION? THIS WAS PROBABLY THE ONLY ROOM THEY KEPT THE MIMIC-27 IN FROM THE DAY THEY BROUGHT IT HERE.>
<THERE'S NOTHING IN HERE.>
<SO IT SEEMS...>
<...BUT WHAT IF A.I.M. DID REPLICATE IT AND JUST MOVED THE NEW ONES SOMEWHERE ELSE?>
<SEEING THIS LAB, I STRONGLY DOUBT IT. I DON'T EVEN THINK THEY KNEW HOW TO USE THE MIMIC-27, LET ALONE HOW TO REPLICATE IT.>

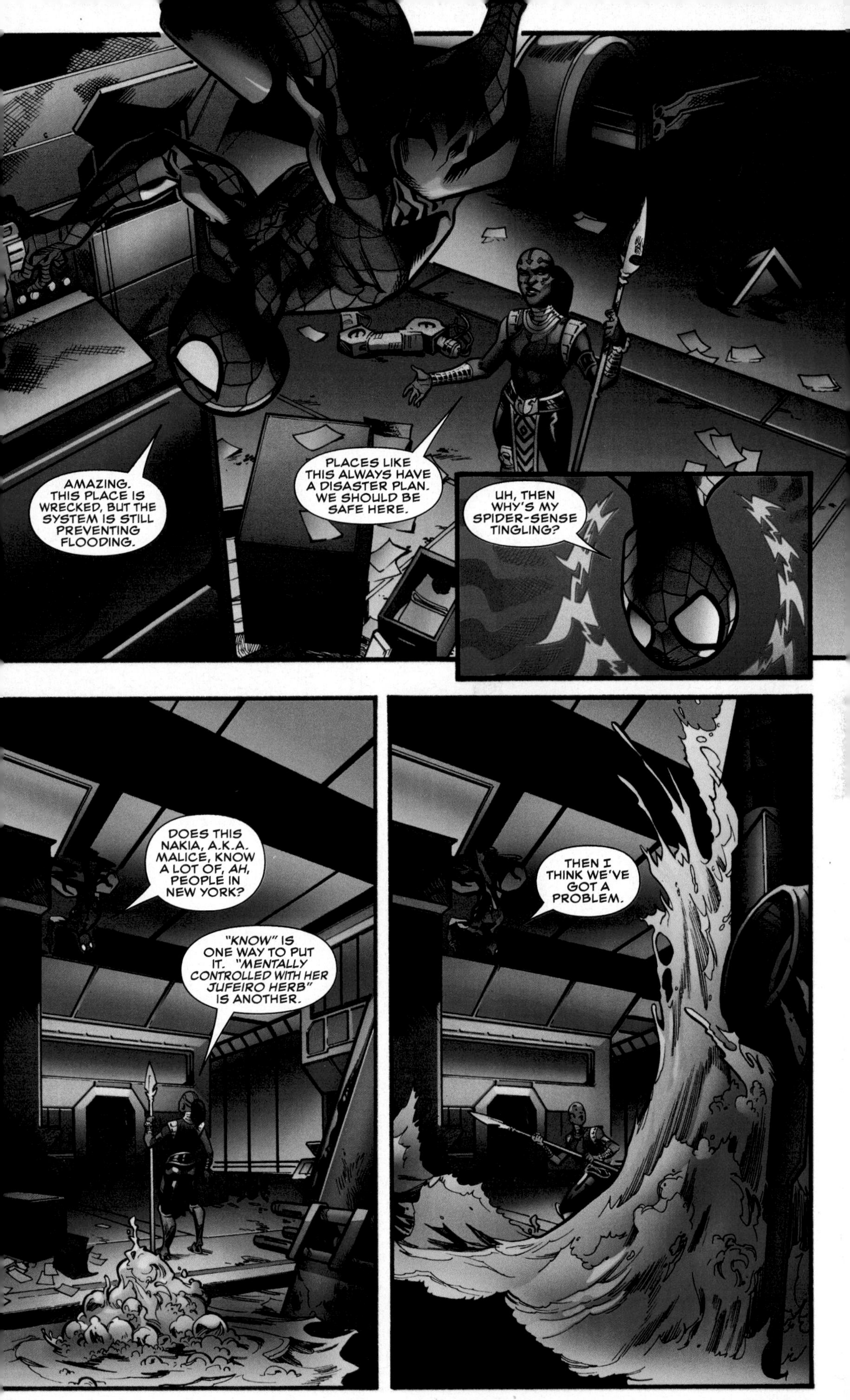
AMAZING. THIS PLACE IS WRECKED, BUT THE SYSTEM IS STILL PREVENTING FLOODING.
PLACES LIKE THIS ALWAYS HAVE A DISASTER PLAN. WE SHOULD BE SAFE HERE.
UH, THEN WHY'S MY SPIDER-SENSE TINGLING?
DOES THIS NAKIA, A.K.A. MALICE, KNOW A LOT OF, AH, PEOPLE IN NEW YORK?
"KNOW" IS ONE WAY TO PUT IT. "MENTALLY CONTROLLED WITH HER JUFEIRO HERB" IS ANOTHER.
THEN I THINK WE'VE GOT A PROBLEM.

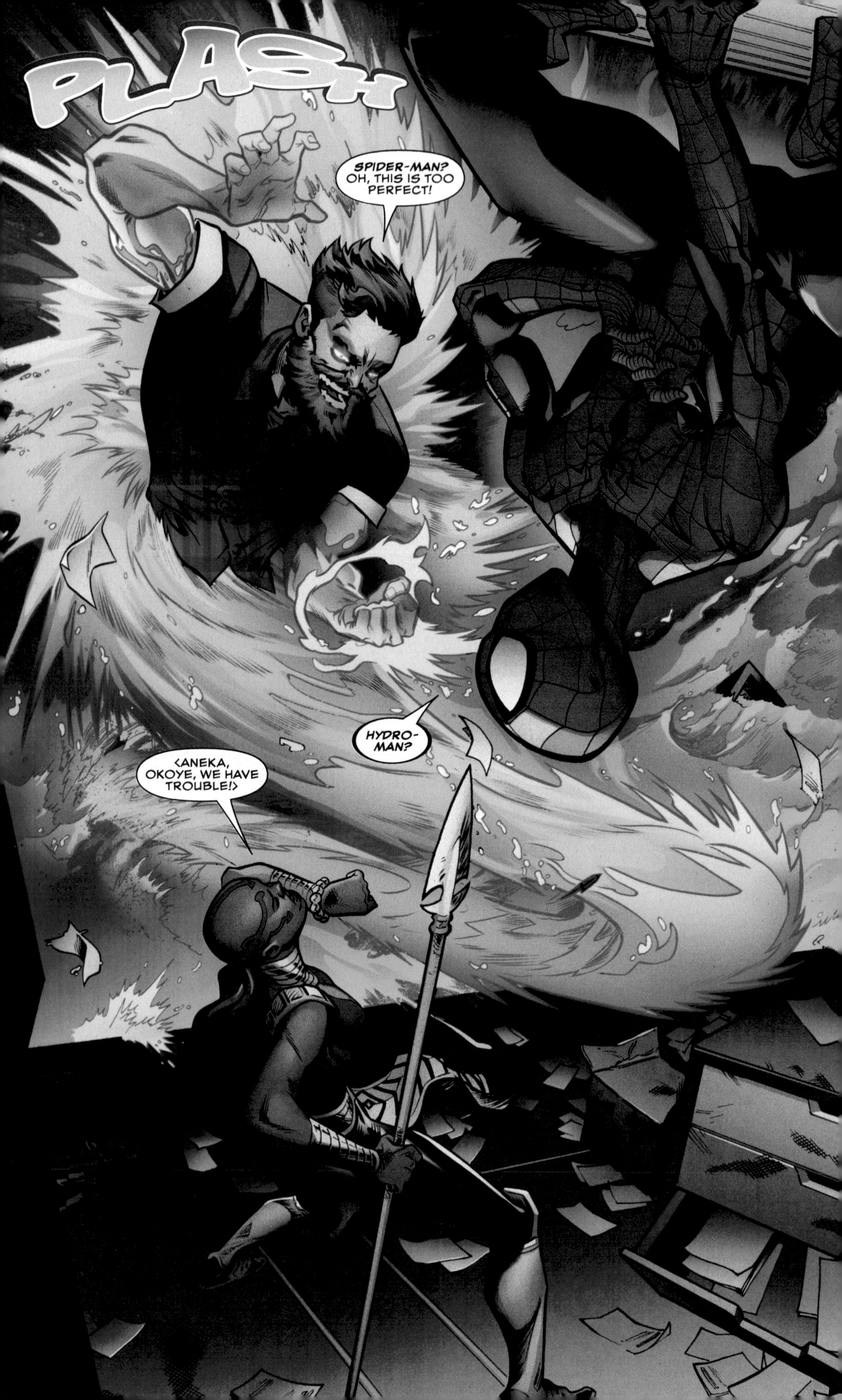
PLASH
SPIDER-MAN? OH, THIS IS TOO PERFECT!
HYDRO-MAN?
<ANEKA, OKOYE, WE HAVE TROUBLE!>

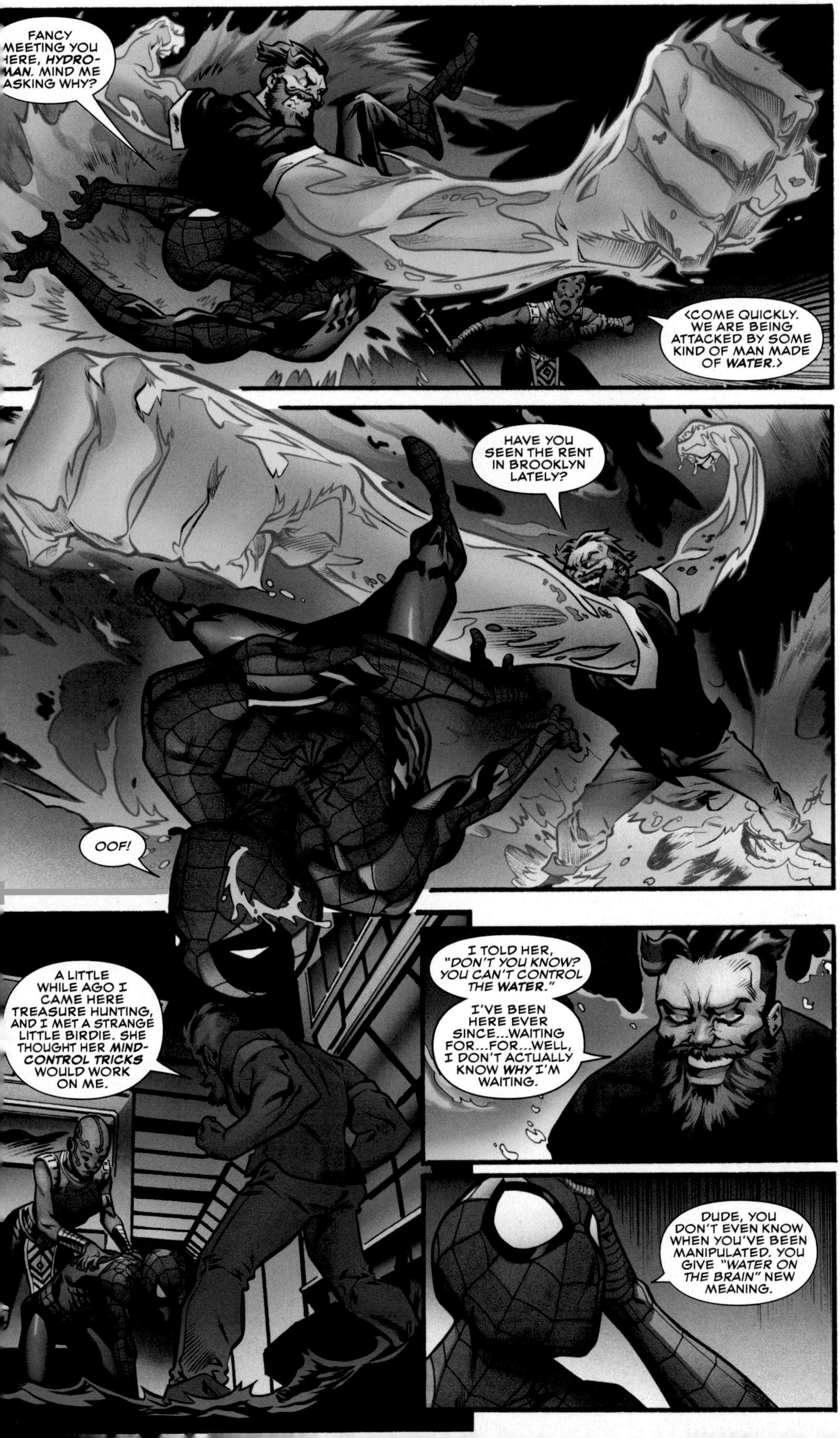

FANCY MEETING YOU HERE, HYDRO-MAN. MIND ME ASKING WHY?
<COME QUICKLY. WE ARE BEING ATTACKED BY SOME KIND OF MAN MADE OF WATER.>
HAVE YOU SEEN THE RENT IN BROOKLYN LATELY?
OOF!
A LITTLE WHILE AGO I CAME HERE TREASURE HUNTING, AND I MET A STRANGE LITTLE BIRDIE. SHE THOUGHT HER MIND-CONTROL TRICKS WOULD WORK ON ME.
I TOLD HER, "DON'T YOU KNOW? YOU CAN'T CONTROL THE WATER."
I'VE BEEN HERE EVER SINCE...WAITING FOR...FOR...WELL, I DON'T ACTUALLY KNOW WHY I'M WAITING.
DUDE, YOU DON'T EVEN KNOW WHEN YOU'VE BEEN MANIPULATED. YOU GIVE "WATER ON THE BRAIN" NEW MEANING.

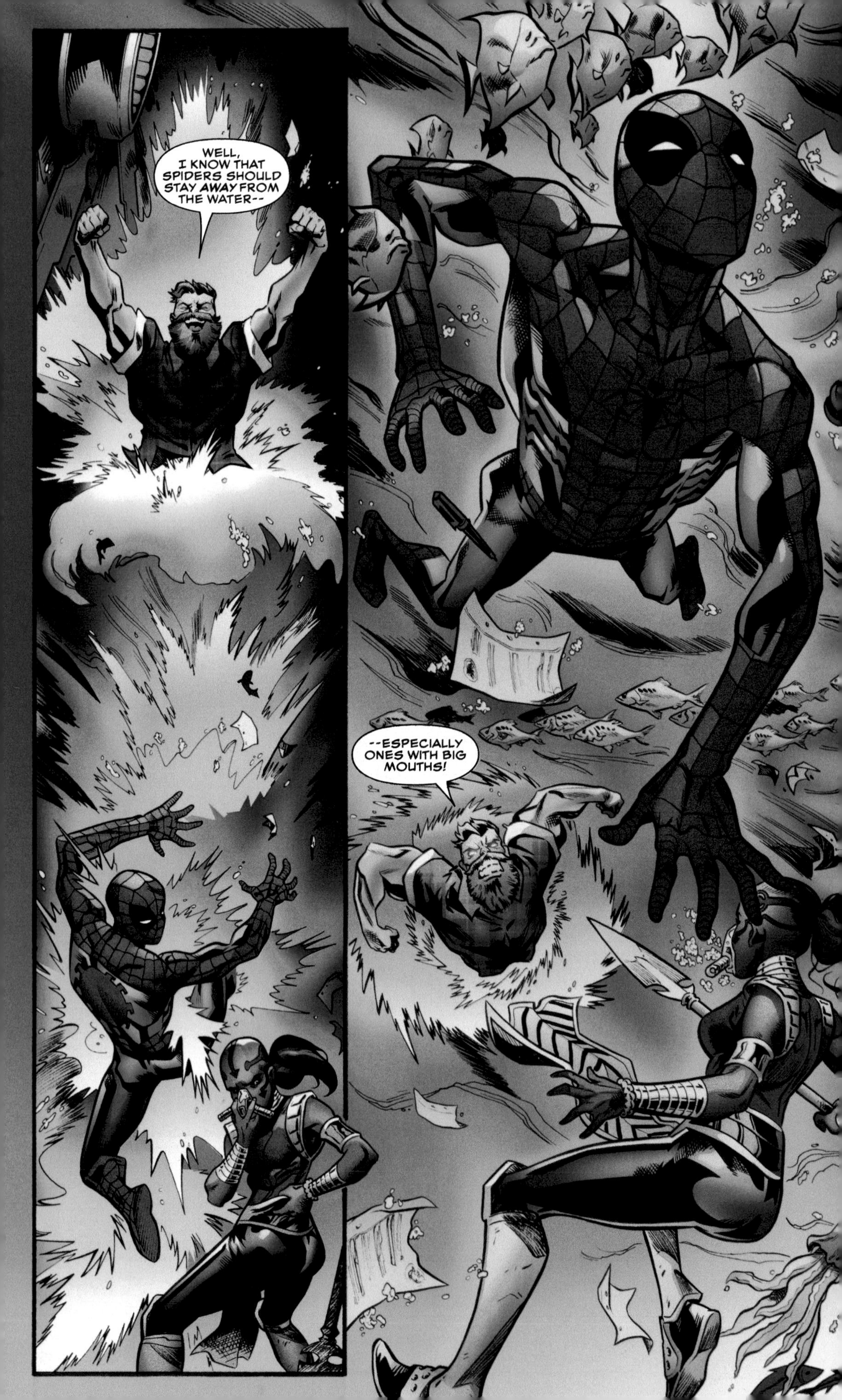
WELL, I KNOW THAT SPIDERS SHOULD STAY AWAY FROM THE WATER--
--ESPECIALLY ONES WITH BIG MOUTHS!

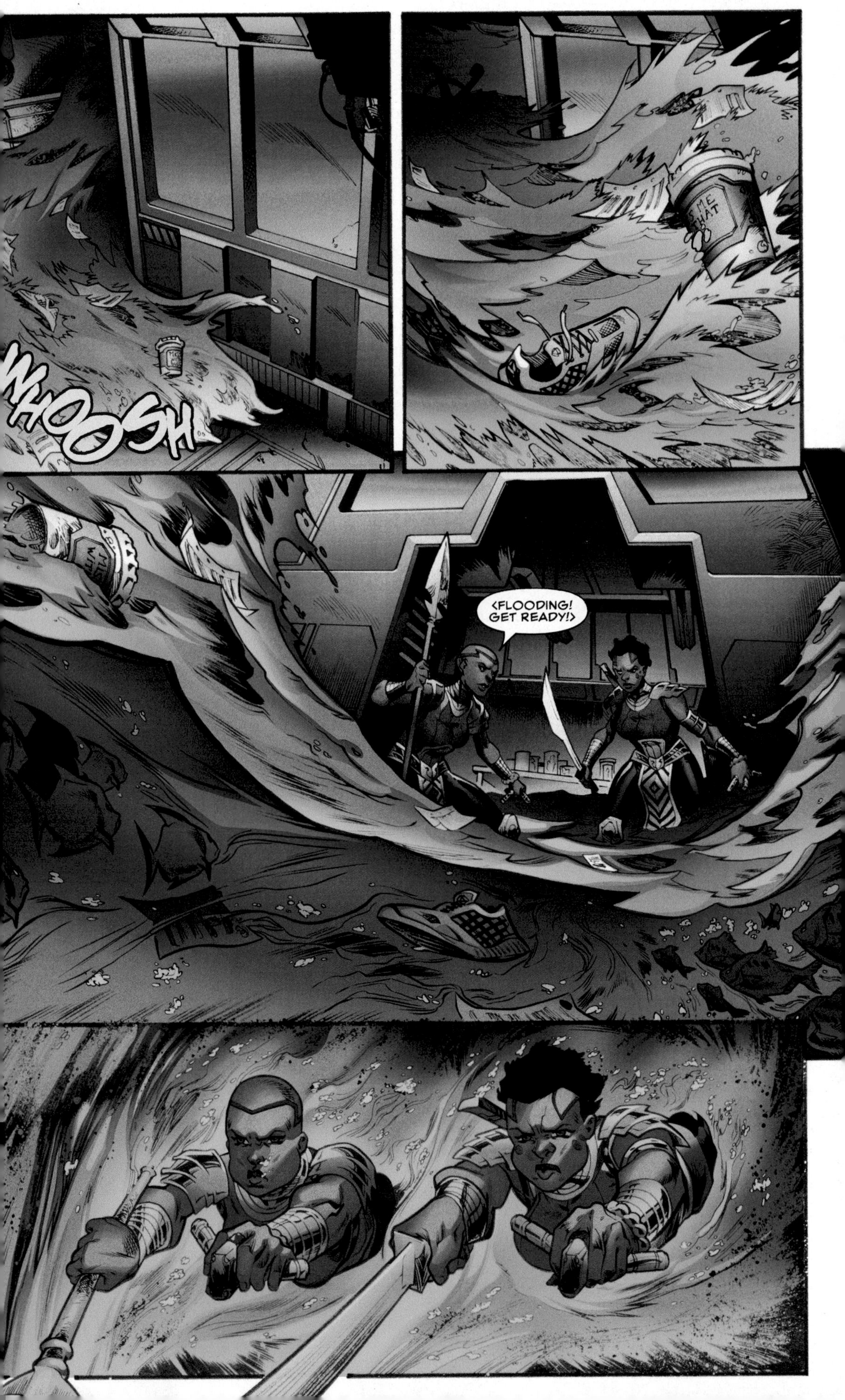
WHOOSH
<FLOODING! GET READY!>

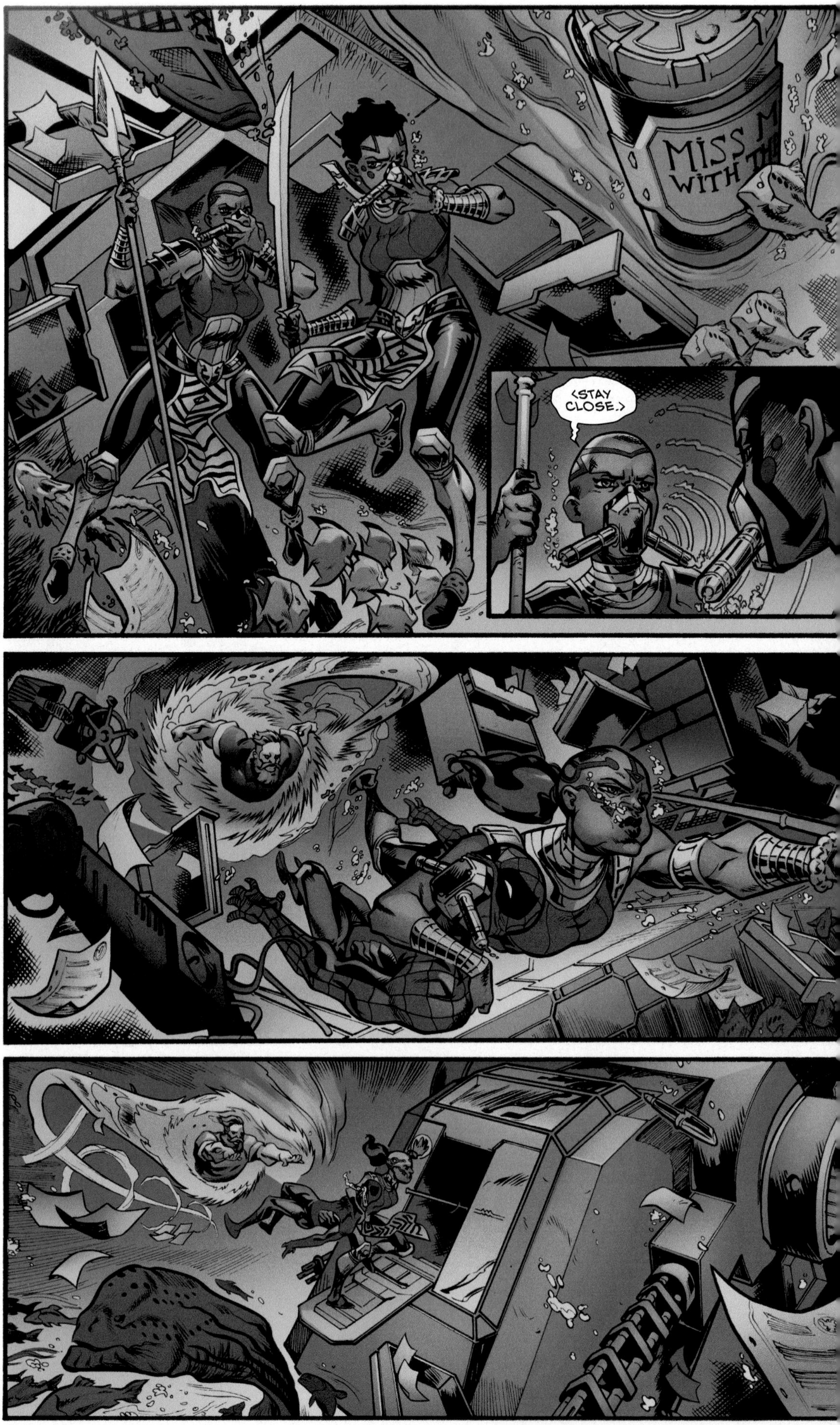
MISS M
WITH TH
<STAY CLOSE.>

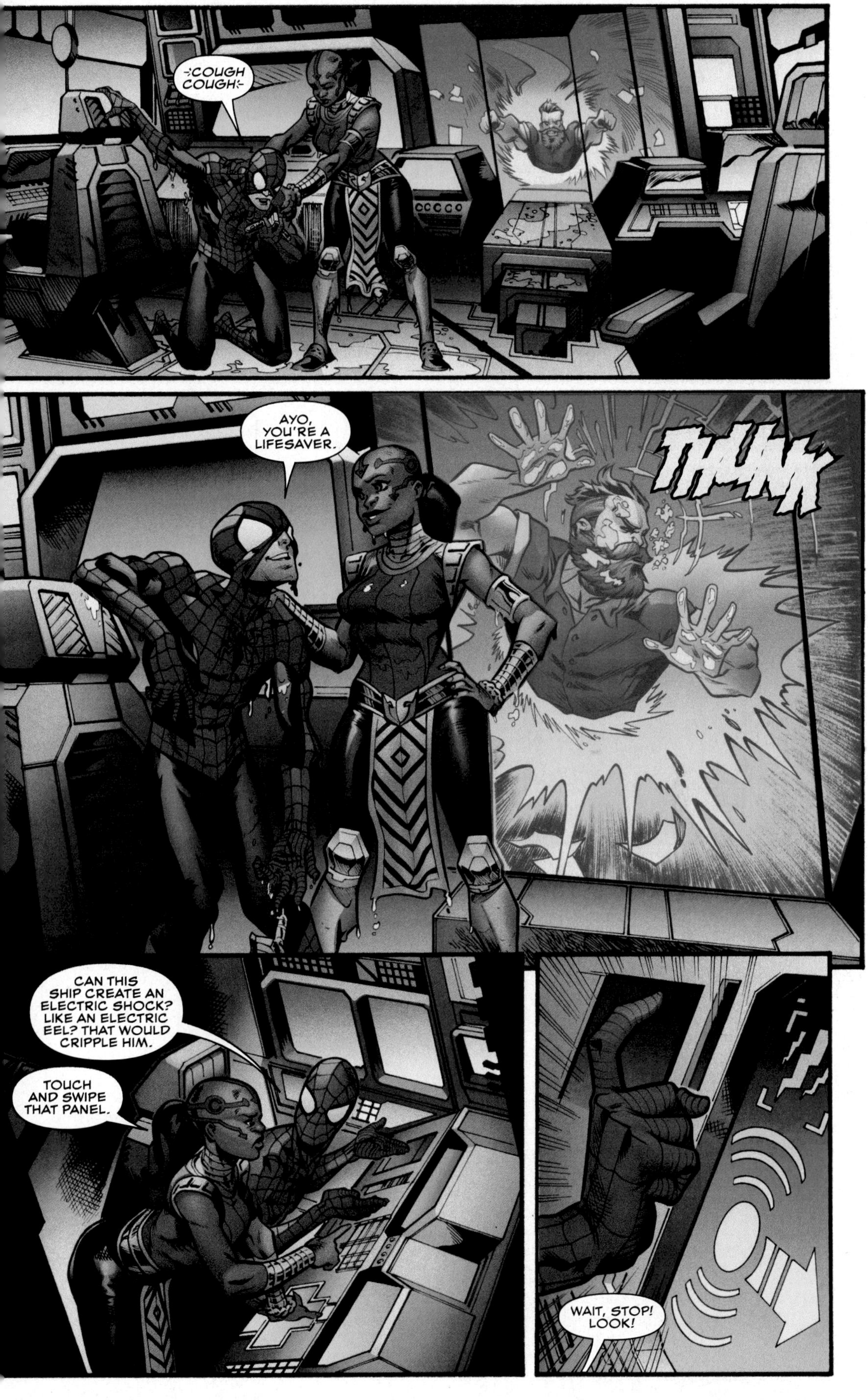
COUGH COUGH
AYO, YOU'RE A LIFESAVER.
THUNK
CAN THIS SHIP CREATE AN ELECTRIC SHOCK? LIKE AN ELECTRIC EEL? THAT WOULD CRIPPLE HIM.
TOUCH AND SWIPE THAT PANEL.
WAIT, STOP! LOOK!

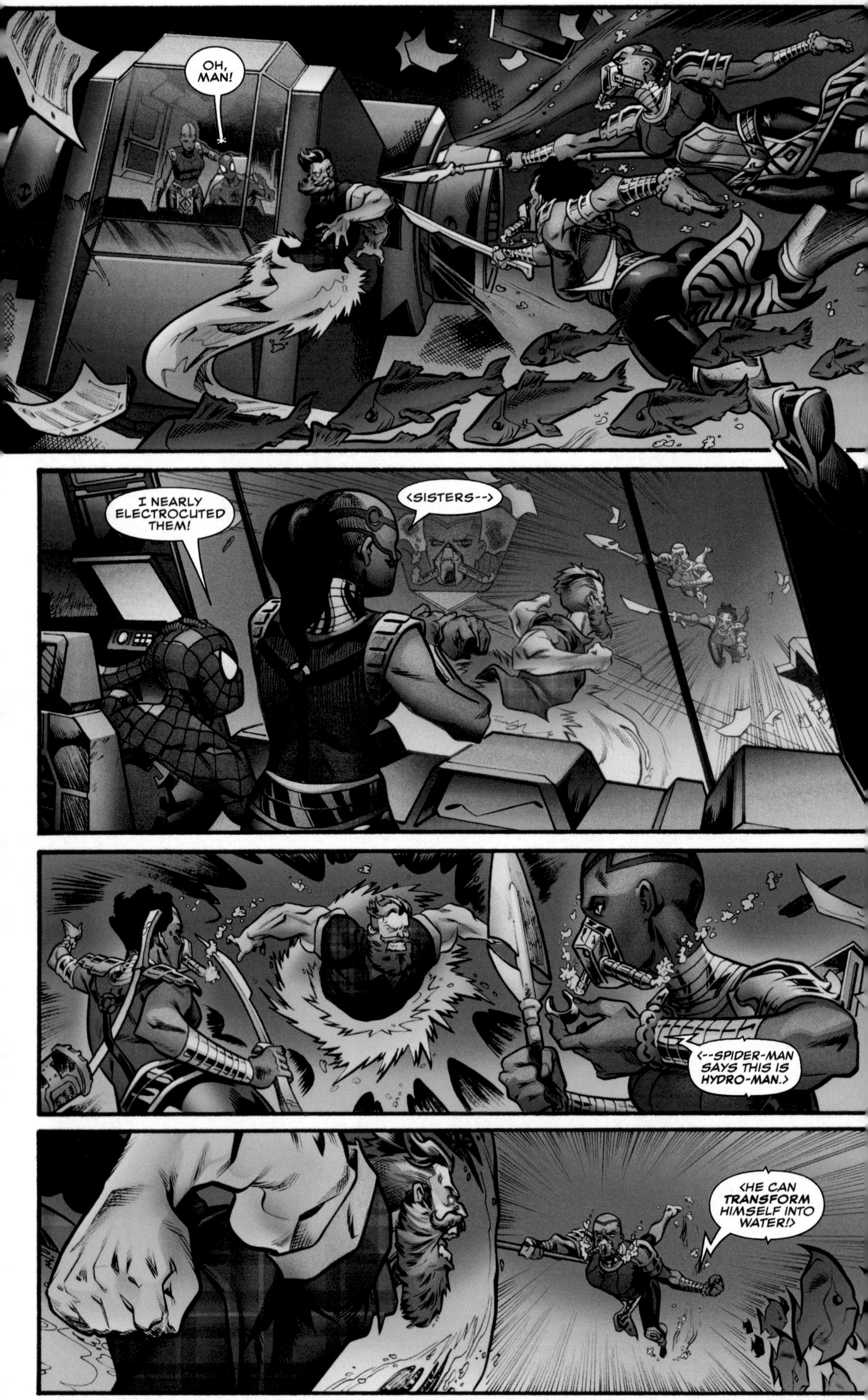
OH, MAN!
I NEARLY ELECTROCUTED THEM!
<SISTERS-->
<--SPIDER-MAN SAYS THIS IS HYDRO-MAN.>
<HE CAN TRANSFORM HIMSELF INTO WATER!>

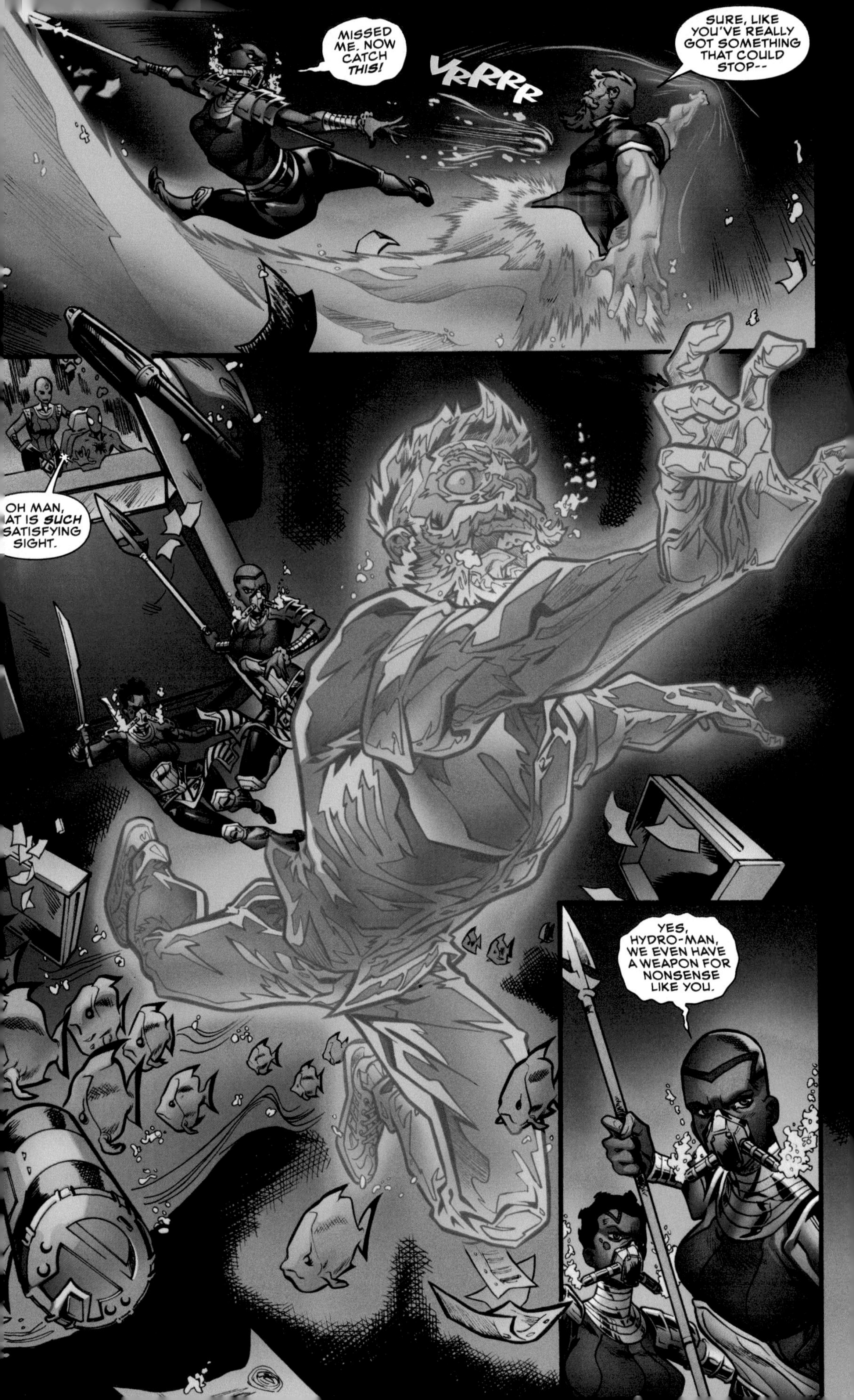
MISSED ME. NOW CATCH *THIS!*
VRRRR
SURE, LIKE YOU'VE REALLY GOT SOMETHING THAT COULD STOP--
OH MAN, AT IS *SUCH* SATISFYING SIGHT.
YES, HYDRO-MAN, WE EVEN HAVE A WEAPON FOR NONSENSE LIKE YOU.

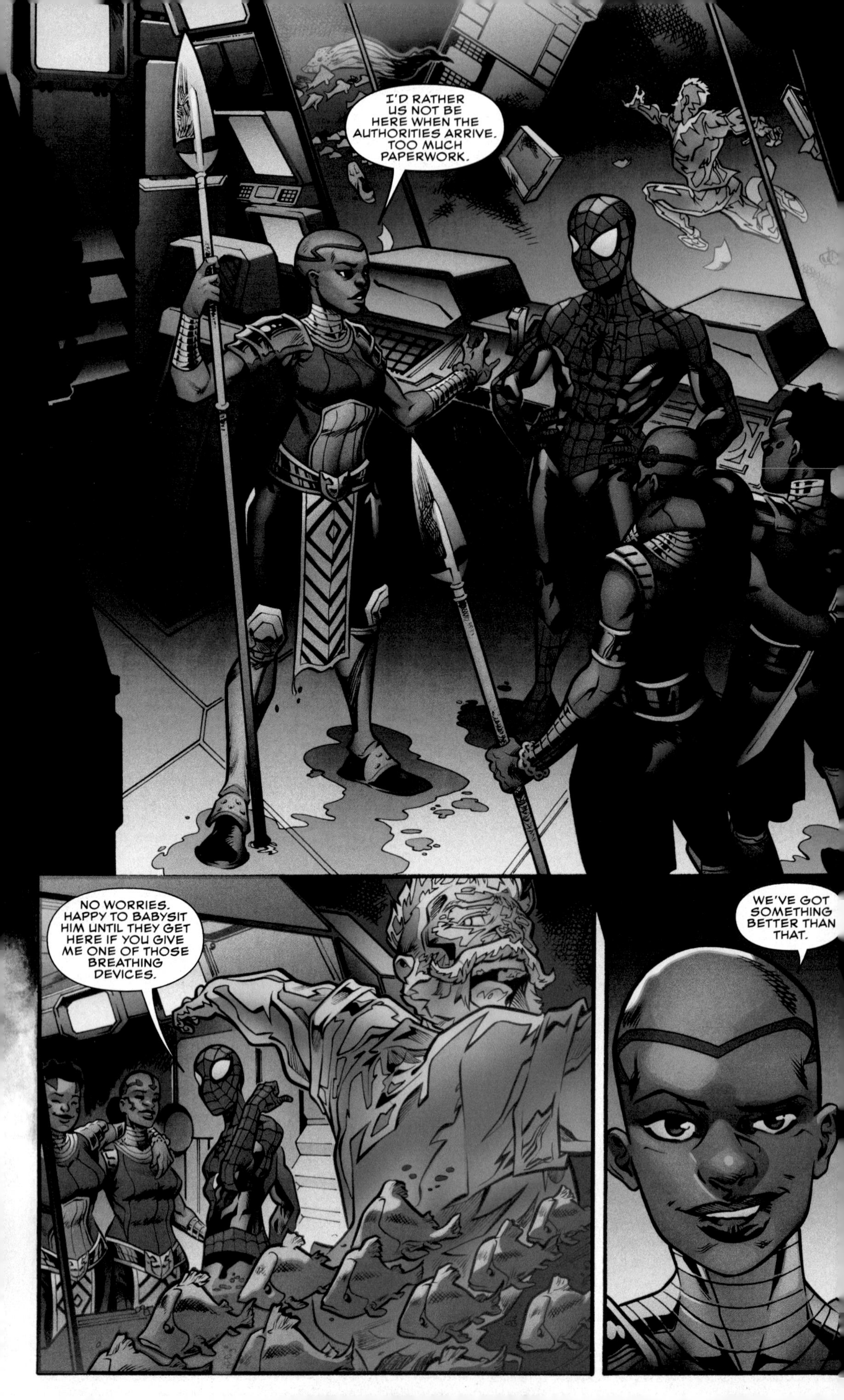
I'D RATHER US NOT BE HERE WHEN THE AUTHORITIES ARRIVE. TOO MUCH PAPERWORK.
NO WORRIES. HAPPY TO BABYSIT HIM UNTIL THEY GET HERE IF YOU GIVE ME ONE OF THOSE BREATHING DEVICES.
WE'VE GOT SOMETHING BETTER THAN THAT.

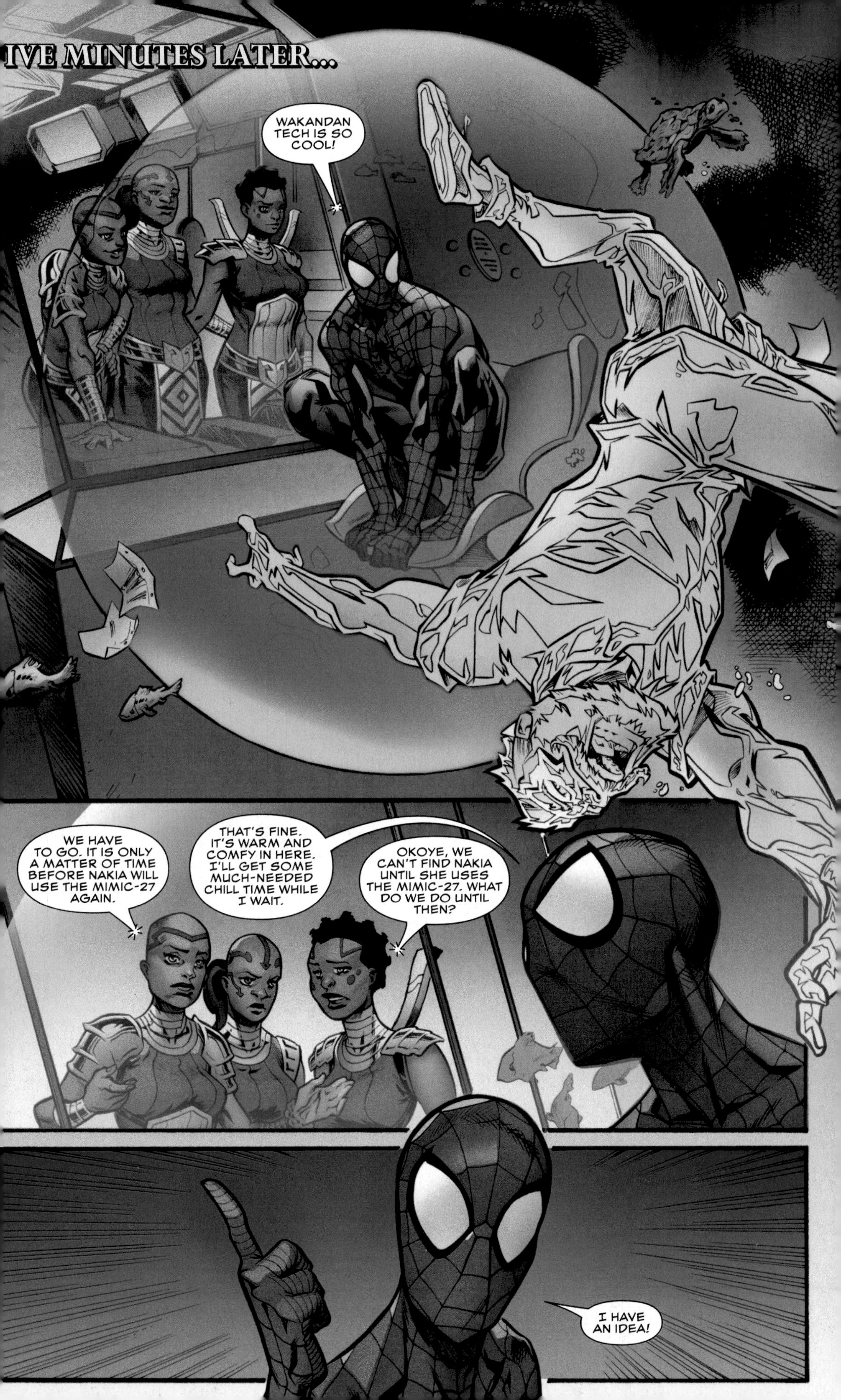

IVE MINUTES LATER...
WAKANDAN TECH IS SO COOL!
WE HAVE TO GO. IT IS ONLY A MATTER OF TIME BEFORE NAKIA WILL USE THE MIMIC-27 AGAIN.
THAT'S FINE. IT'S WARM AND COMFY IN HERE. I'LL GET SOME MUCH-NEEDED CHILL TIME WHILE I WAIT.
OKOYE, WE CAN'T FIND NAKIA UNTIL SHE USES THE MIMIC-27. WHAT DO WE DO UNTIL THEN?
I HAVE AN IDEA!

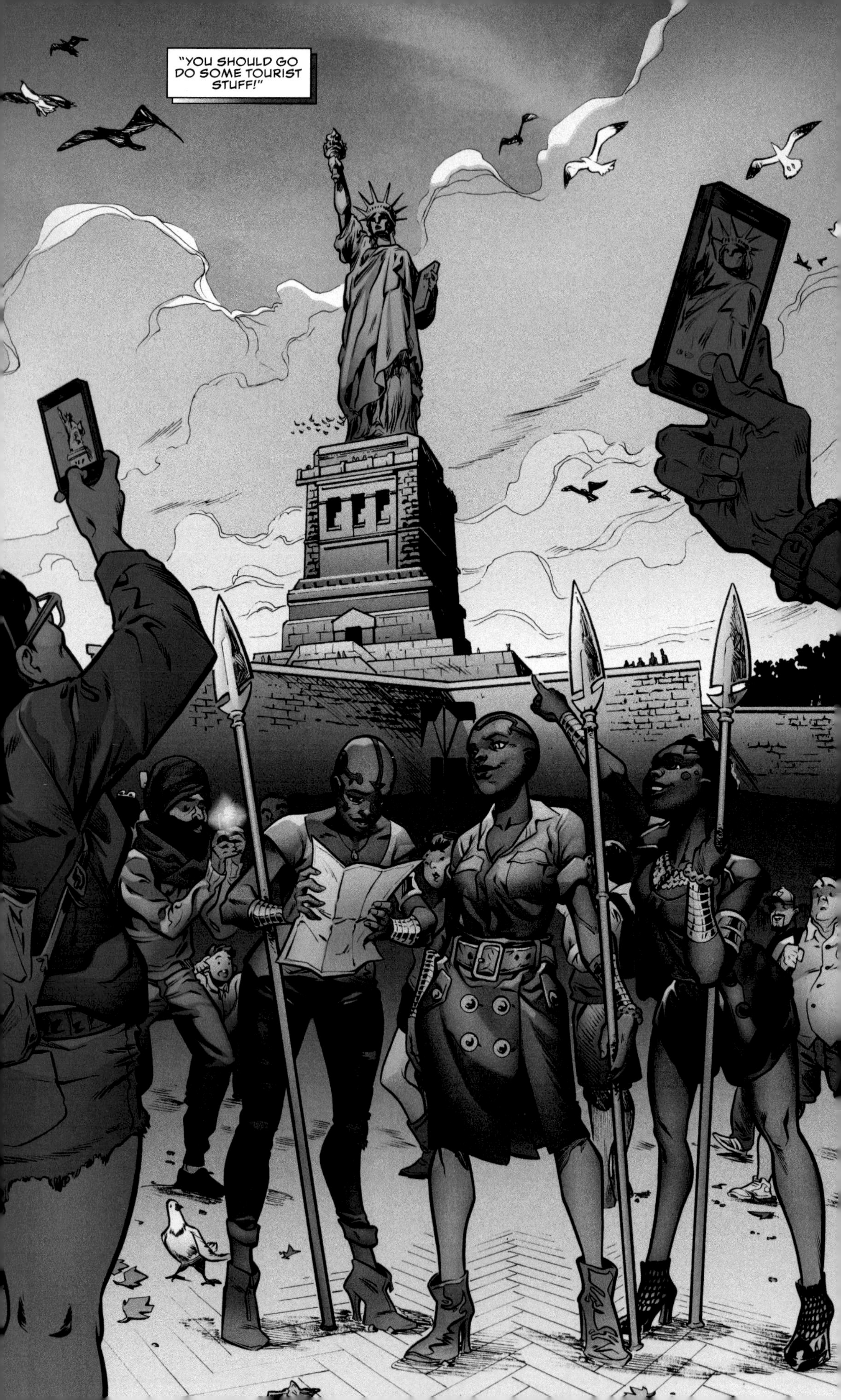
"YOU SHOULD GO DO SOME TOURIST STUFF!"

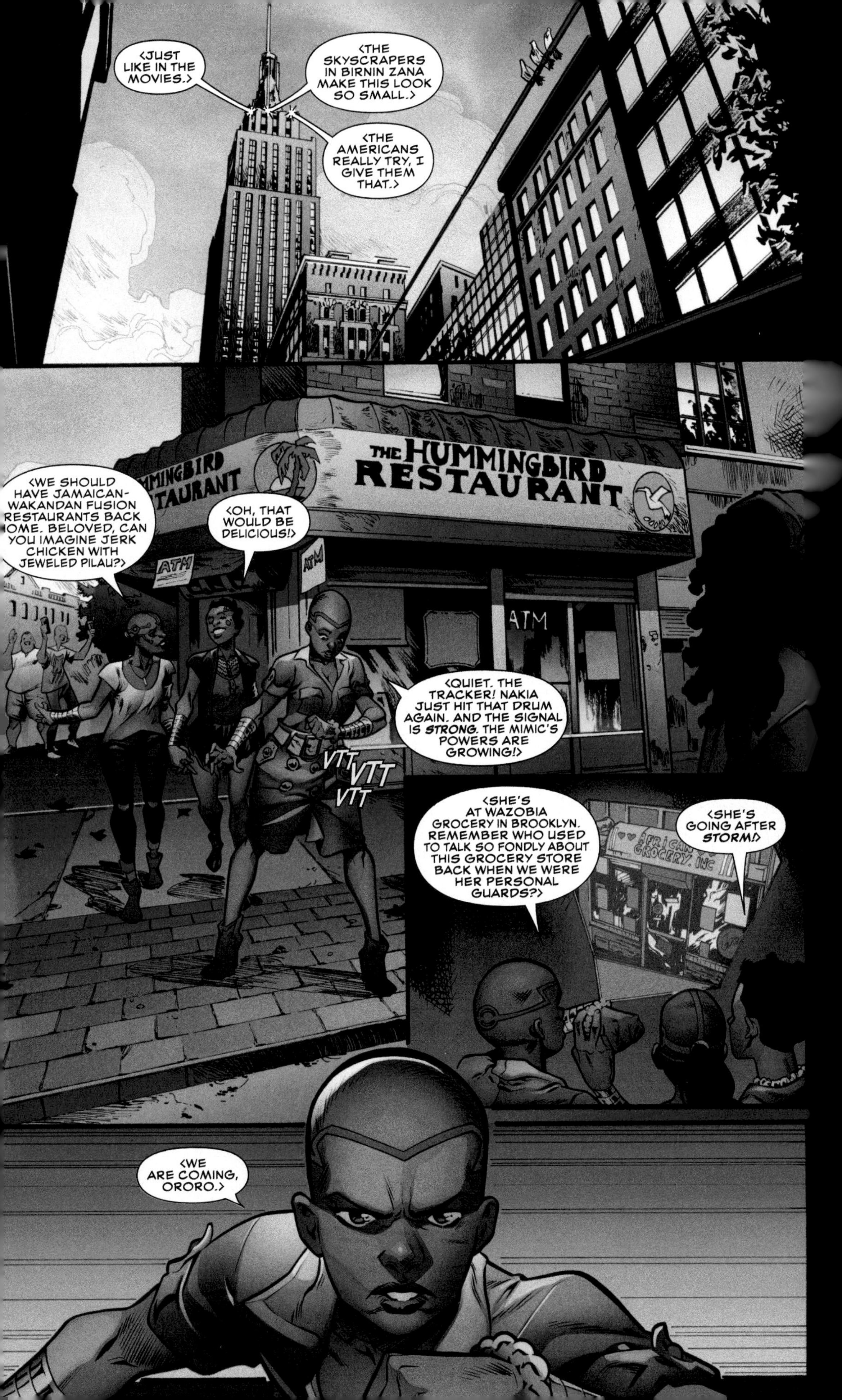
<JUST LIKE IN THE MOVIES.>
<THE SKYSCRAPERS IN BIRNIN ZANA MAKE THIS LOOK SO SMALL.>
<THE AMERICANS REALLY TRY, I GIVE THEM THAT.>
THE HUMMINGBIRD RESTAURANT
<WE SHOULD HAVE JAMAICAN-WAKANDAN FUSION RESTAURANTS BACK HOME. BELOVED, CAN YOU IMAGINE JERK CHICKEN WITH JEWELED PILAU?>
<OH, THAT WOULD BE DELICIOUS!>
ATM
<QUIET. THE TRACKER! NAKIA JUST HIT THAT DRUM AGAIN. AND THE SIGNAL IS STRONG. THE MIMIC'S POWERS ARE GROWING!>
VTT VTT VTT
<SHE'S AT WAZOBIA GROCERY IN BROOKLYN. REMEMBER WHO USED TO TALK SO FONDLY ABOUT THIS GROCERY STORE BACK WHEN WE WERE HER PERSONAL GUARDS?>
<SHE'S GOING AFTER STORM!>
<WE ARE COMING, ORORO.>

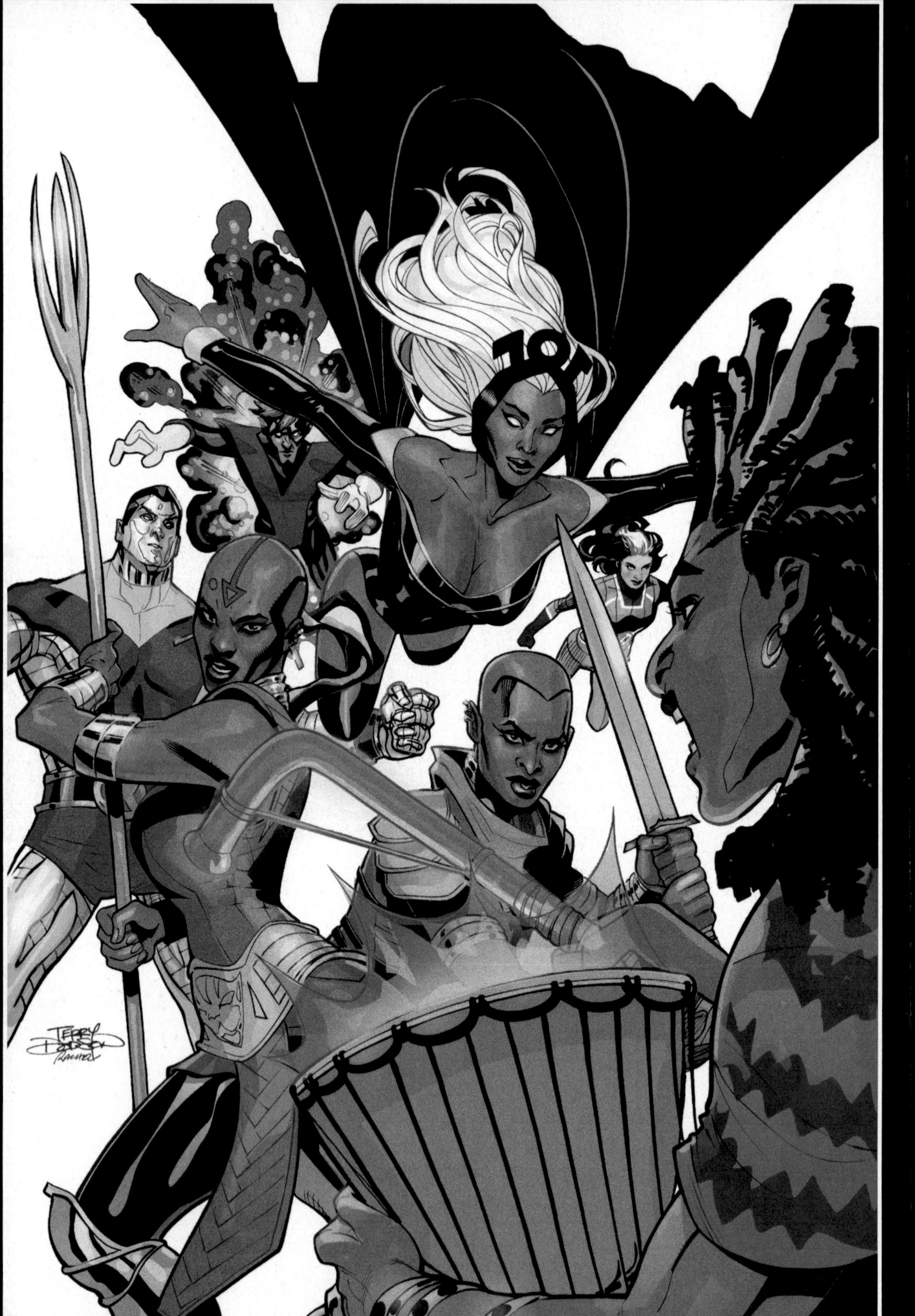

WAKANDA FOREVER: X-MEN

ECHO CHAMBER

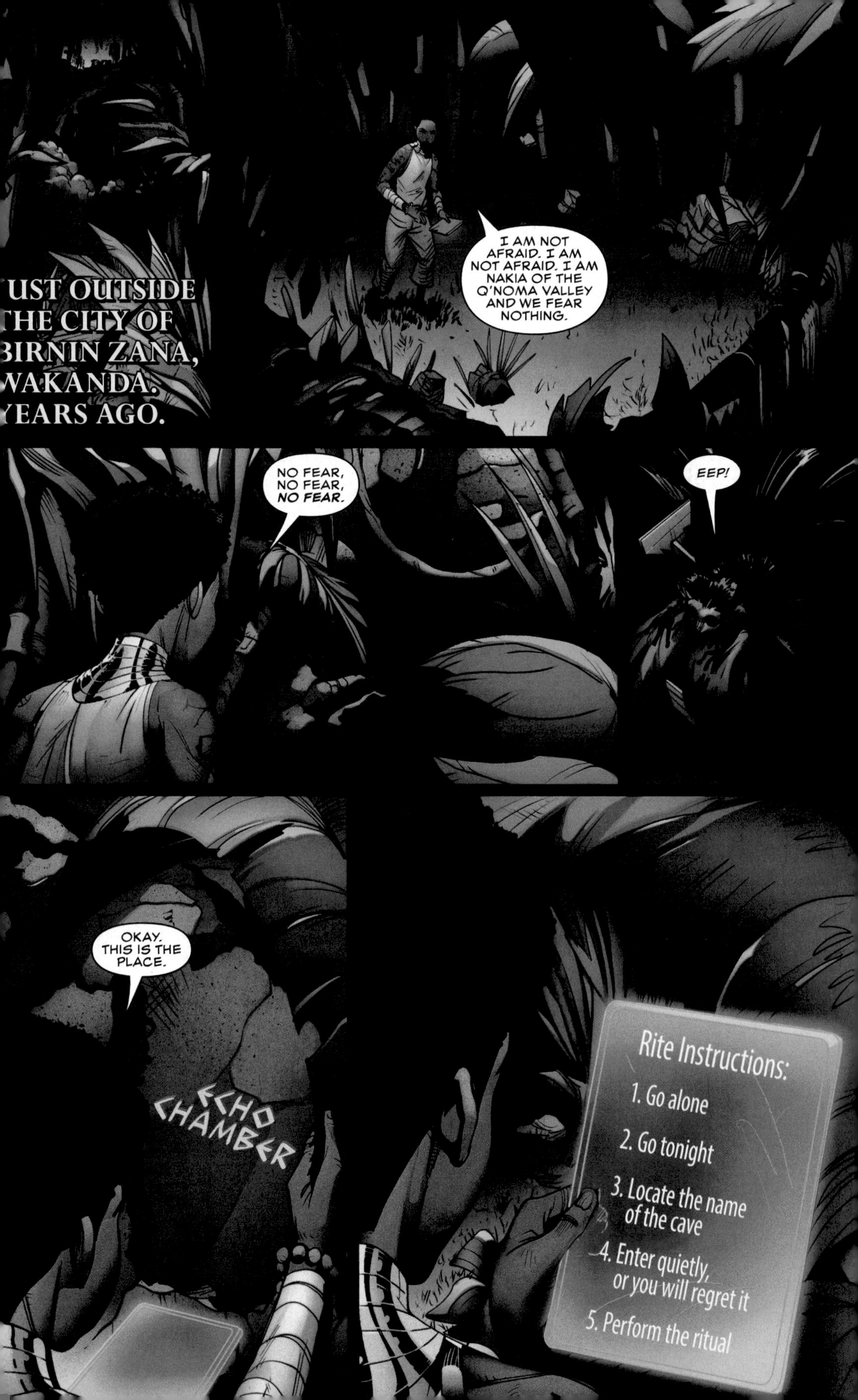

JUST OUTSIDE THE CITY OF BIRNIN ZANA, WAKANDA. YEARS AGO.
I AM NOT AFRAID. I AM NOT AFRAID. I AM NAKIA OF THE Q'NOMA VALLEY AND WE FEAR NOTHING.
NO FEAR, NO FEAR, NO FEAR.
EEP!
OKAY. THIS IS THE PLACE.
ECHO CHAMBER
Rite Instructions:
1. Go alone
2. Go tonight
3. Locate the name of the cave
4. Enter quietly, or you will regret it
5. Perform the ritual

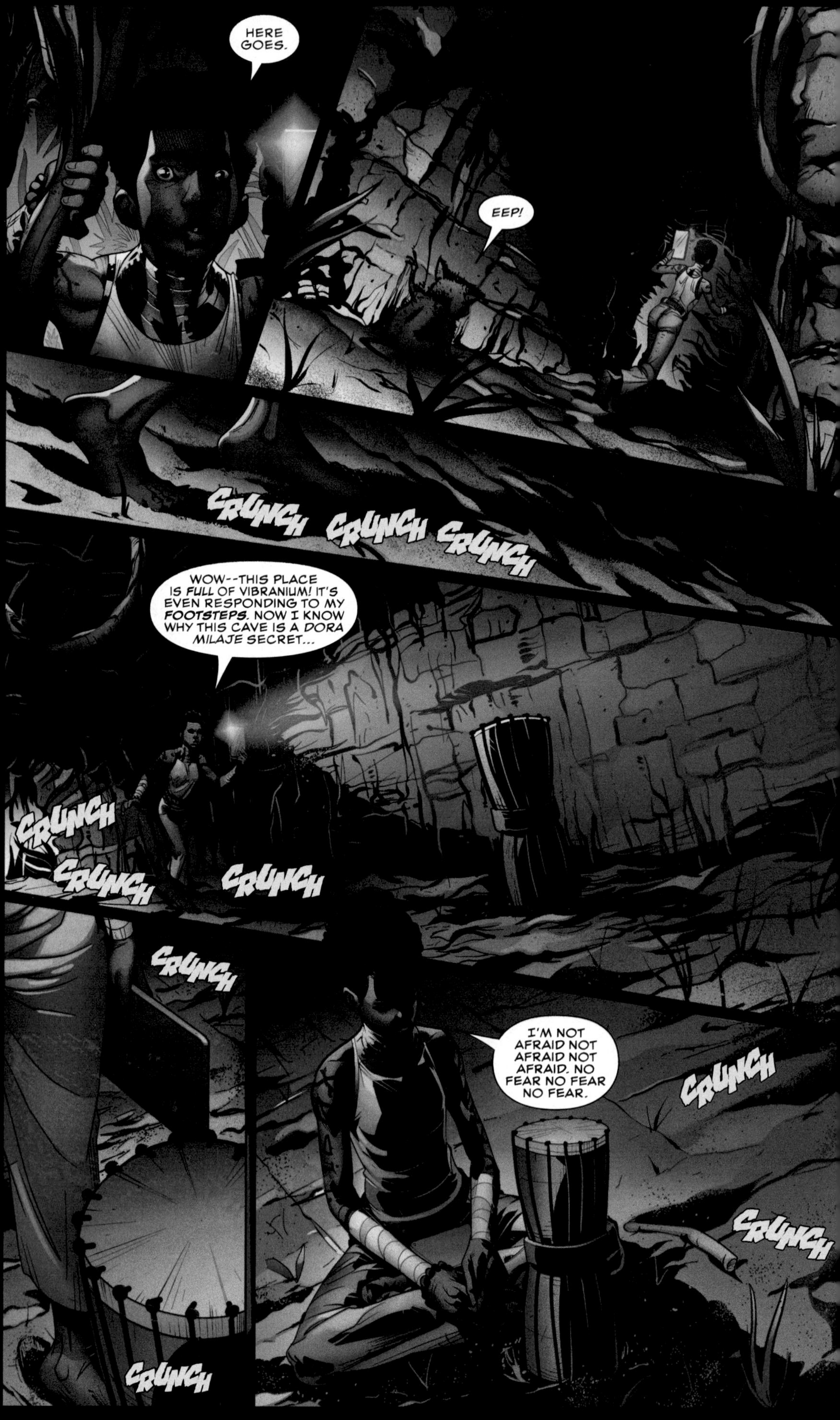
HERE GOES.
EEP!
CRUNCH CRUNCH CRUNCH
WOW--THIS PLACE IS FULL OF VIBRANIUM! IT'S EVEN RESPONDING TO MY FOOTSTEPS. NOW I KNOW WHY THIS CAVE IS A DORA MILAJE SECRET...
CRUNCH
CRUNCH
CRUNCH
CRUNCH
I'M NOT AFRAID NOT AFRAID NOT AFRAID. NO FEAR NO FEAR NO FEAR.
CRUNCH
CRUNCH
CRUNCH

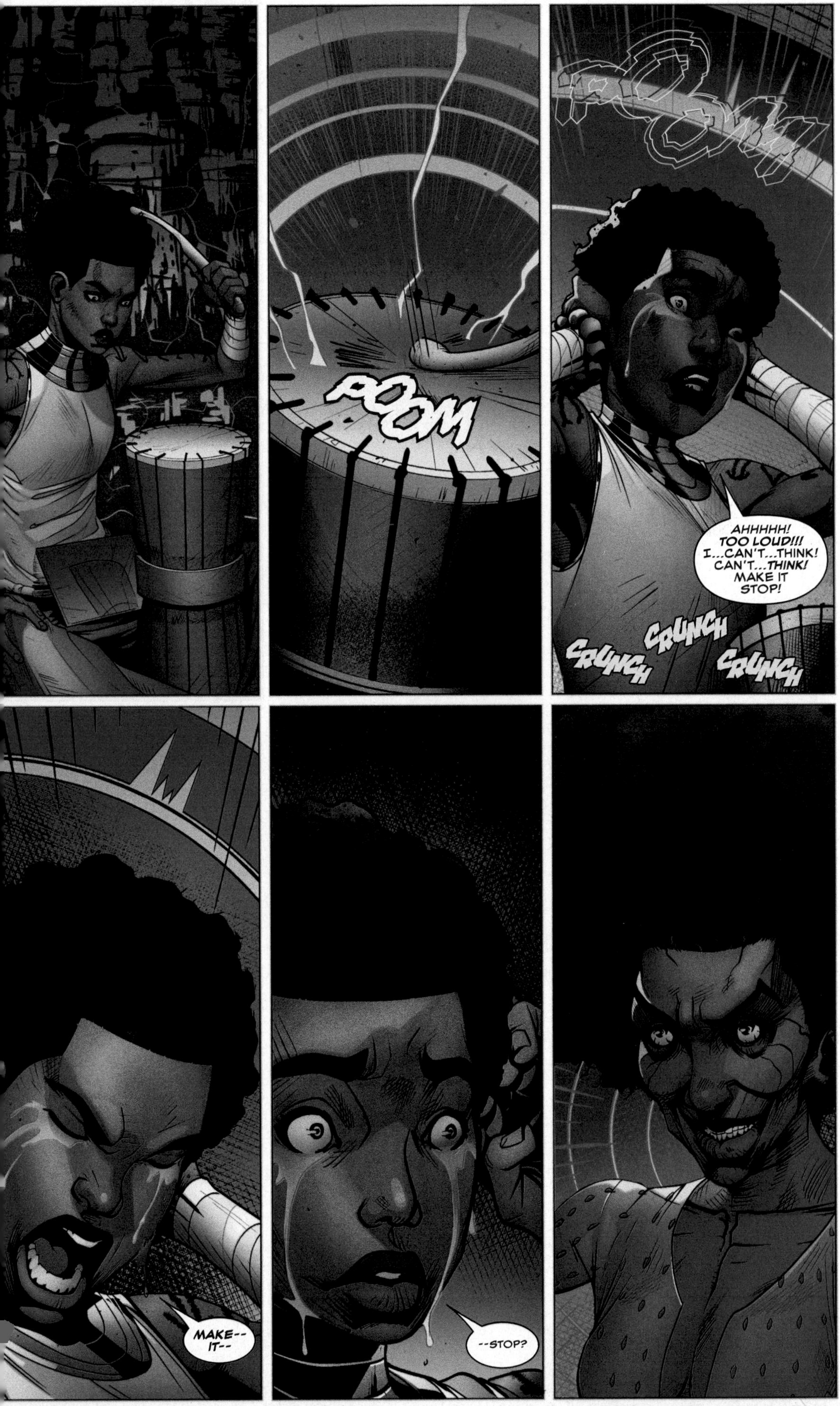
POOM
POOM
AHHHHH! TOO LOUD!!! I...CAN'T...THINK! CAN'T...THINK! MAKE IT STOP!
CRUNCH
CRUNCH
CRUNCH
MAKE-- IT--
--STOP?

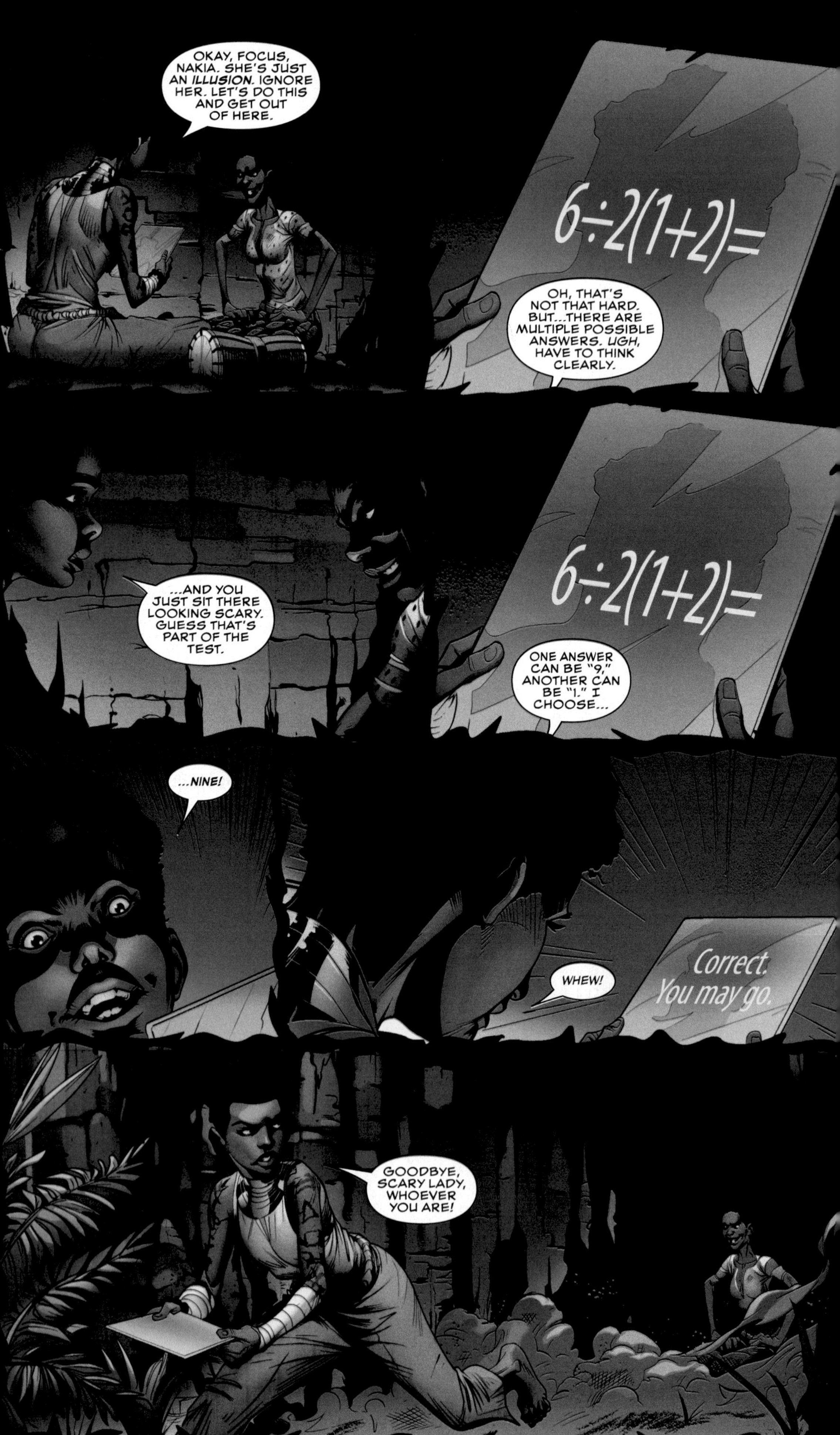

OKAY, FOCUS, NAKIA. SHE'S JUST AN *ILLUSION*. IGNORE HER. LET'S DO THIS AND GET OUT OF HERE.
6÷2(1+2)=
OH, THAT'S NOT THAT HARD. BUT...THERE ARE MULTIPLE POSSIBLE ANSWERS. *UGH*, HAVE TO THINK CLEARLY.
...AND YOU JUST SIT THERE LOOKING SCARY. GUESS THAT'S PART OF THE TEST.
6÷2(1+2)=
ONE ANSWER CAN BE "9," ANOTHER CAN BE "1." I CHOOSE...
...NINE!
WHEW!
Correct. You may go.
GOODBYE, SCARY LADY, WHOEVER YOU ARE!

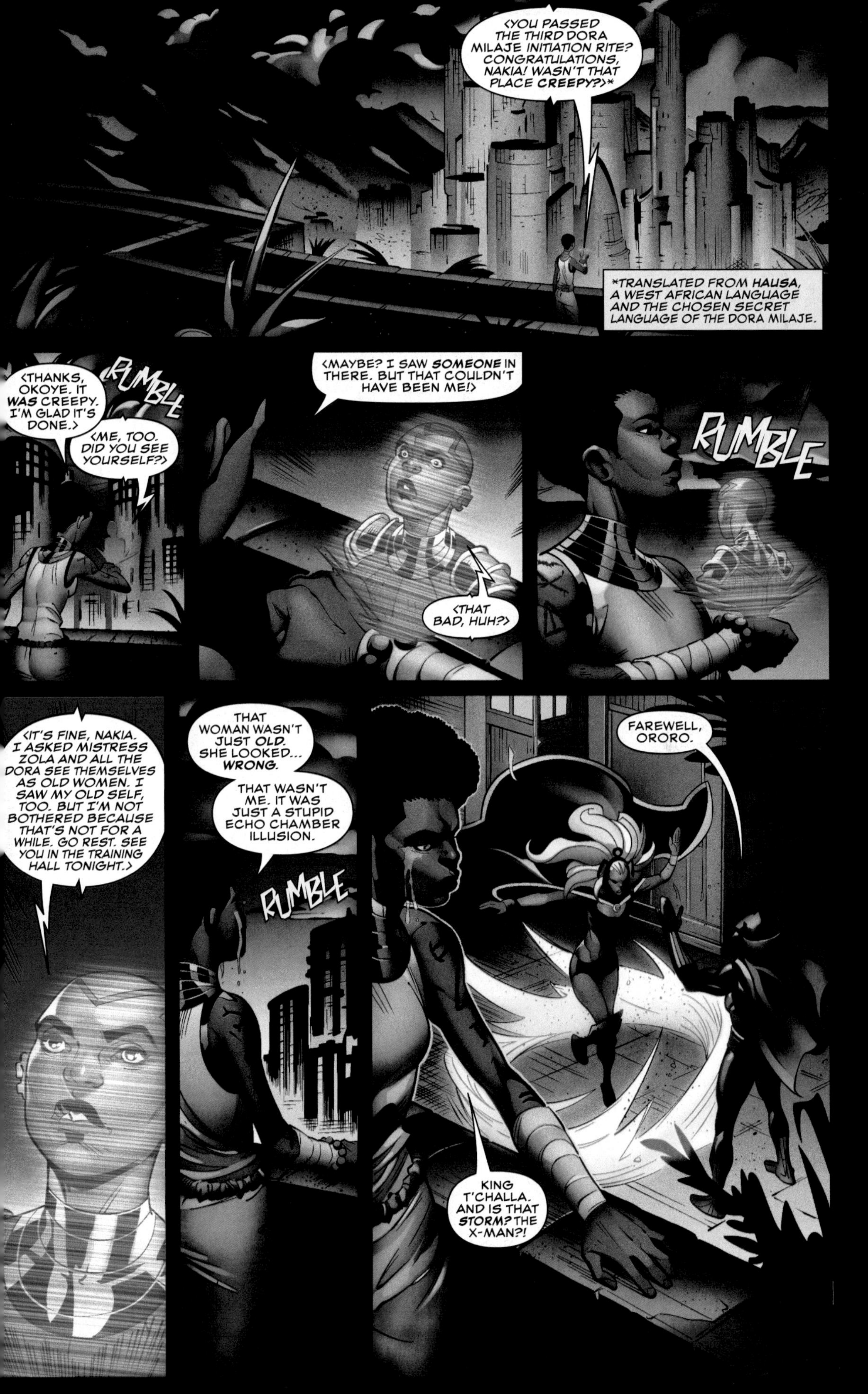

<YOU PASSED THE THIRD DORA MILAJE INITIATION RITE? CONGRATULATIONS, NAKIA! WASN'T THAT PLACE CREEPY?>*
*TRANSLATED FROM HAUSA, A WEST AFRICAN LANGUAGE AND THE CHOSEN SECRET LANGUAGE OF THE DORA MILAJE.
<THANKS, OKOYE. IT WAS CREEPY. I'M GLAD IT'S DONE.>
RUMBLE
<ME, TOO. DID YOU SEE YOURSELF?>
<MAYBE? I SAW SOMEONE IN THERE. BUT THAT COULDN'T HAVE BEEN ME!>
<THAT BAD, HUH?>
RUMBLE
<IT'S FINE, NAKIA. I ASKED MISTRESS ZOLA AND ALL THE DORA SEE THEMSELVES AS OLD WOMEN. I SAW MY OLD SELF, TOO. BUT I'M NOT BOTHERED BECAUSE THAT'S NOT FOR A WHILE. GO REST. SEE YOU IN THE TRAINING HALL TONIGHT.>
THAT WOMAN WASN'T JUST OLD. SHE LOOKED... WRONG.
THAT WASN'T ME. IT WAS JUST A STUPID ECHO CHAMBER ILLUSION.
RUMBLE
FAREWELL, ORORO.
KING T'CHALLA. AND IS THAT STORM? THE X-MAN?!

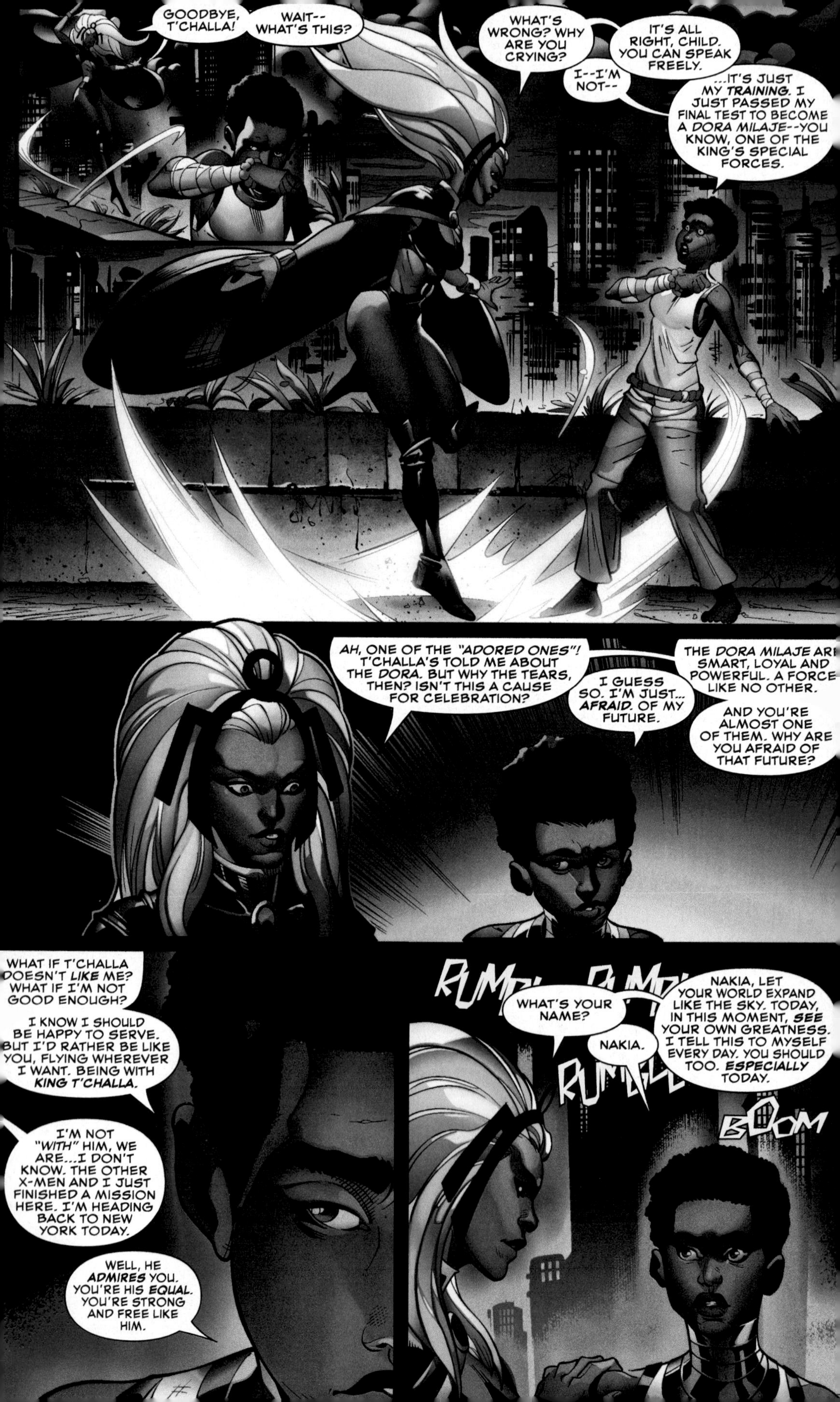
GOODBYE, T'CHALLA!
WAIT-- WHAT'S THIS?
WHAT'S WRONG? WHY ARE YOU CRYING?
I--I'M NOT--
IT'S ALL RIGHT, CHILD. YOU CAN SPEAK FREELY.
...IT'S JUST MY TRAINING. I JUST PASSED MY FINAL TEST TO BECOME A DORA MILAJE--YOU KNOW, ONE OF THE KING'S SPECIAL FORCES.
AH, ONE OF THE "ADORED ONES"! T'CHALLA'S TOLD ME ABOUT THE DORA. BUT WHY THE TEARS, THEN? ISN'T THIS A CAUSE FOR CELEBRATION?
I GUESS SO. I'M JUST... AFRAID. OF MY FUTURE.
THE DORA MILAJE ARE SMART, LOYAL AND POWERFUL. A FORCE LIKE NO OTHER.
AND YOU'RE ALMOST ONE OF THEM. WHY ARE YOU AFRAID OF THAT FUTURE?
WHAT IF T'CHALLA DOESN'T LIKE ME? WHAT IF I'M NOT GOOD ENOUGH?
I KNOW I SHOULD BE HAPPY TO SERVE. BUT I'D RATHER BE LIKE YOU, FLYING WHEREVER I WANT. BEING WITH KING T'CHALLA.
I'M NOT "WITH" HIM, WE ARE...I DON'T KNOW. THE OTHER X-MEN AND I JUST FINISHED A MISSION HERE. I'M HEADING BACK TO NEW YORK TODAY.
WELL, HE ADMIRES YOU. YOU'RE HIS EQUAL. YOU'RE STRONG AND FREE LIKE HIM.
WHAT'S YOUR NAME?
NAKIA.
NAKIA, LET YOUR WORLD EXPAND LIKE THE SKY. TODAY, IN THIS MOMENT, SEE YOUR OWN GREATNESS. I TELL THIS TO MYSELF EVERY DAY. YOU SHOULD TOO. ESPECIALLY TODAY.
BOOM

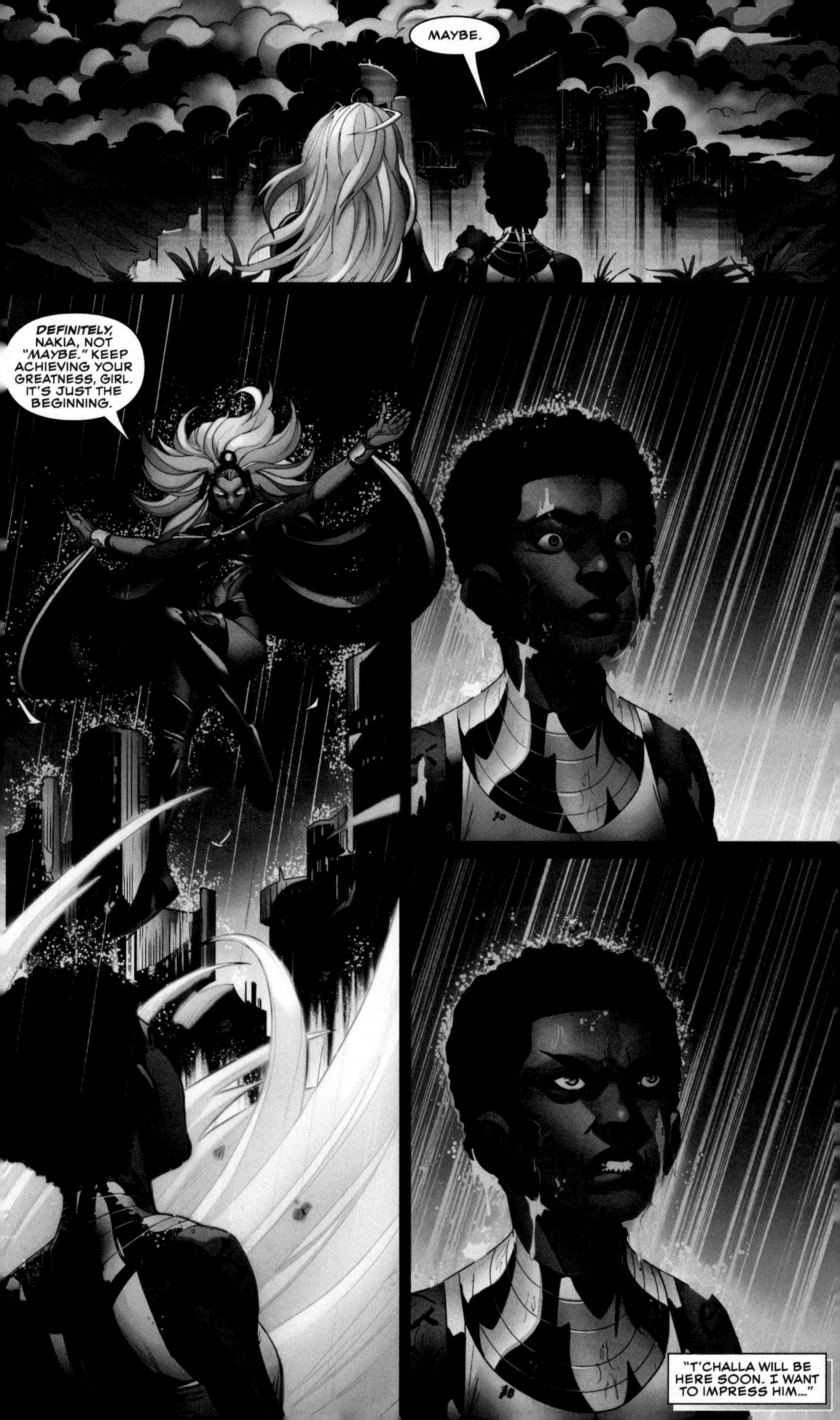
MAYBE.
DEFINITELY, NAKIA, NOT "*MAYBE.*" KEEP ACHIEVING YOUR GREATNESS, GIRL. IT'S JUST THE BEGINNING.
"T'CHALLA WILL BE HERE SOON. I WANT TO IMPRESS HIM..."

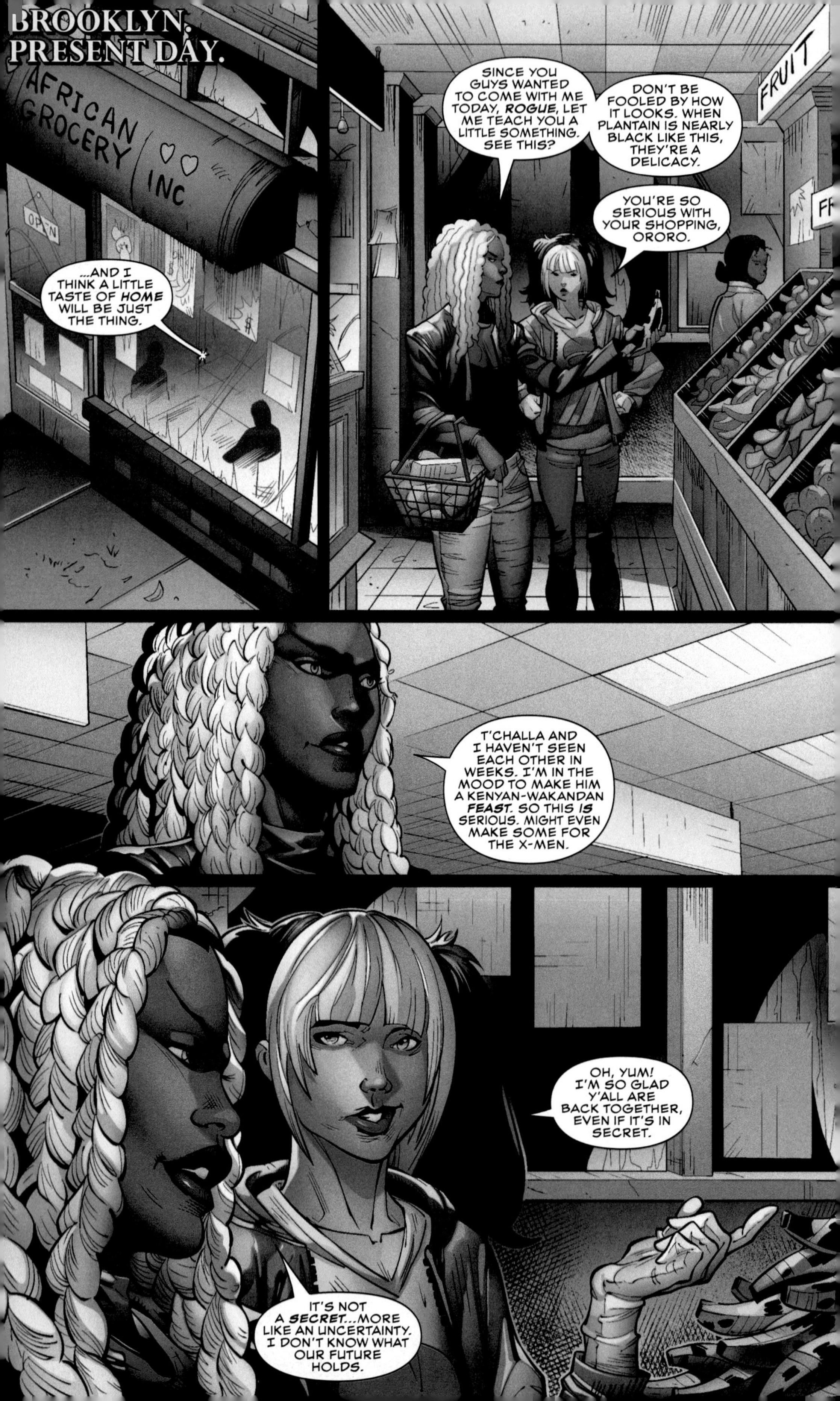
BROOKLYN. PRESENT DAY.
AFRICAN GROCERY INC
OPEN
...AND I THINK A LITTLE TASTE OF HOME WILL BE JUST THE THING.
FRUIT
SINCE YOU GUYS WANTED TO COME WITH ME TODAY, ROGUE, LET ME TEACH YOU A LITTLE SOMETHING. SEE THIS?
DON'T BE FOOLED BY HOW IT LOOKS. WHEN PLANTAIN IS NEARLY BLACK LIKE THIS, THEY'RE A DELICACY.
YOU'RE SO SERIOUS WITH YOUR SHOPPING, ORORO.
T'CHALLA AND I HAVEN'T SEEN EACH OTHER IN WEEKS. I'M IN THE MOOD TO MAKE HIM A KENYAN-WAKANDAN FEAST. SO THIS IS SERIOUS. MIGHT EVEN MAKE SOME FOR THE X-MEN.
OH, YUM! I'M SO GLAD Y'ALL ARE BACK TOGETHER, EVEN IF IT'S IN SECRET.
IT'S NOT A SECRET...MORE LIKE AN UNCERTAINTY. I DON'T KNOW WHAT OUR FUTURE HOLDS.

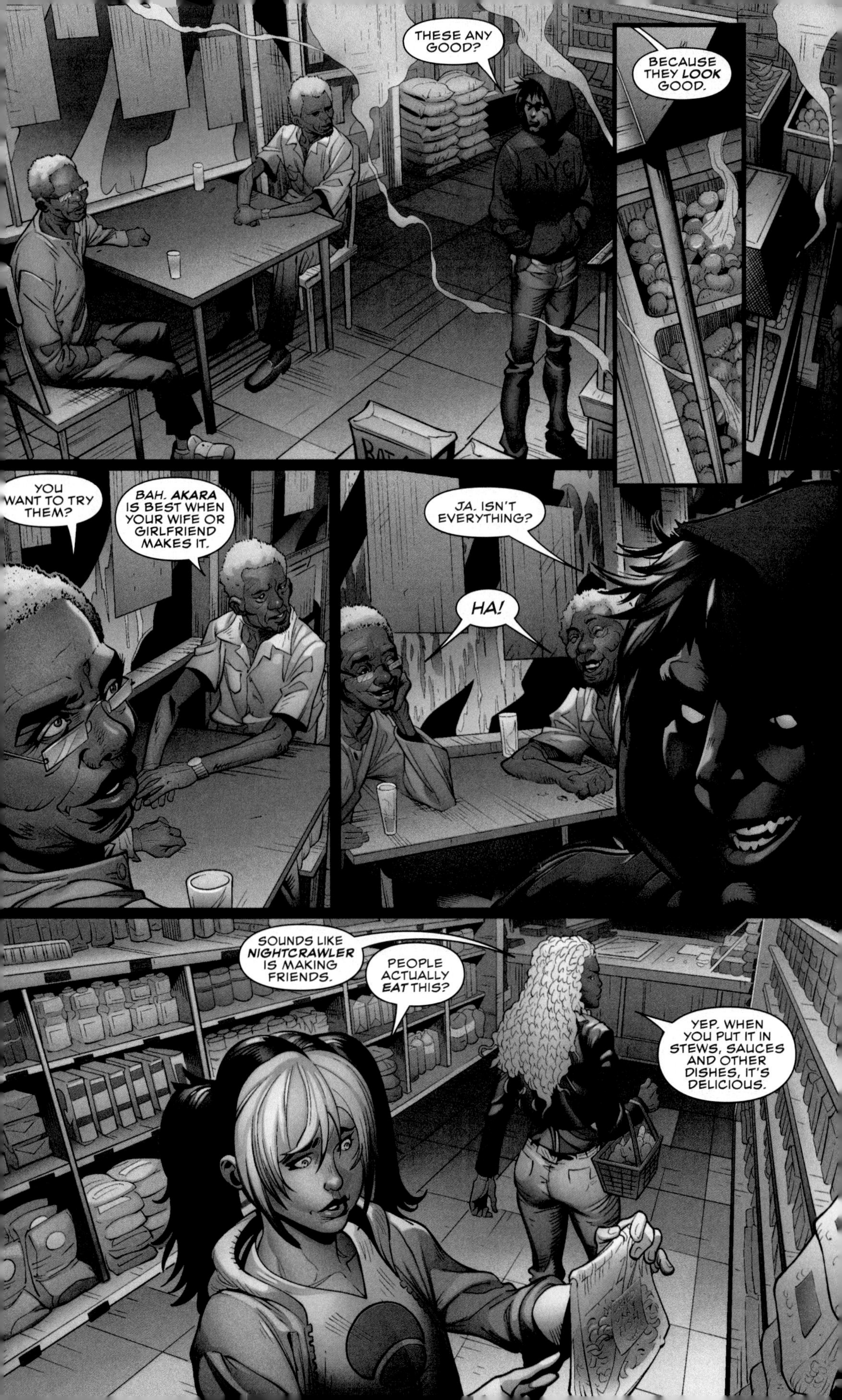

THESE ANY GOOD?
BECAUSE THEY LOOK GOOD.
YOU WANT TO TRY THEM?
BAH. AKARA IS BEST WHEN YOUR WIFE OR GIRLFRIEND MAKES IT.
JA. ISN'T EVERYTHING?
HA!
SOUNDS LIKE NIGHTCRAWLER IS MAKING FRIENDS.
PEOPLE ACTUALLY EAT THIS?
YEP. WHEN YOU PUT IT IN STEWS, SAUCES AND OTHER DISHES, IT'S DELICIOUS.

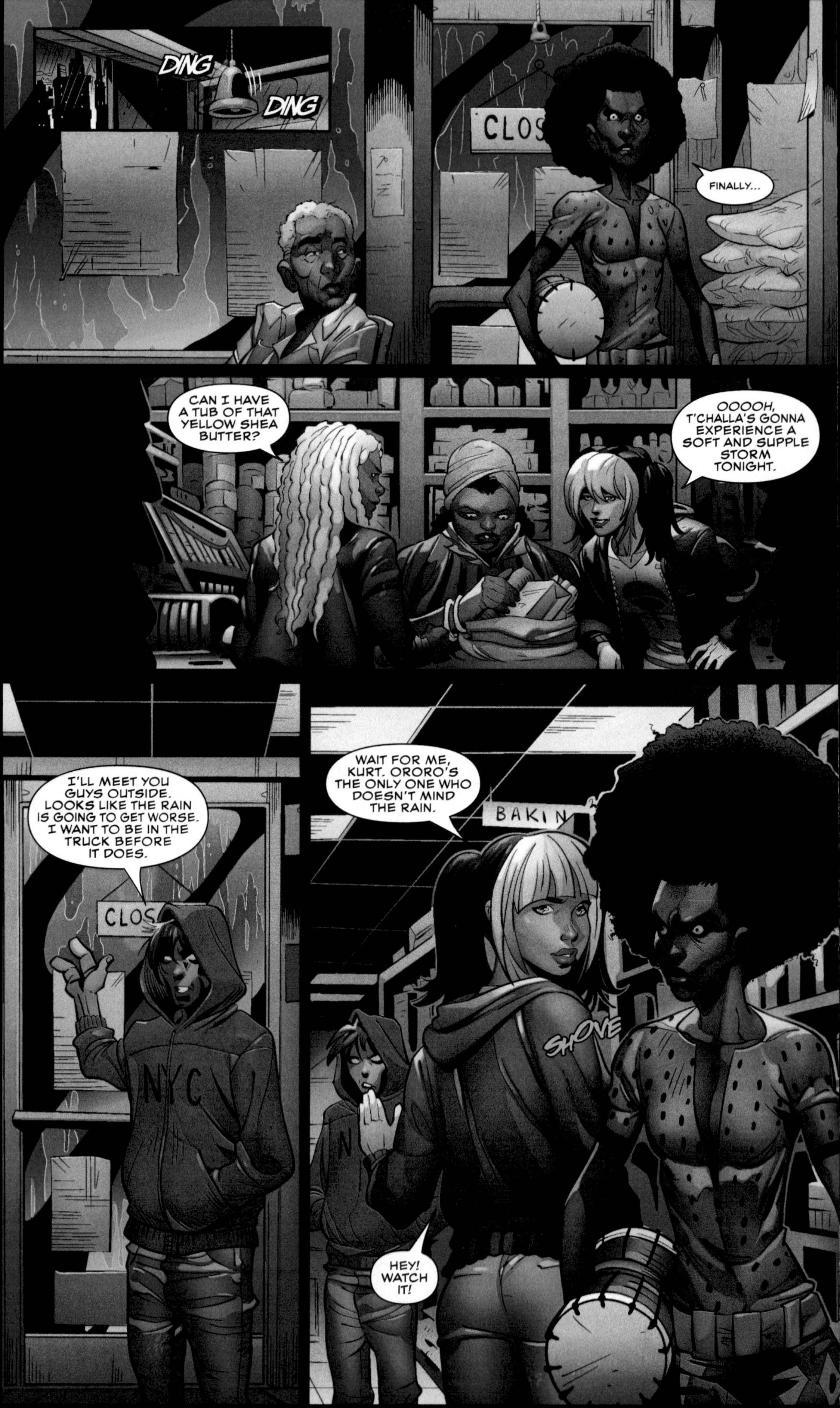
DING
DING
CLOS
FINALLY...
CAN I HAVE A TUB OF THAT YELLOW SHEA BUTTER?
OOOOH, T'CHALLA'S GONNA EXPERIENCE A SOFT AND SUPPLE STORM TONIGHT.
I'LL MEET YOU GUYS OUTSIDE. LOOKS LIKE THE RAIN IS GOING TO GET WORSE. I WANT TO BE IN THE TRUCK BEFORE IT DOES.
CLOS
WAIT FOR ME, KURT. ORORO'S THE ONLY ONE WHO DOESN'T MIND THE RAIN.
BAKIN
SHOVE
HEY! WATCH IT!

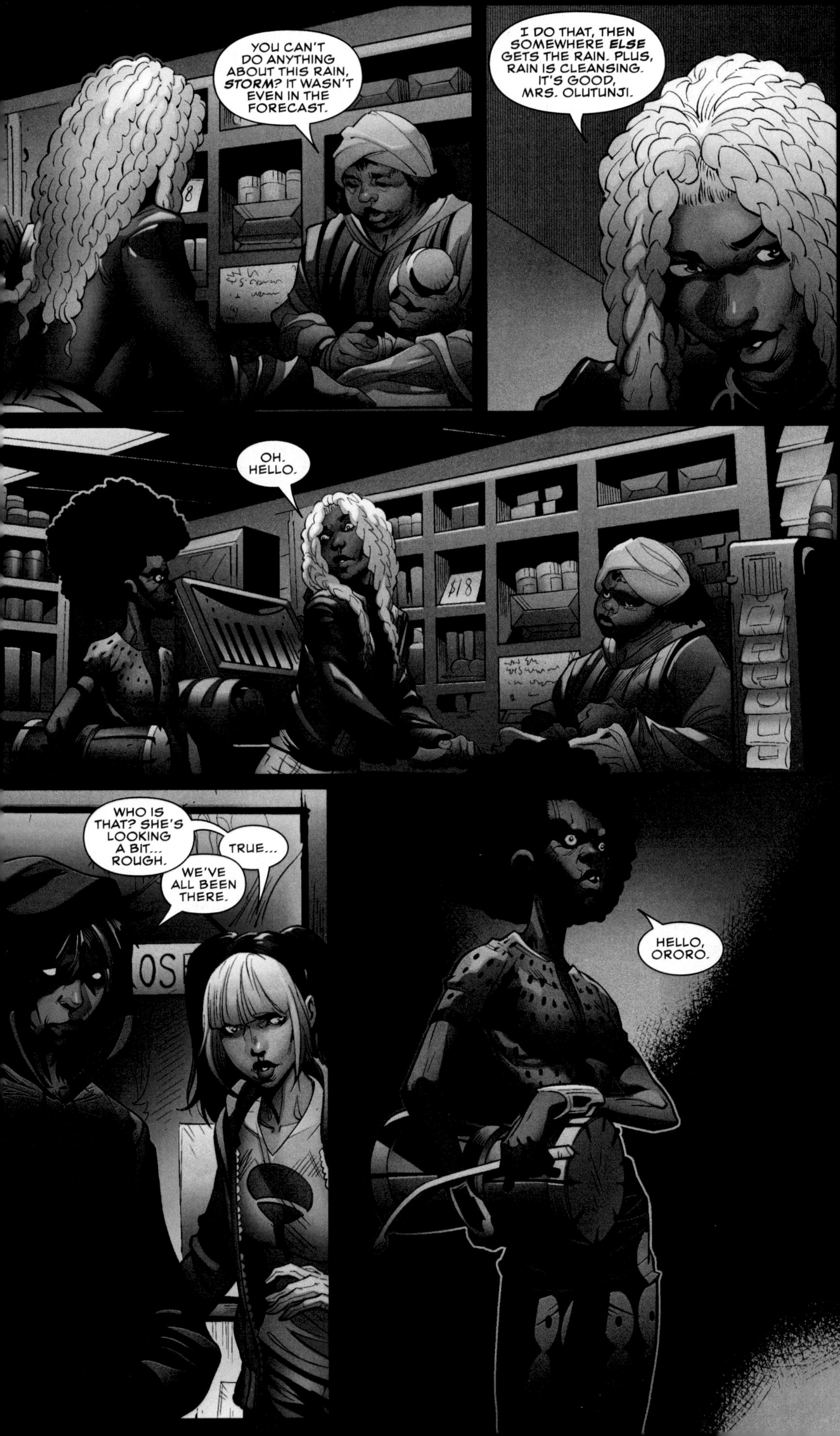
YOU CAN'T DO ANYTHING ABOUT THIS RAIN, STORM? IT WASN'T EVEN IN THE FORECAST.
I DO THAT, THEN SOMEWHERE ELSE GETS THE RAIN. PLUS, RAIN IS CLEANSING. IT'S GOOD, MRS. OLUTUNJI.
$18
OH. HELLO.
WHO IS THAT? SHE'S LOOKING A BIT... ROUGH.
TRUE...
WE'VE ALL BEEN THERE.
HELLO, ORORO.

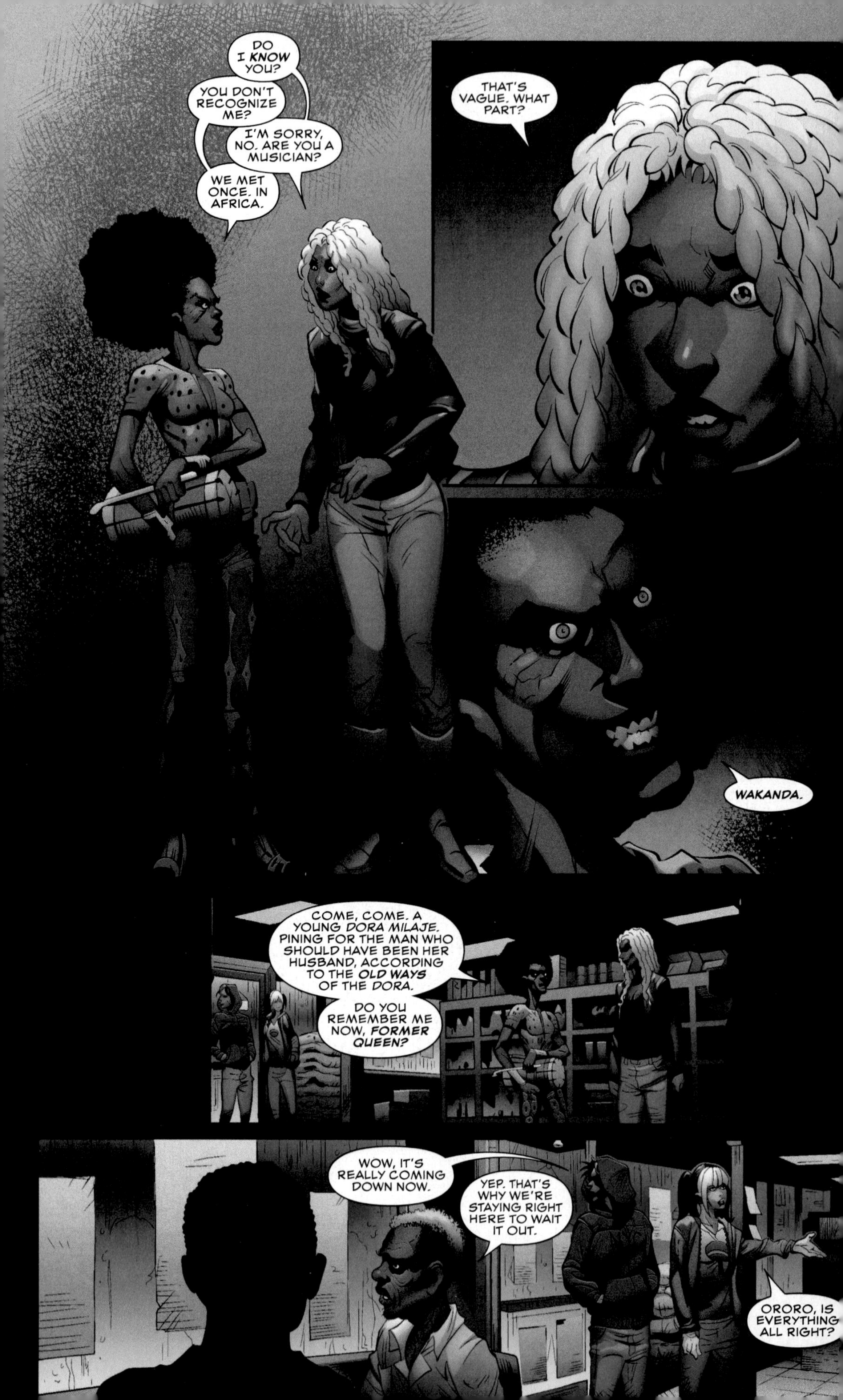
DO I KNOW YOU?
YOU DON'T RECOGNIZE ME?
I'M SORRY, NO. ARE YOU A MUSICIAN?
WE MET ONCE. IN AFRICA.
THAT'S VAGUE. WHAT PART?
WAKANDA.
COME, COME. A YOUNG DORA MILAJE. PINING FOR THE MAN WHO SHOULD HAVE BEEN HER HUSBAND, ACCORDING TO THE OLD WAYS OF THE DORA.
DO YOU REMEMBER ME NOW, FORMER QUEEN?
WOW, IT'S REALLY COMING DOWN NOW.
YEP. THAT'S WHY WE'RE STAYING RIGHT HERE TO WAIT IT OUT.
ORORO, IS EVERYTHING ALL RIGHT?

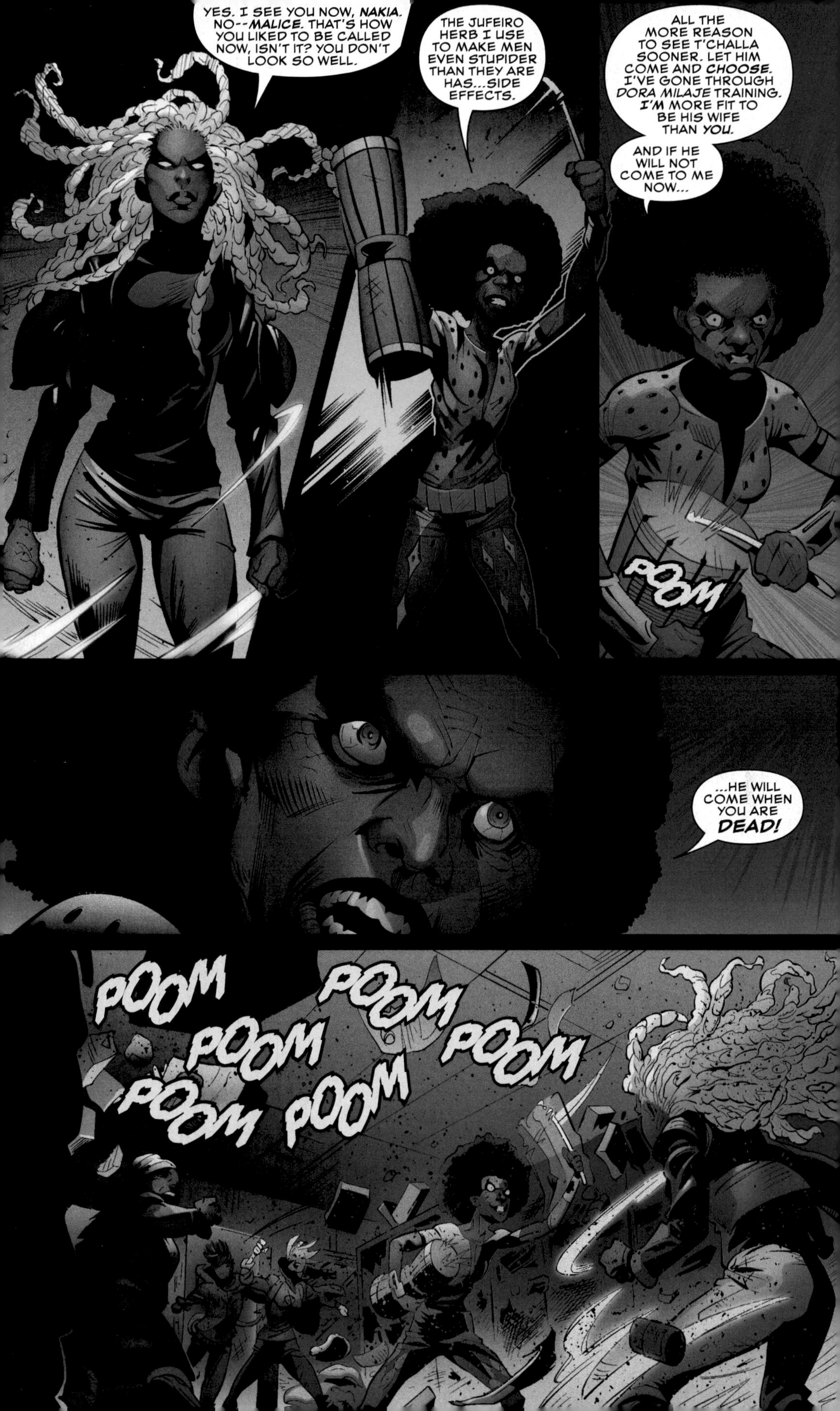

YES. I SEE YOU NOW, NAKIA. NO--MALICE. THAT'S HOW YOU LIKED TO BE CALLED NOW, ISN'T IT? YOU DON'T LOOK SO WELL.
THE JUFEIRO HERB I USE TO MAKE MEN EVEN STUPIDER THAN THEY ARE HAS...SIDE EFFECTS.
ALL THE MORE REASON TO SEE T'CHALLA SOONER. LET HIM COME AND CHOOSE. I'VE GONE THROUGH DORA MILAJE TRAINING. I'M MORE FIT TO BE HIS WIFE THAN YOU.
AND IF HE WILL NOT COME TO ME NOW...
POOM
...HE WILL COME WHEN YOU ARE DEAD!
POOM
POOM
POOM
POOM
POOM
POOM

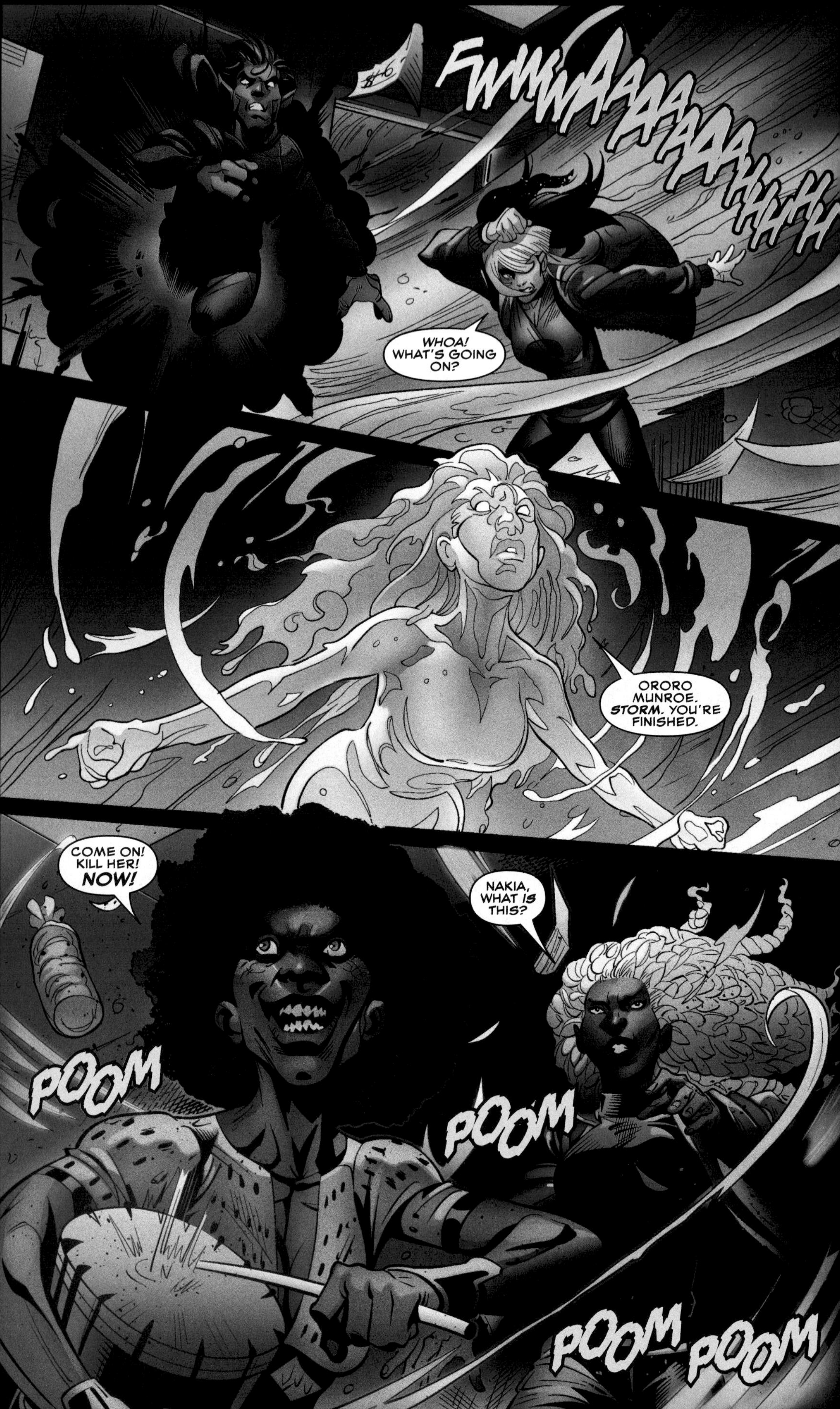
FWWWAAAAAAAAHHHHH
WHOA! WHAT'S GOING ON?
ORORO MUNROE. STORM. YOU'RE FINISHED.
COME ON! KILL HER! NOW!
NAKIA, WHAT IS THIS?
POOM
POOM
POOM POOM

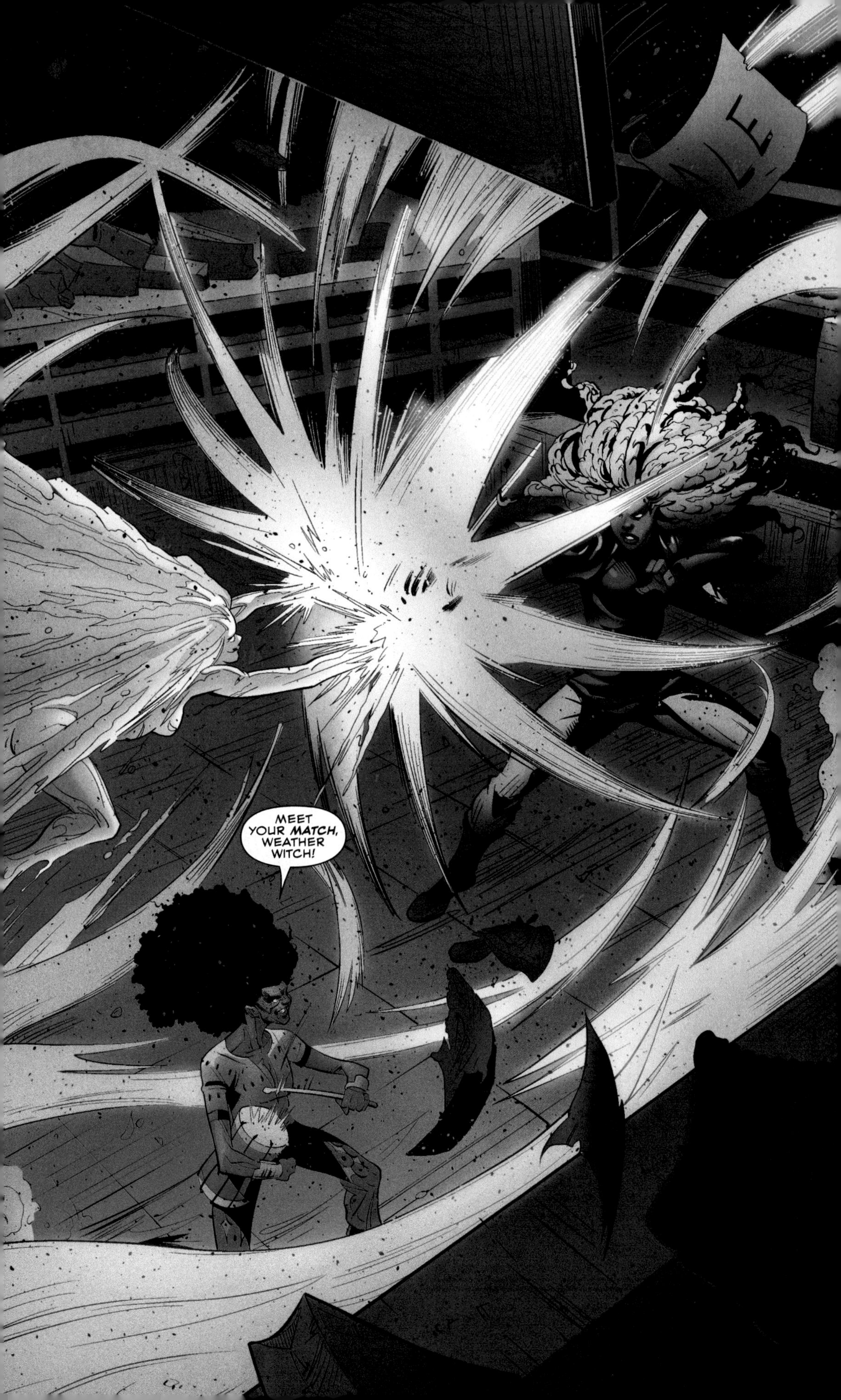
MEET YOUR *MATCH*, WEATHER WITCH!

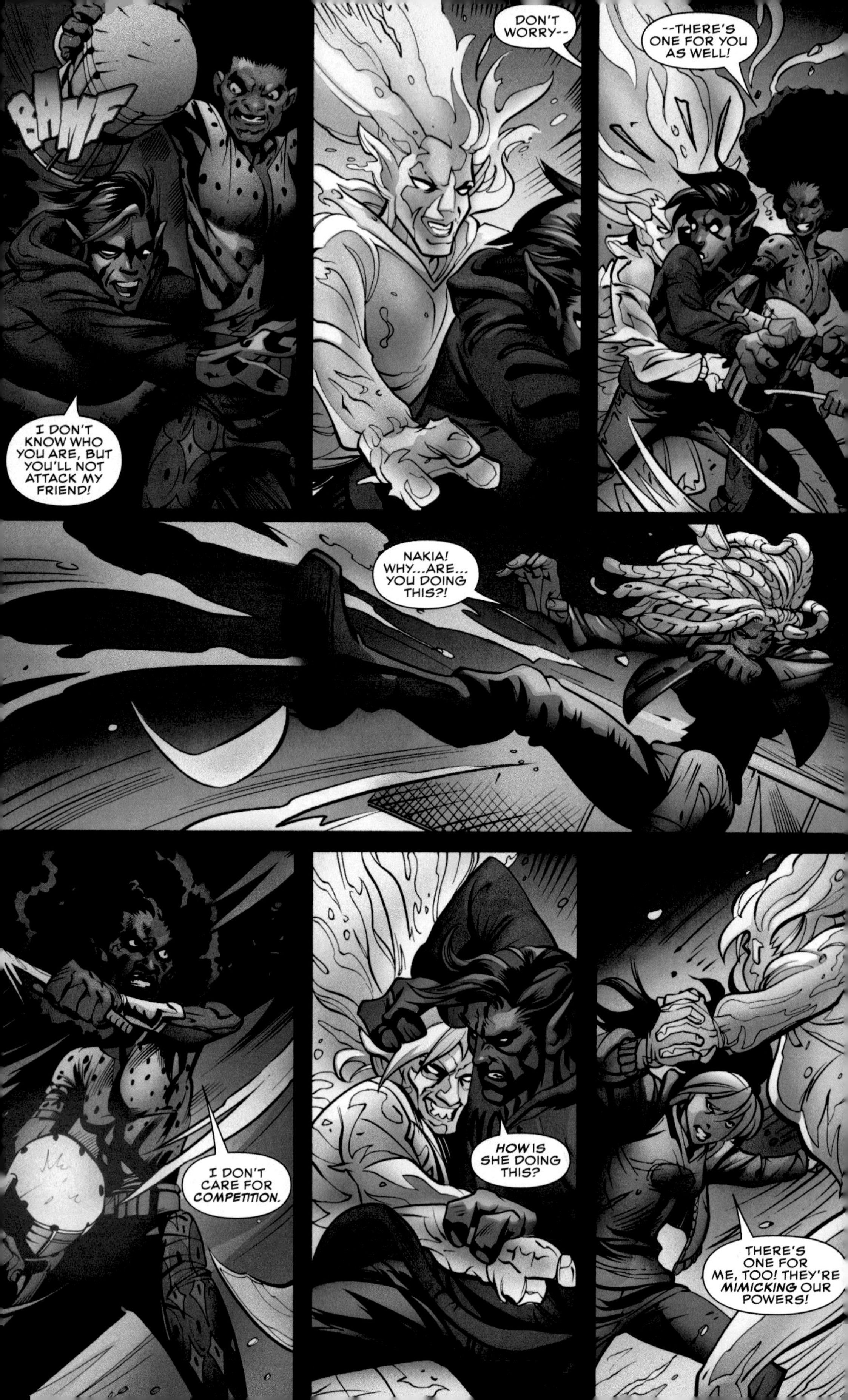
BAMF
I DON'T KNOW WHO YOU ARE, BUT YOU'LL NOT ATTACK MY FRIEND!
DON'T WORRY--
--THERE'S ONE FOR YOU AS WELL!
NAKIA! WHY...ARE... YOU DOING THIS?!
I DON'T CARE FOR COMPETITION.
HOW IS SHE DOING THIS?
THERE'S ONE FOR ME, TOO! THEY'RE MIMICKING OUR POWERS!

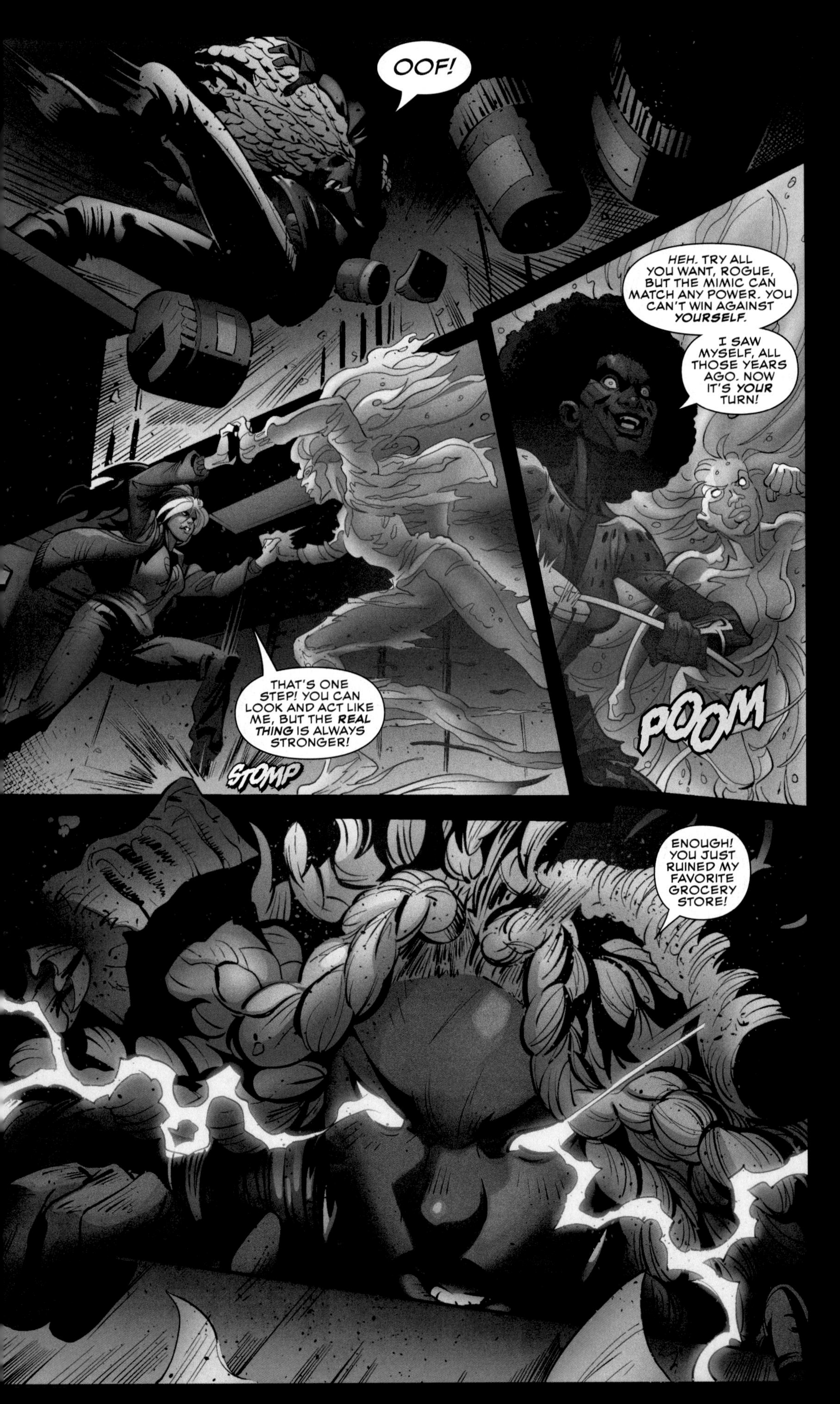
OOF!
HEH. TRY ALL YOU WANT, ROGUE, BUT THE MIMIC CAN MATCH ANY POWER. YOU CAN'T WIN AGAINST YOURSELF.
I SAW MYSELF, ALL THOSE YEARS AGO. NOW IT'S YOUR TURN!
THAT'S ONE STEP! YOU CAN LOOK AND ACT LIKE ME, BUT THE REAL THING IS ALWAYS STRONGER!
STOMP
POOM
ENOUGH! YOU JUST RUINED MY FAVORITE GROCERY STORE!

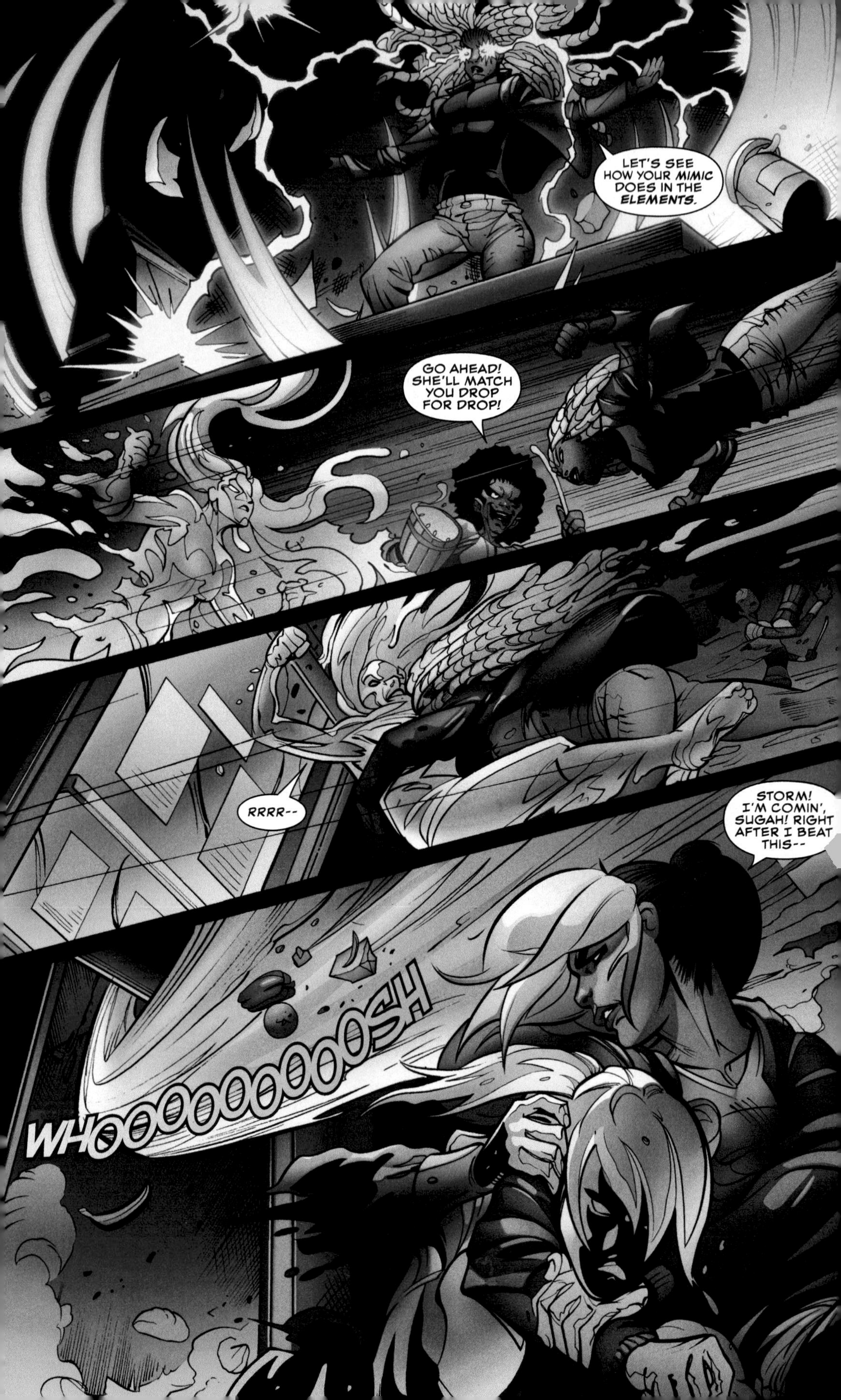
LET'S SEE HOW YOUR MIMIC DOES IN THE ELEMENTS.
GO AHEAD! SHE'LL MATCH YOU DROP FOR DROP!
RRRR--
STORM! I'M COMIN', SUGAH! RIGHT AFTER I BEAT THIS--
WHOOOOOOOOOOOSH

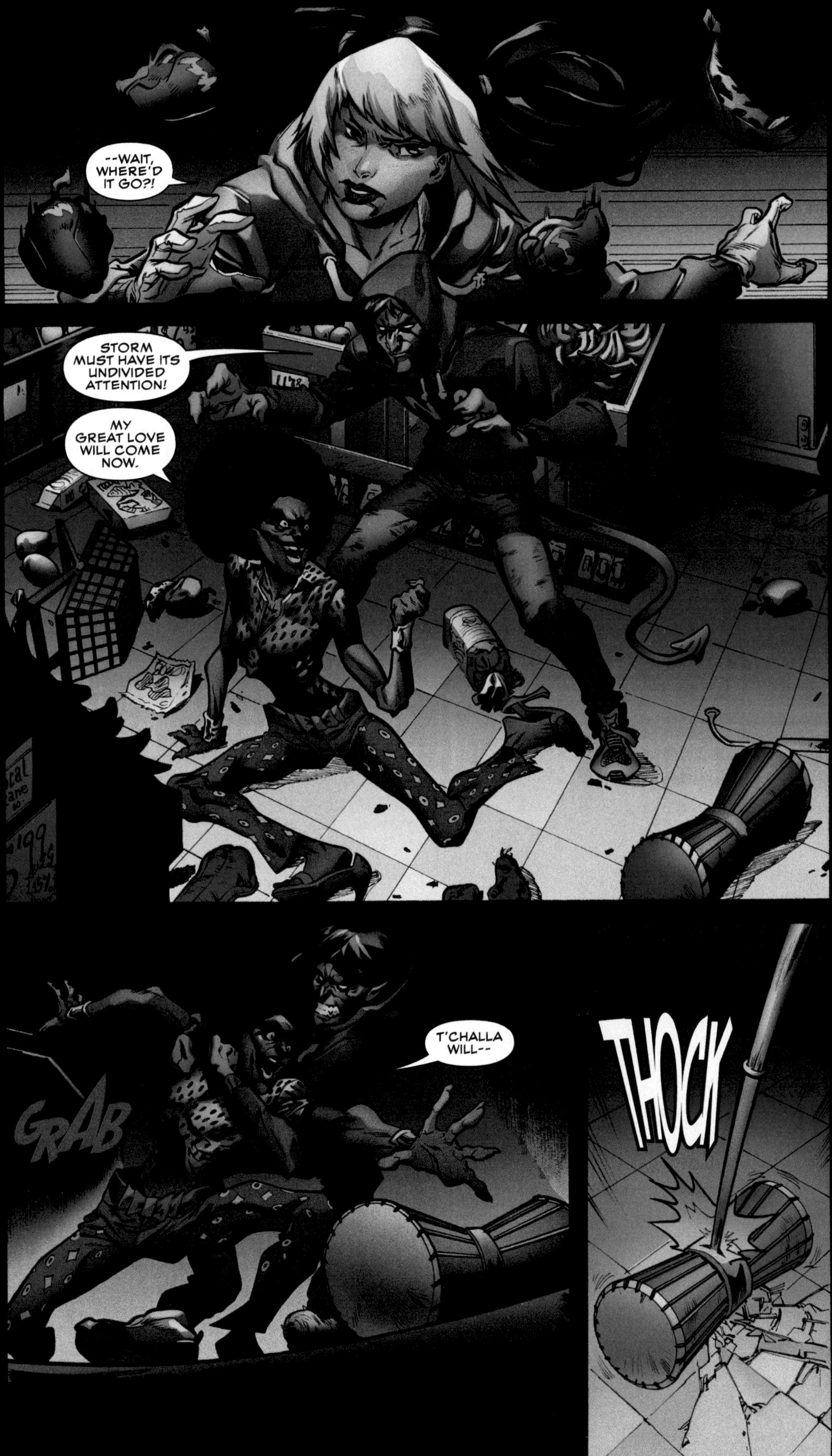
--WAIT, WHERE'D IT GO?!
STORM MUST HAVE ITS UNDIVIDED ATTENTION!
MY GREAT LOVE WILL COME NOW.
GRAB
T'CHALLA WILL--
THOCK

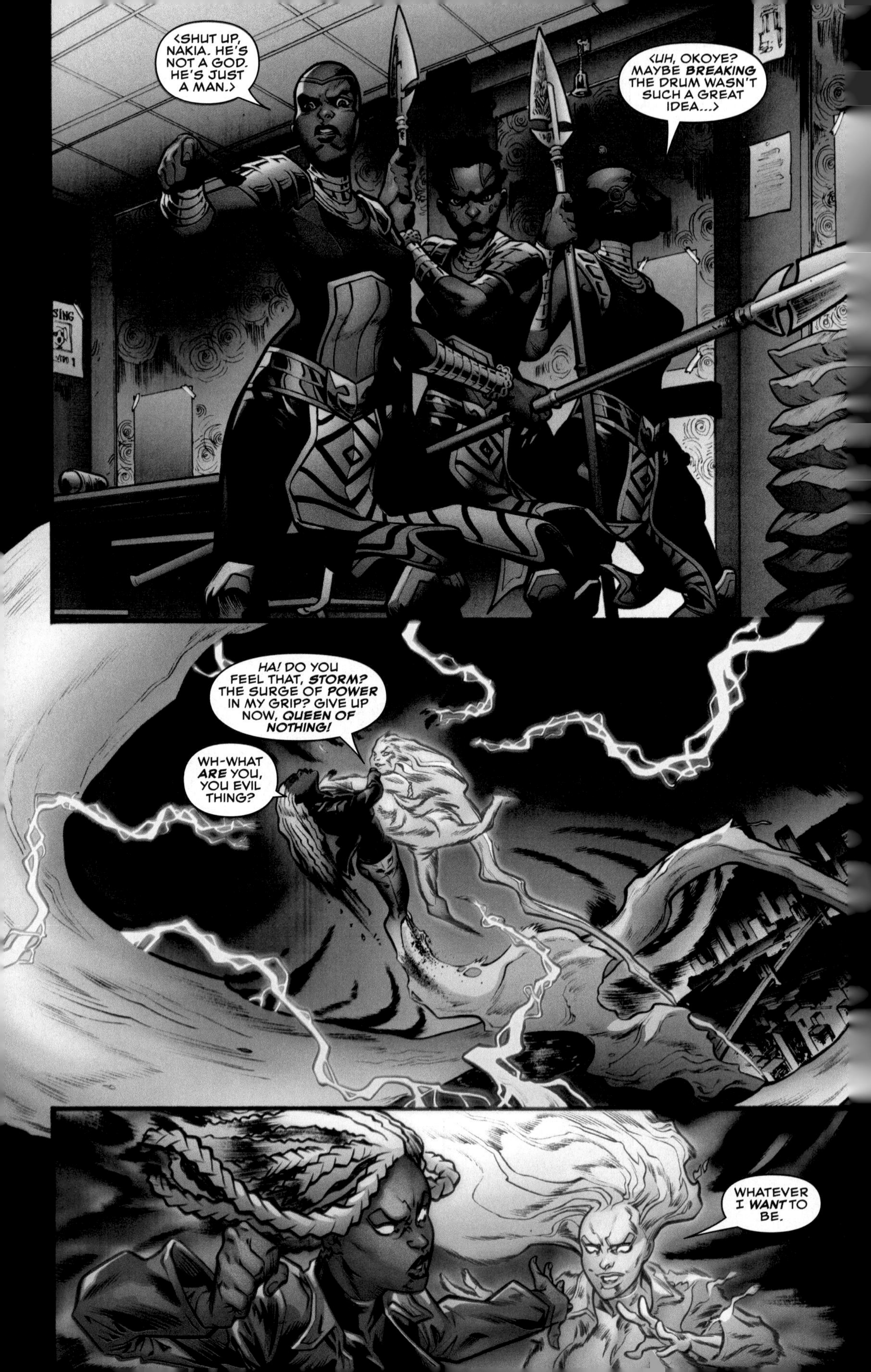
<SHUT UP, NAKIA. HE'S NOT A GOD. HE'S JUST A MAN.>
<UH, OKOYE? MAYBE BREAKING THE DRUM WASN'T SUCH A GREAT IDEA...>
HA! DO YOU FEEL THAT, STORM? THE SURGE OF POWER IN MY GRIP? GIVE UP NOW, QUEEN OF NOTHING!
WH-WHAT ARE YOU, YOU EVIL THING?
WHATEVER I WANT TO BE.

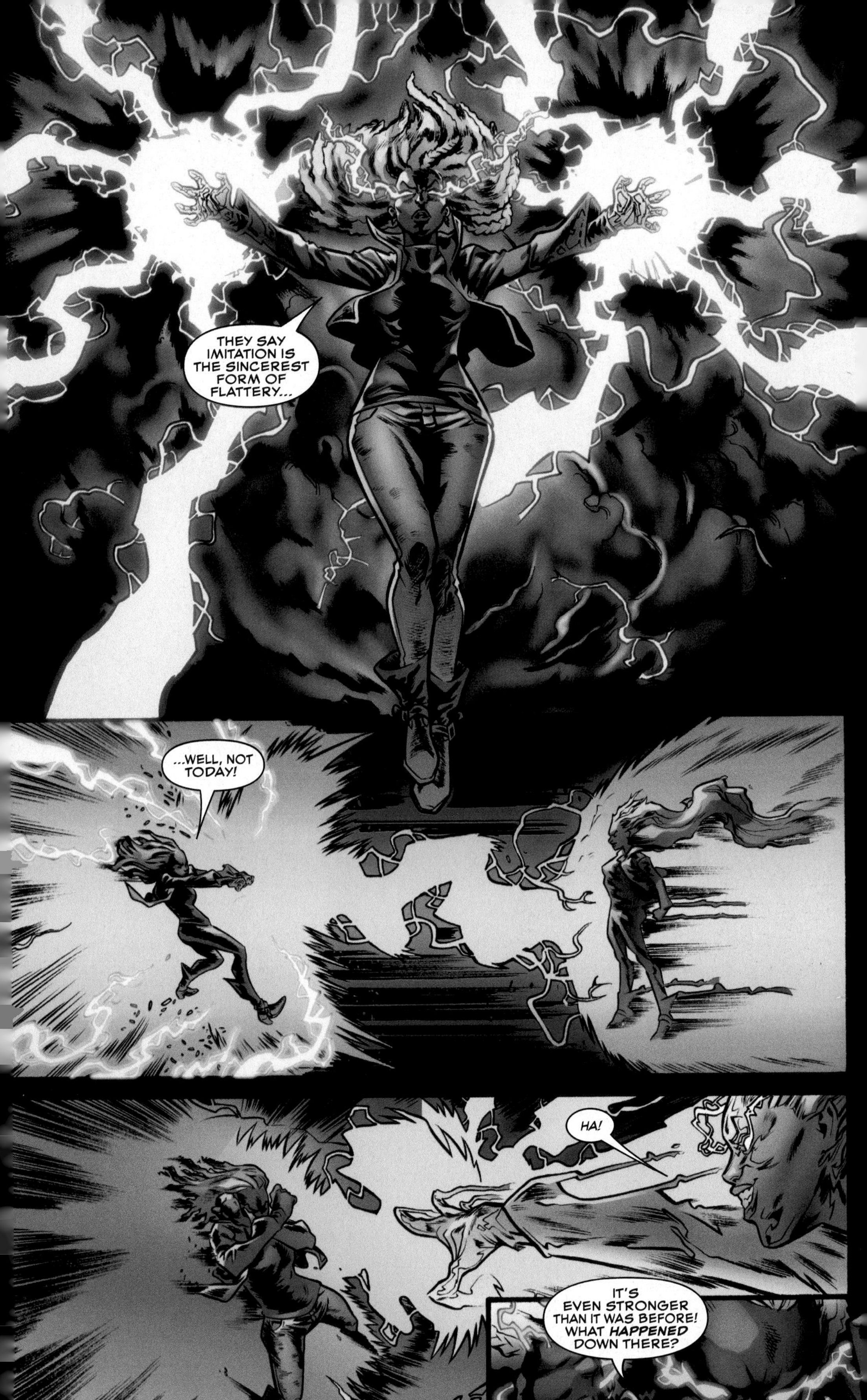
THEY SAY IMITATION IS THE SINCEREST FORM OF FLATTERY...
...WELL, NOT TODAY!
HA!
IT'S EVEN STRONGER THAN IT WAS BEFORE! WHAT HAPPENED DOWN THERE?

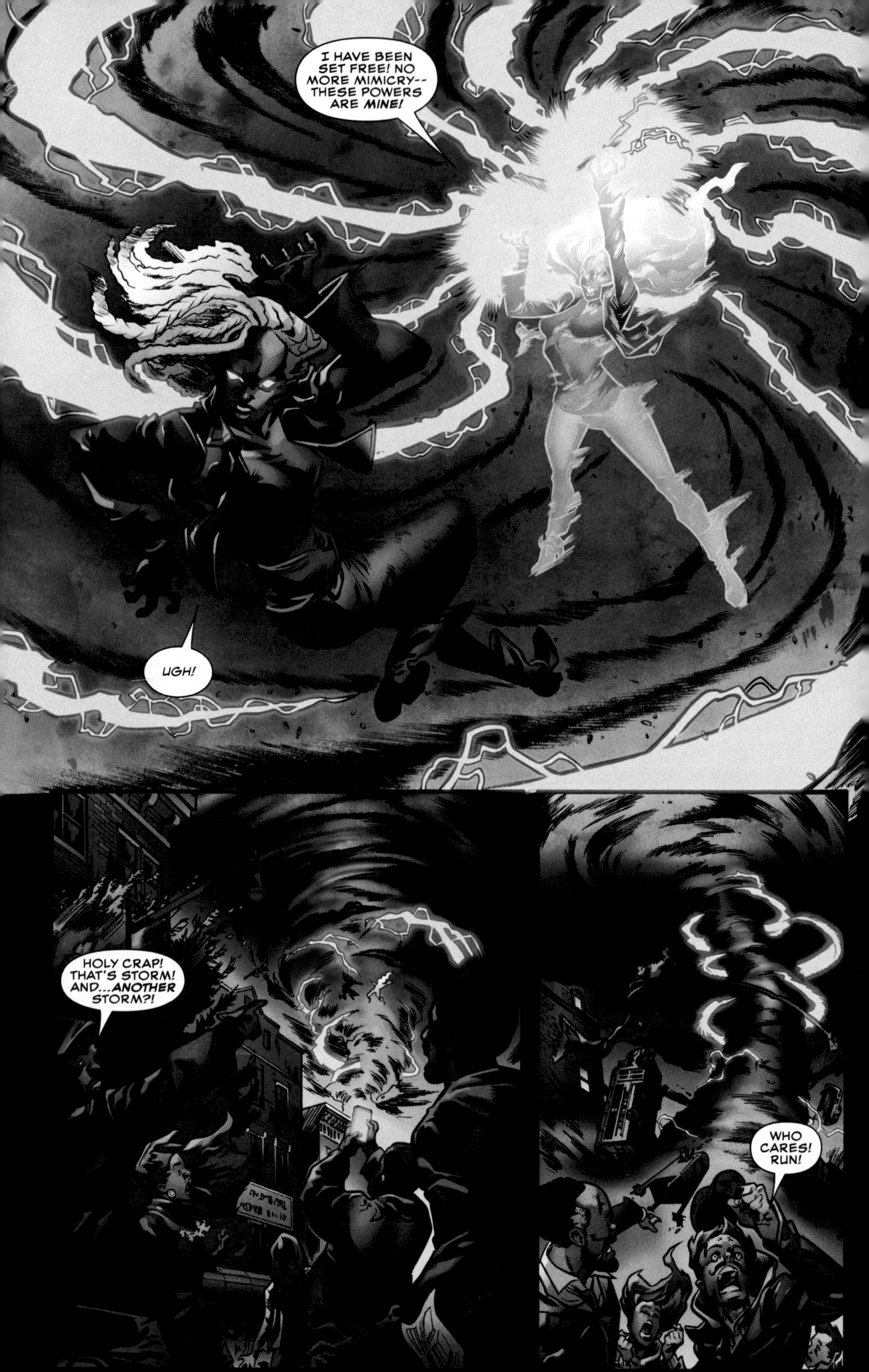

I HAVE BEEN SET FREE! NO MORE MIMICRY-- THESE POWERS ARE *MINE!*
UGH!
HOLY CRAP! THAT'S STORM! AND... *ANOTHER* STORM?!
WHO CARES! RUN!

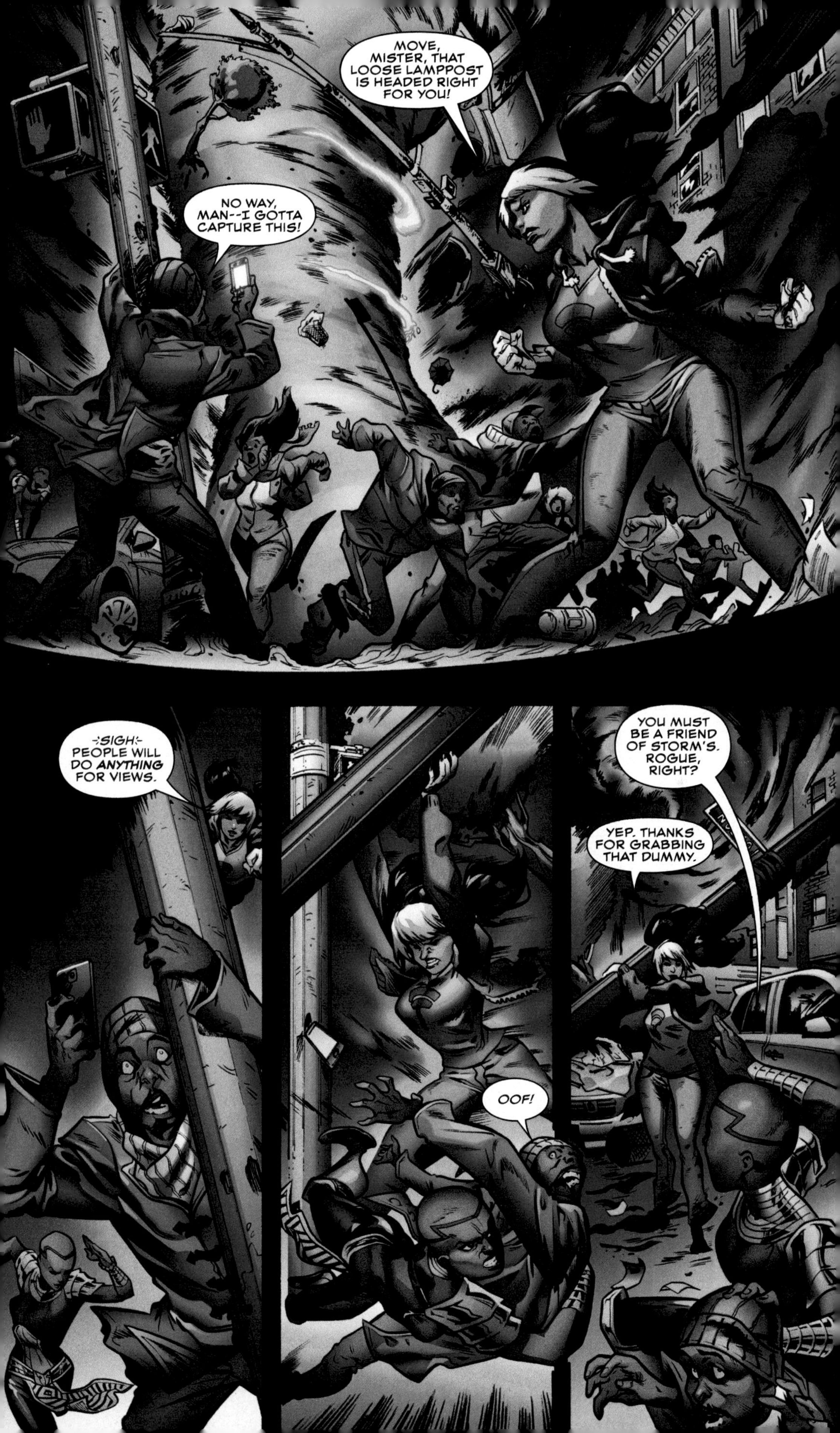
MOVE, MISTER, THAT LOOSE LAMPPOST IS HEADED RIGHT FOR YOU!
NO WAY, MAN--I GOTTA CAPTURE THIS!
-SIGH- PEOPLE WILL DO *ANYTHING* FOR VIEWS.
OOF!
YOU MUST BE A FRIEND OF STORM'S. ROGUE, RIGHT?
YEP. THANKS FOR GRABBING THAT DUMMY.

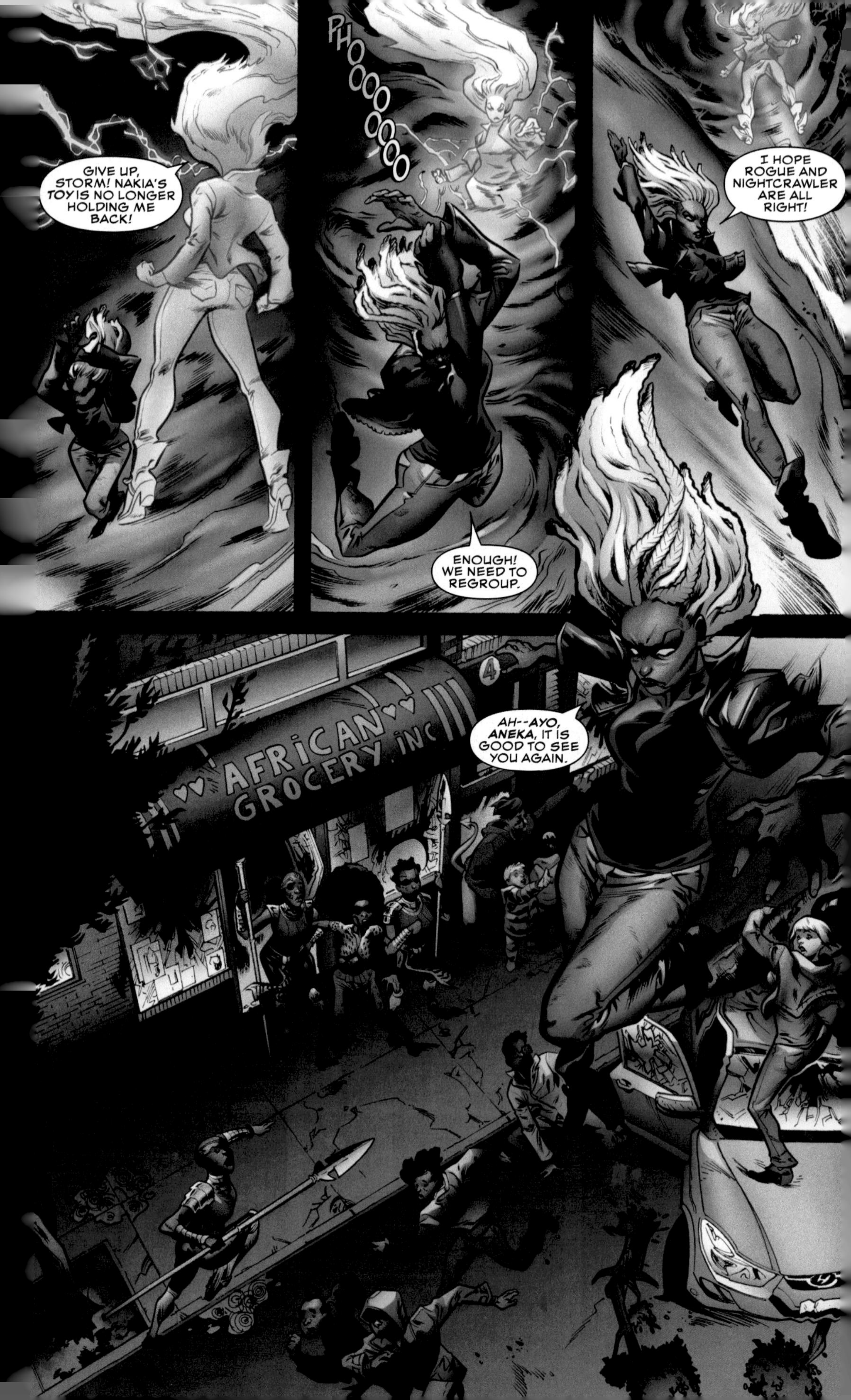
GIVE UP, STORM! NAKIA'S *TOY* IS NO LONGER HOLDING ME BACK!
PHOOOOOOOO
ENOUGH! WE NEED TO REGROUP.
I HOPE ROGUE AND NIGHTCRAWLER ARE ALL RIGHT!
AFRICAN GROCERY, INC
4
AH--*AYO*, *ANEKA*, IT IS GOOD TO SEE YOU AGAIN.

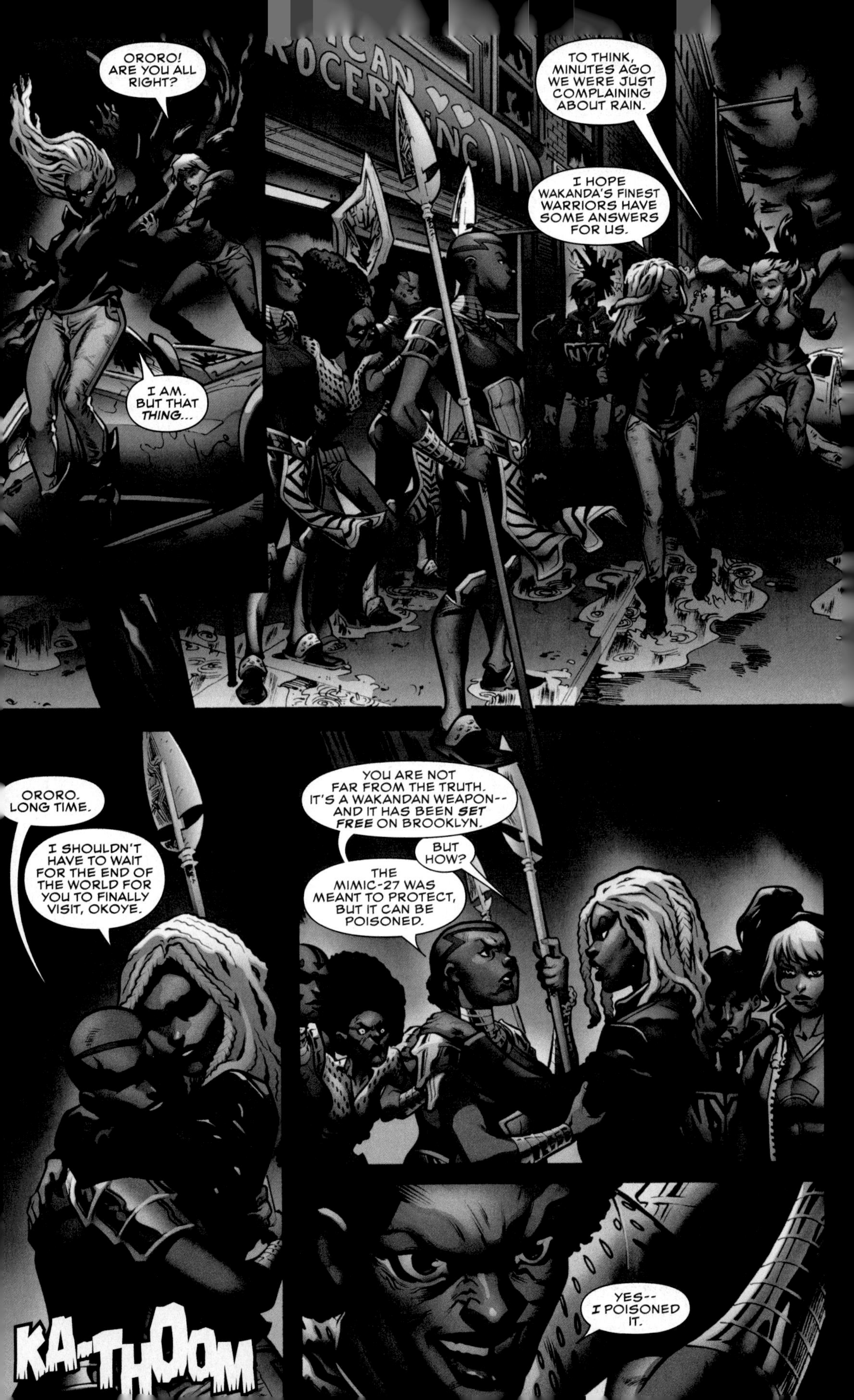
ORORO! ARE YOU ALL RIGHT?
I AM. BUT THAT THING...
TO THINK, MINUTES AGO WE WERE JUST COMPLAINING ABOUT RAIN.
I HOPE WAKANDA'S FINEST WARRIORS HAVE SOME ANSWERS FOR US.
ORORO. LONG TIME.
I SHOULDN'T HAVE TO WAIT FOR THE END OF THE WORLD FOR YOU TO FINALLY VISIT, OKOYE.
YOU ARE NOT FAR FROM THE TRUTH. IT'S A WAKANDAN WEAPON-- AND IT HAS BEEN SET FREE ON BROOKLYN.
BUT HOW?
THE MIMIC-27 WAS MEANT TO PROTECT, BUT IT CAN BE POISONED.
KA-THOOM
YES-- I POISONED IT.

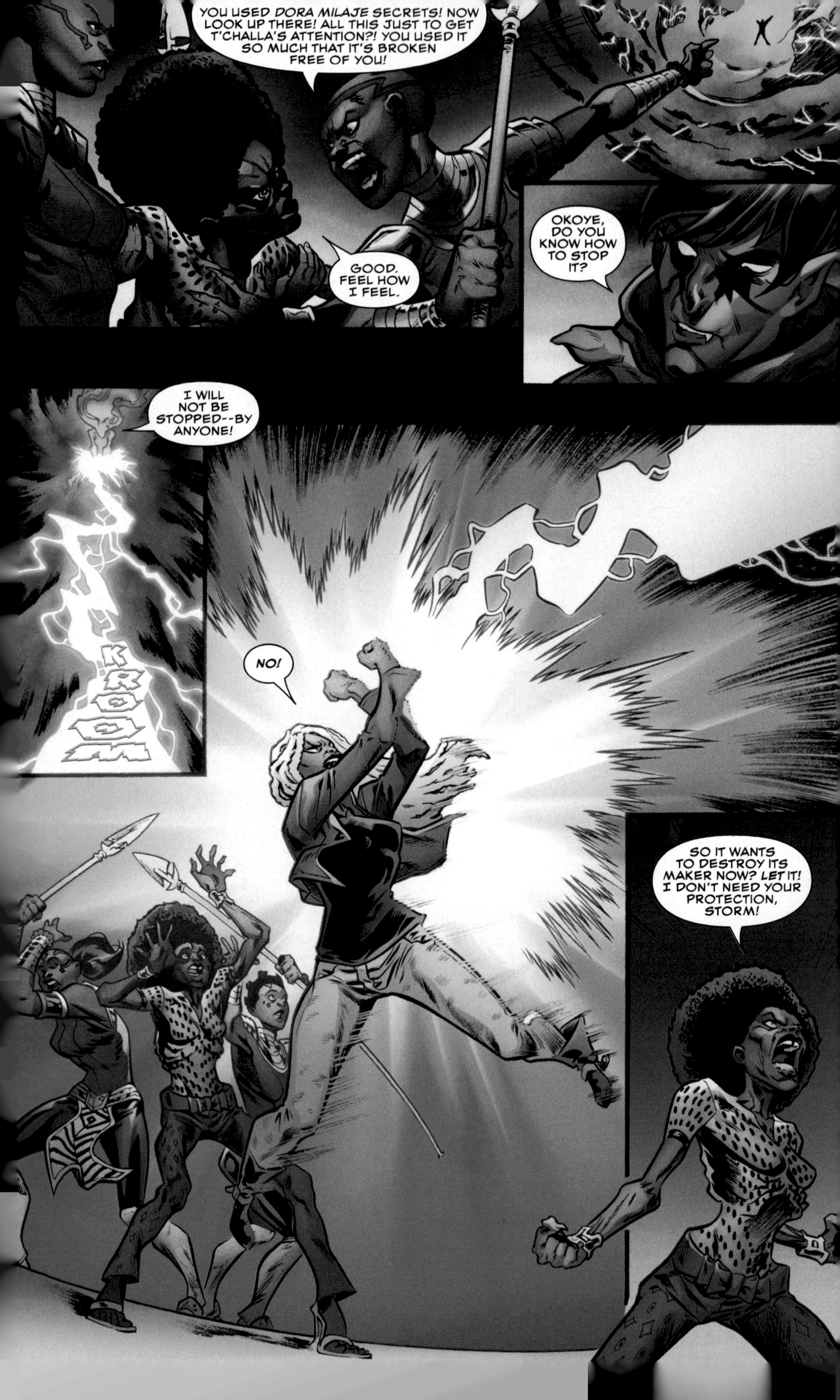
YOU USED DORA MILAJE SECRETS! NOW LOOK UP THERE! ALL THIS JUST TO GET T'CHALLA'S ATTENTION?! YOU USED IT SO MUCH THAT IT'S BROKEN FREE OF YOU!
GOOD. FEEL HOW I FEEL.
OKOYE, DO YOU KNOW HOW TO STOP IT?
I WILL NOT BE STOPPED--BY ANYONE!
KROOM
NO!
SO IT WANTS TO DESTROY ITS MAKER NOW? LET IT! I DON'T NEED YOUR PROTECTION, STORM!

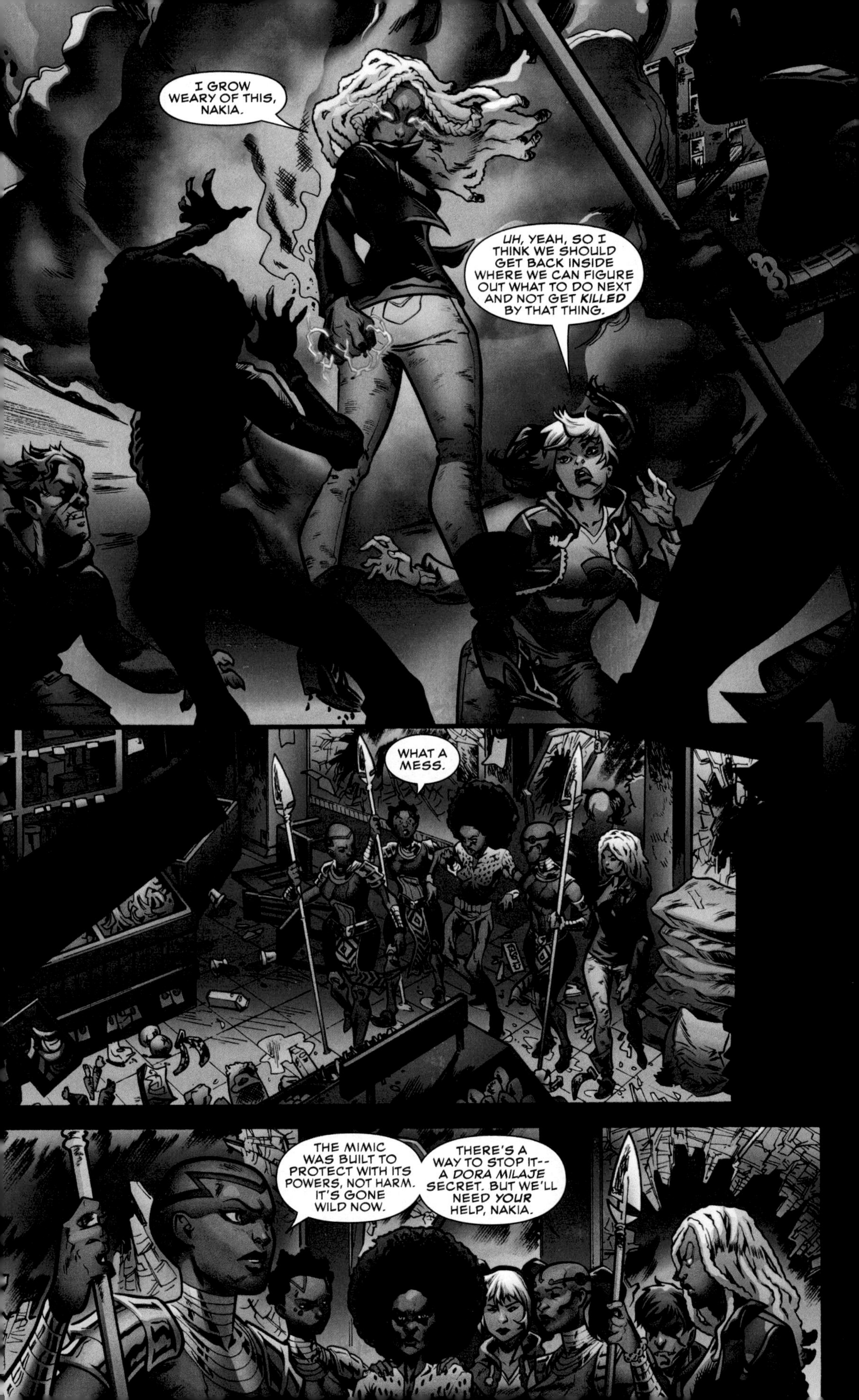

I GROW WEARY OF THIS, NAKIA.
UH, YEAH, SO I THINK WE SHOULD GET BACK INSIDE WHERE WE CAN FIGURE OUT WHAT TO DO NEXT AND NOT GET *KILLED* BY THAT THING.
WHAT A MESS.
THE MIMIC WAS BUILT TO PROTECT WITH ITS POWERS, NOT HARM. IT'S GONE WILD NOW.
THERE'S A WAY TO STOP IT-- A *DORA MILAJE* SECRET. BUT WE'LL NEED *YOUR* HELP, NAKIA.

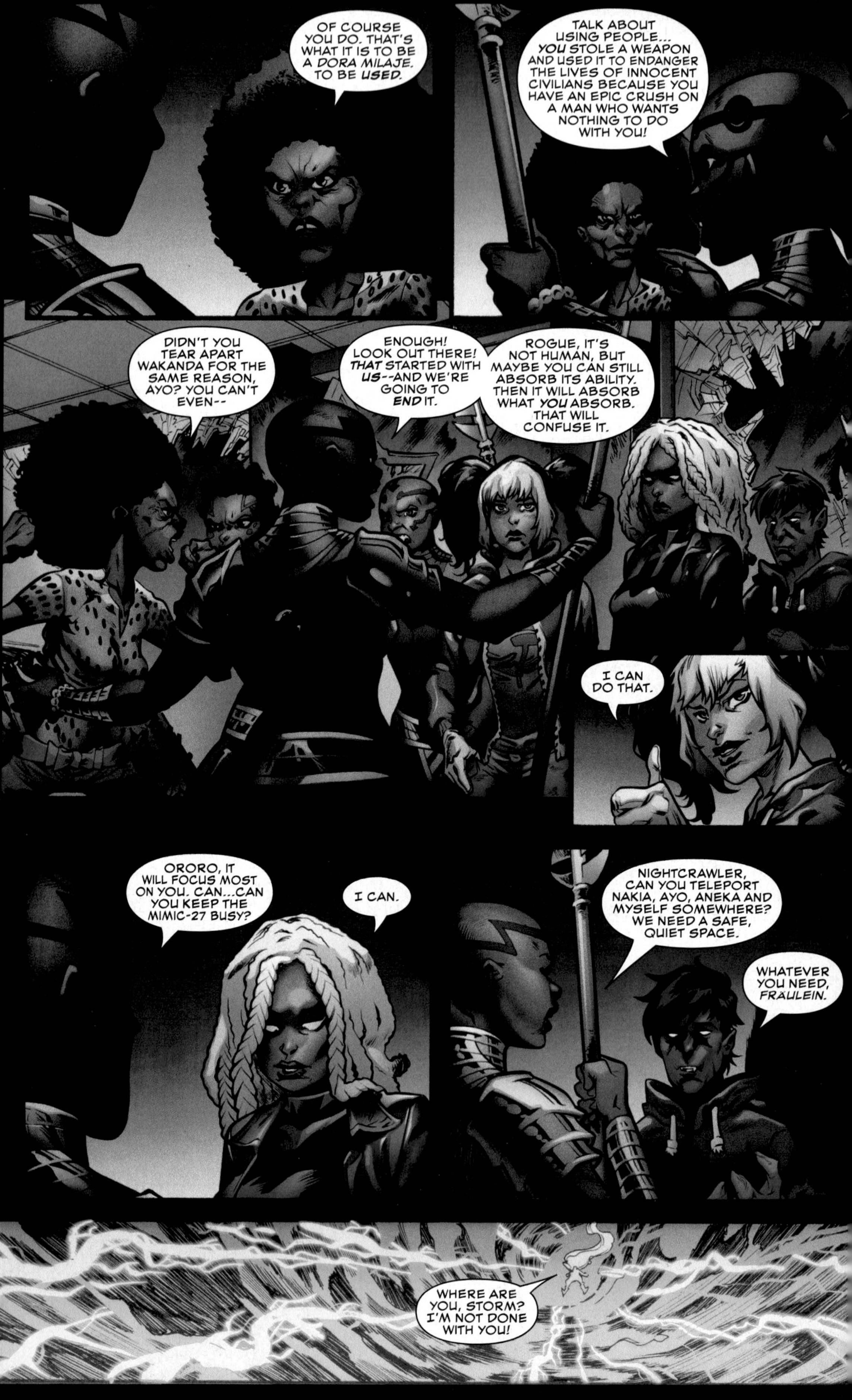
OF COURSE YOU DO. THAT'S WHAT IT IS TO BE A *DORA MILAJE.* TO BE *USED.*
TALK ABOUT USING PEOPLE... *YOU* STOLE A WEAPON AND USED IT TO ENDANGER THE LIVES OF INNOCENT CIVILIANS BECAUSE YOU HAVE AN EPIC CRUSH ON A MAN WHO WANTS NOTHING TO DO WITH YOU!
DIDN'T YOU TEAR APART WAKANDA FOR THE SAME REASON, AYO? YOU CAN'T EVEN--
ENOUGH! LOOK OUT THERE! *THAT* STARTED WITH *US*--AND WE'RE GOING TO *END* IT.
ROGUE, IT'S NOT HUMAN, BUT MAYBE YOU CAN STILL ABSORB ITS ABILITY. THEN IT WILL ABSORB WHAT *YOU* ABSORB. THAT WILL CONFUSE IT.
I CAN DO THAT.
ORORO, IT WILL FOCUS MOST ON YOU. CAN...CAN YOU KEEP THE MIMIC-27 BUSY?
I CAN.
NIGHTCRAWLER, CAN YOU TELEPORT NAKIA, AYO, ANEKA AND MYSELF SOMEWHERE? WE NEED A SAFE, QUIET SPACE.
WHATEVER YOU NEED, *FRÄULEIN.*
WHERE ARE YOU, STORM? I'M NOT DONE WITH YOU!

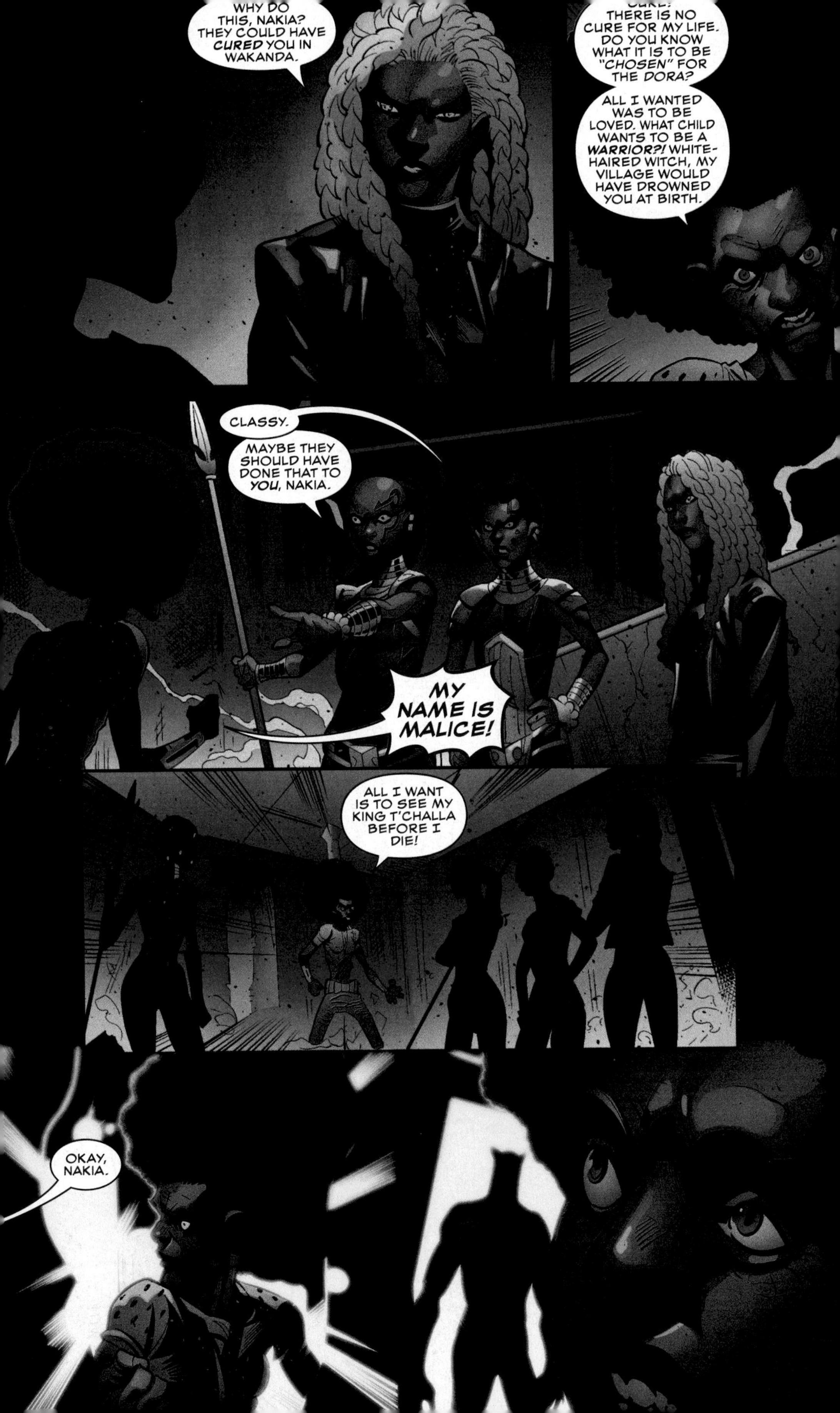
WHY DO THIS, NAKIA? THEY COULD HAVE CURED YOU IN WAKANDA.
THERE IS NO CURE FOR MY LIFE. DO YOU KNOW WHAT IT IS TO BE "CHOSEN" FOR THE DORA?
ALL I WANTED WAS TO BE LOVED. WHAT CHILD WANTS TO BE A WARRIOR?! WHITE-HAIRED WITCH, MY VILLAGE WOULD HAVE DROWNED YOU AT BIRTH.
CLASSY.
MAYBE THEY SHOULD HAVE DONE THAT TO YOU, NAKIA.
MY NAME IS MALICE!
ALL I WANT IS TO SEE MY KING T'CHALLA BEFORE I DIE!
OKAY, NAKIA.

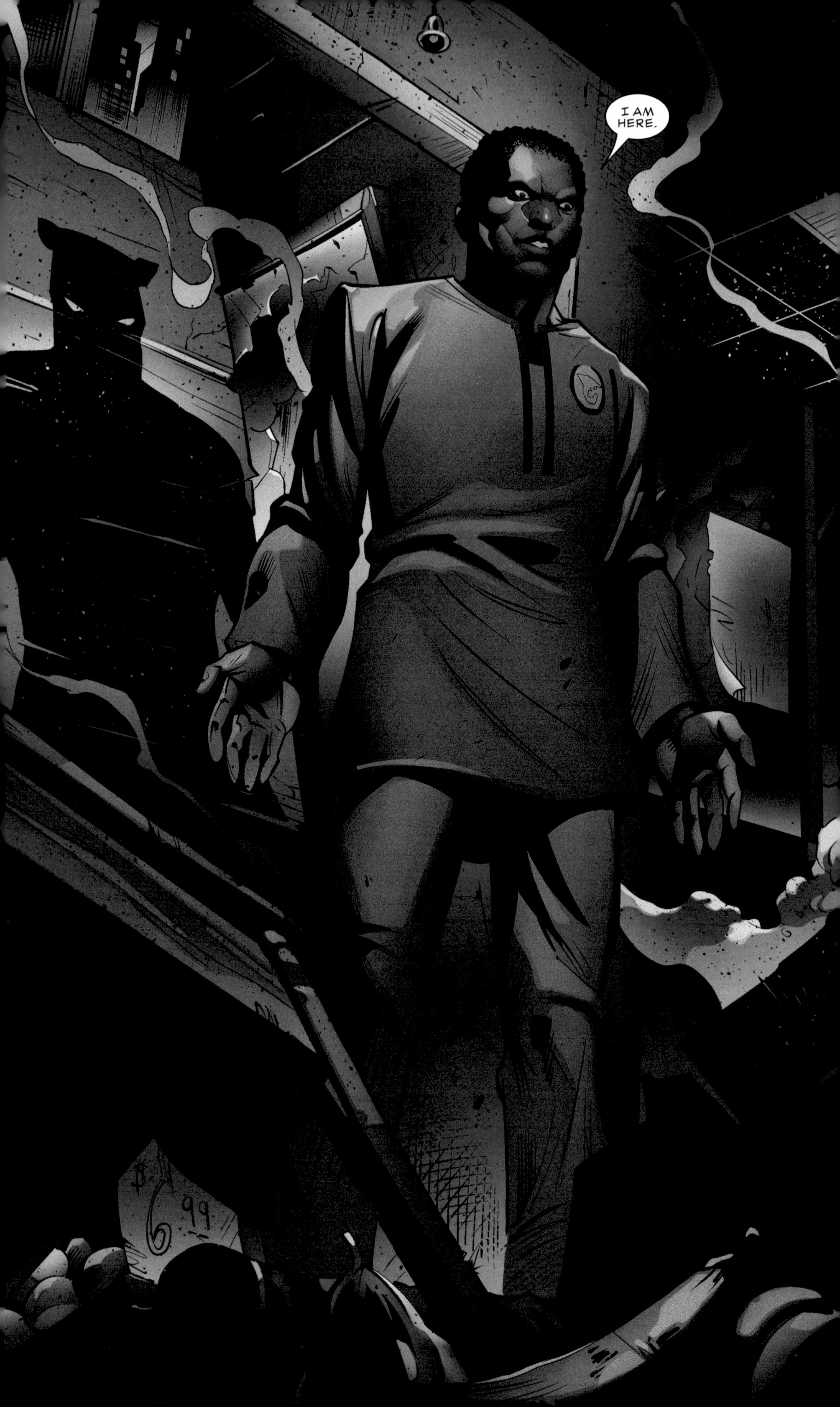
I AM HERE.

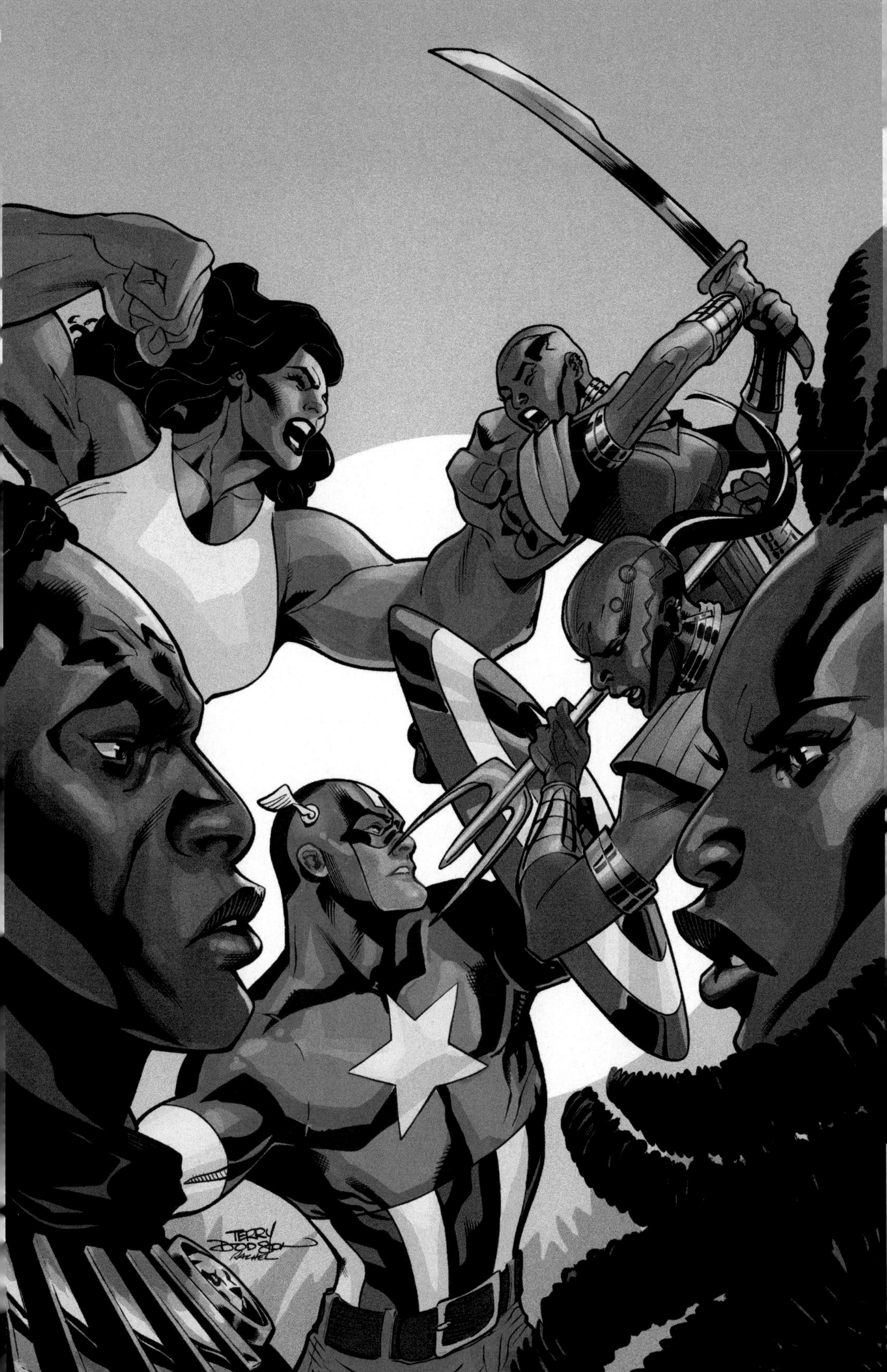
TERRY DODSON RACHEL

WAKANDA FOREVER: AVENGERS

REFLECTIONS

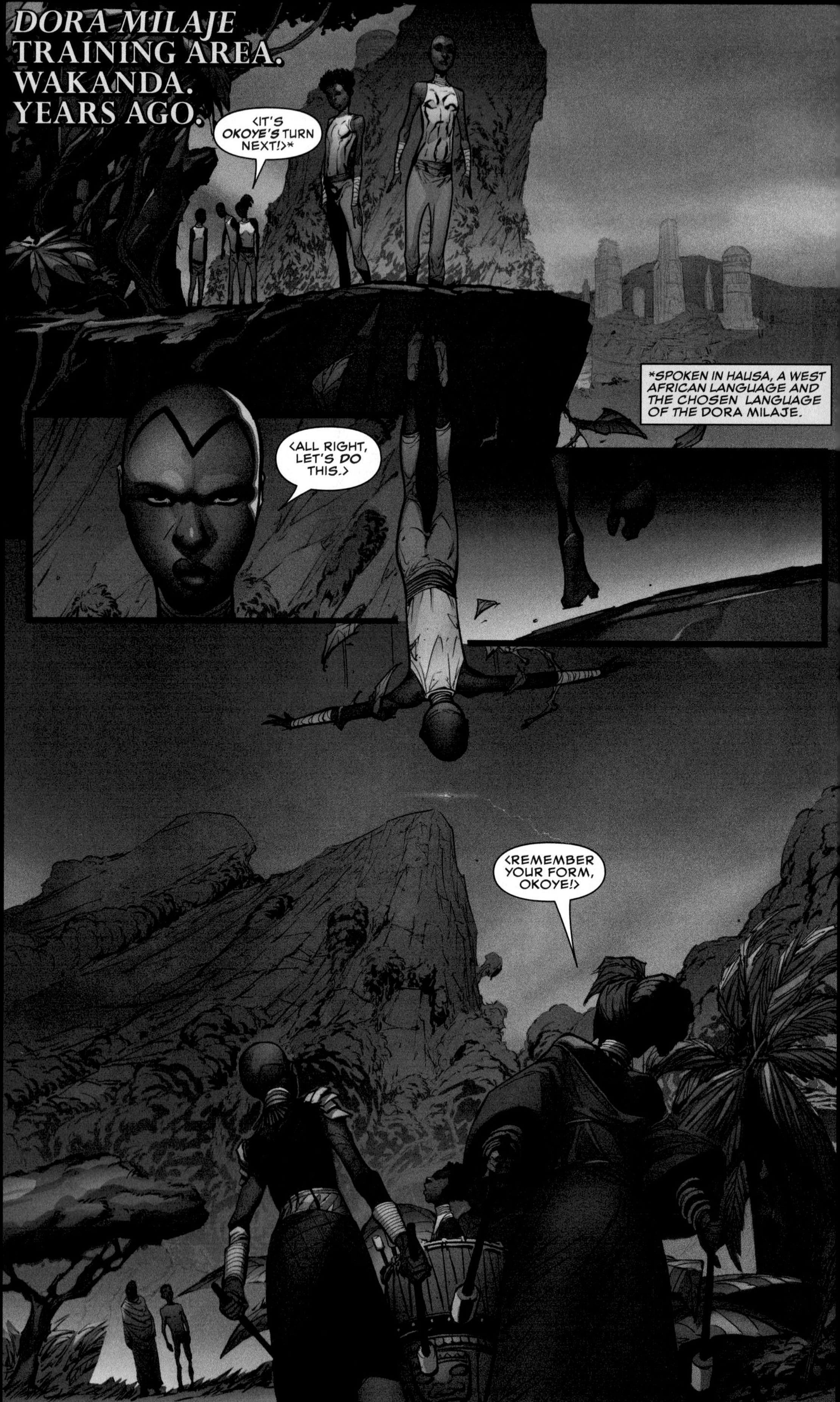
DORA MILAJE TRAINING AREA. WAKANDA. YEARS AGO.
<IT'S OKOYE'S TURN NEXT!>*
*SPOKEN IN HAUSA, A WEST AFRICAN LANGUAGE AND THE CHOSEN LANGUAGE OF THE DORA MILAJE.
<ALL RIGHT, LET'S DO THIS.>
<REMEMBER YOUR FORM, OKOYE!>

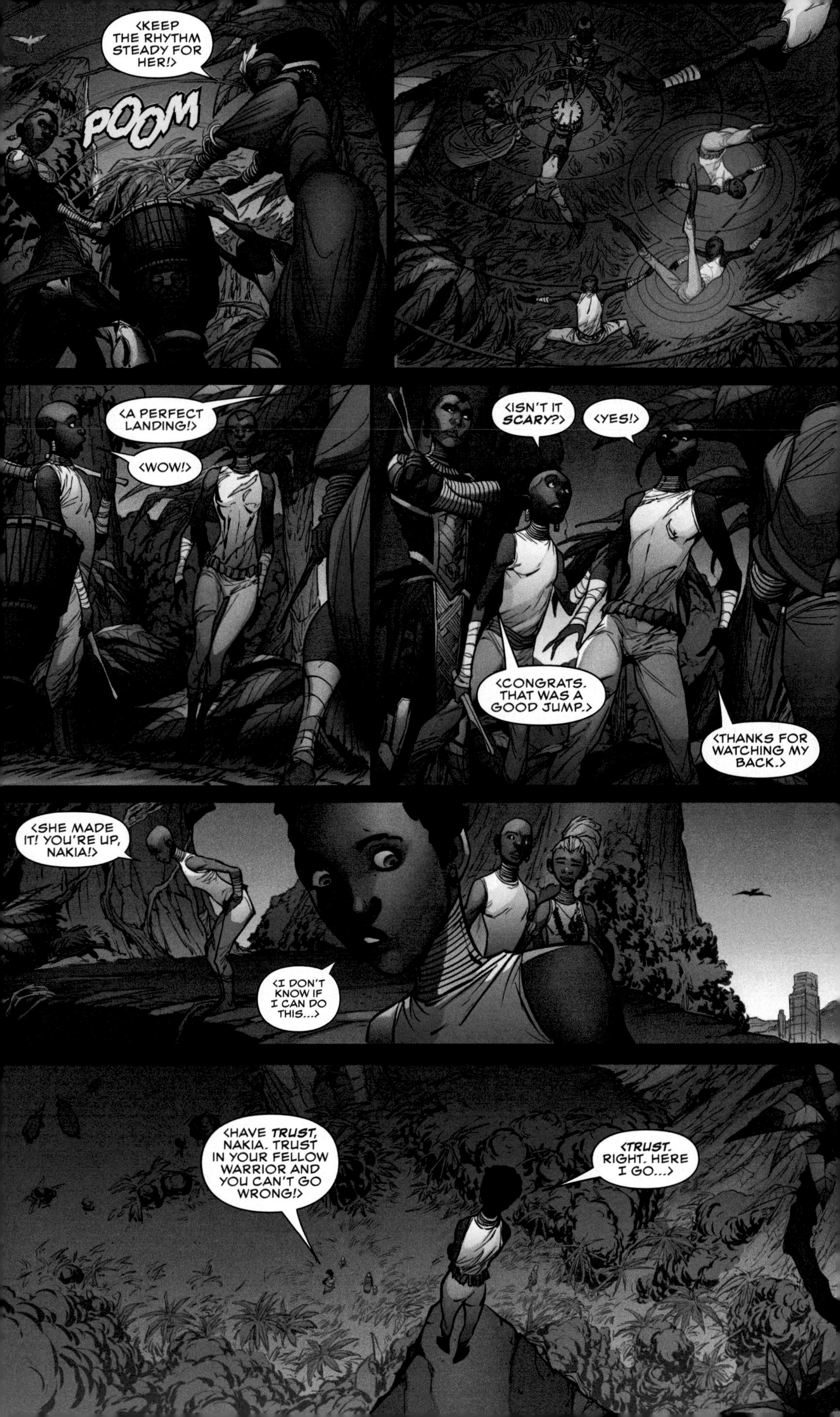
<KEEP THE RHYTHM STEADY FOR HER!>
POOM
<A PERFECT LANDING!>
<WOW!>
<ISN'T IT SCARY?>
<YES!>
<CONGRATS. THAT WAS A GOOD JUMP.>
<THANKS FOR WATCHING MY BACK.>
<SHE MADE IT! YOU'RE UP, NAKIA!>
<I DON'T KNOW IF I CAN DO THIS...>
<HAVE TRUST, NAKIA. TRUST IN YOUR FELLOW WARRIOR AND YOU CAN'T GO WRONG!>
<TRUST. RIGHT. HERE I GO...>

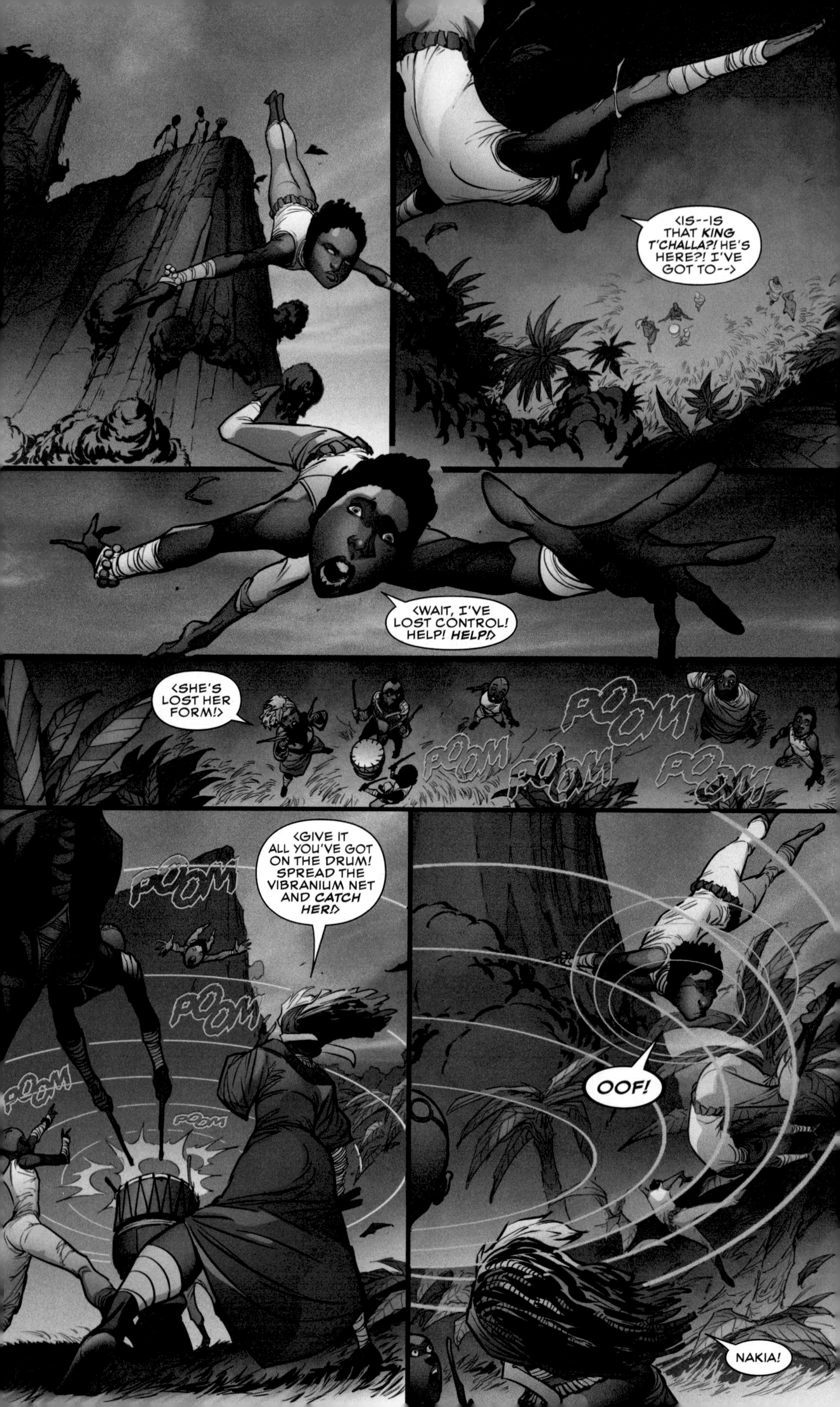

<IS--IS THAT KING T'CHALLA?! HE'S HERE?! I'VE GOT TO-->
<WAIT, I'VE LOST CONTROL! HELP! HELP!>
<SHE'S LOST HER FORM!>
POOM
POOM
POOM
POOM
<GIVE IT ALL YOU'VE GOT ON THE DRUM! SPREAD THE VIBRANIUM NET AND CATCH HER!>
POOM
POOM
POOM
POOM
OOF!
NAKIA!

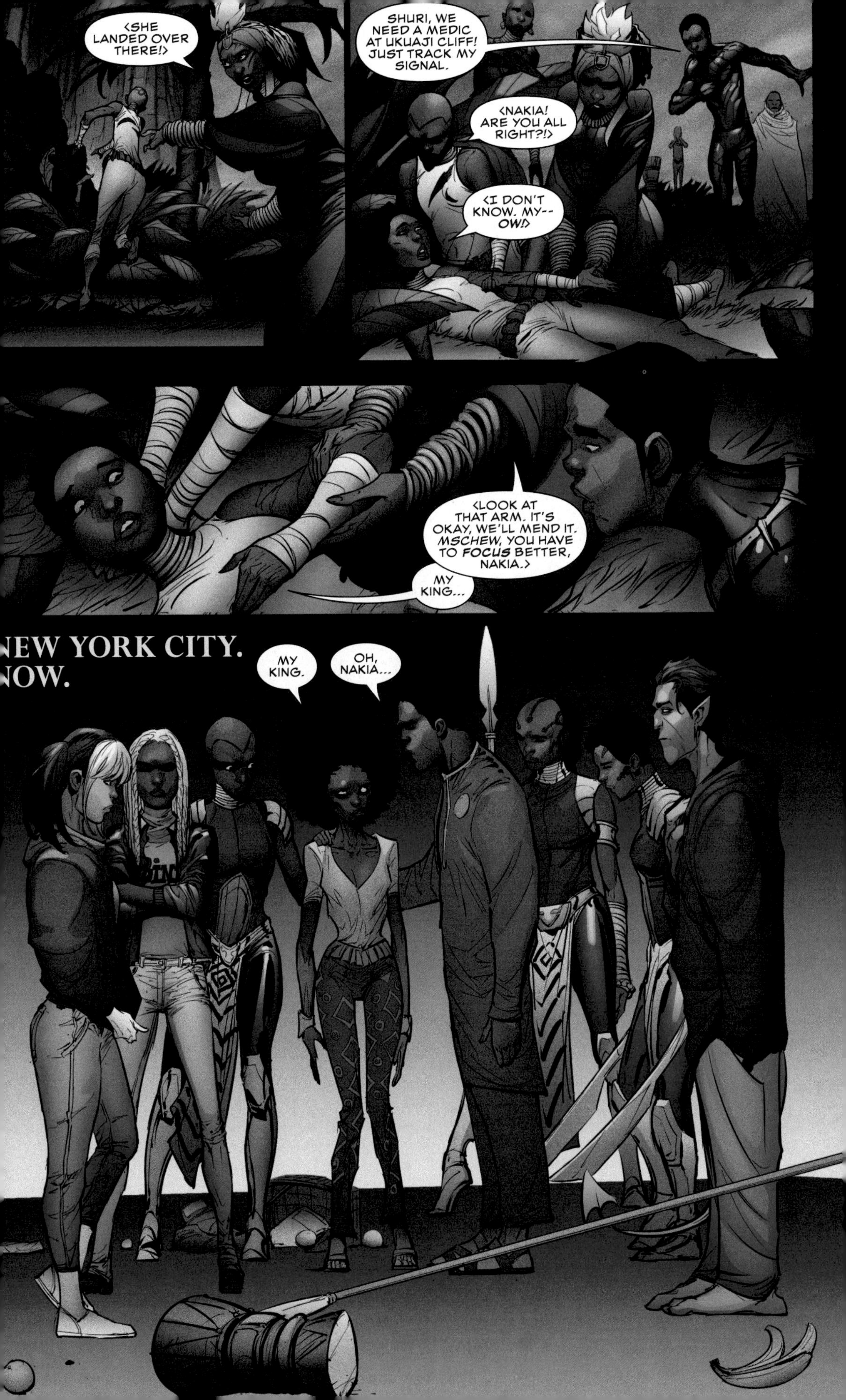

<SHE LANDED OVER THERE!>
SHURI, WE NEED A MEDIC AT UKUAJI CLIFF! JUST TRACK MY SIGNAL.
<NAKIA! ARE YOU ALL RIGHT?!>
<I DON'T KNOW. MY-- OW!>
<LOOK AT THAT ARM. IT'S OKAY, WE'LL MEND IT. MSCHEW, YOU HAVE TO FOCUS BETTER, NAKIA.>
MY KING...
NEW YORK CITY. NOW.
MY KING.
OH, NAKIA...

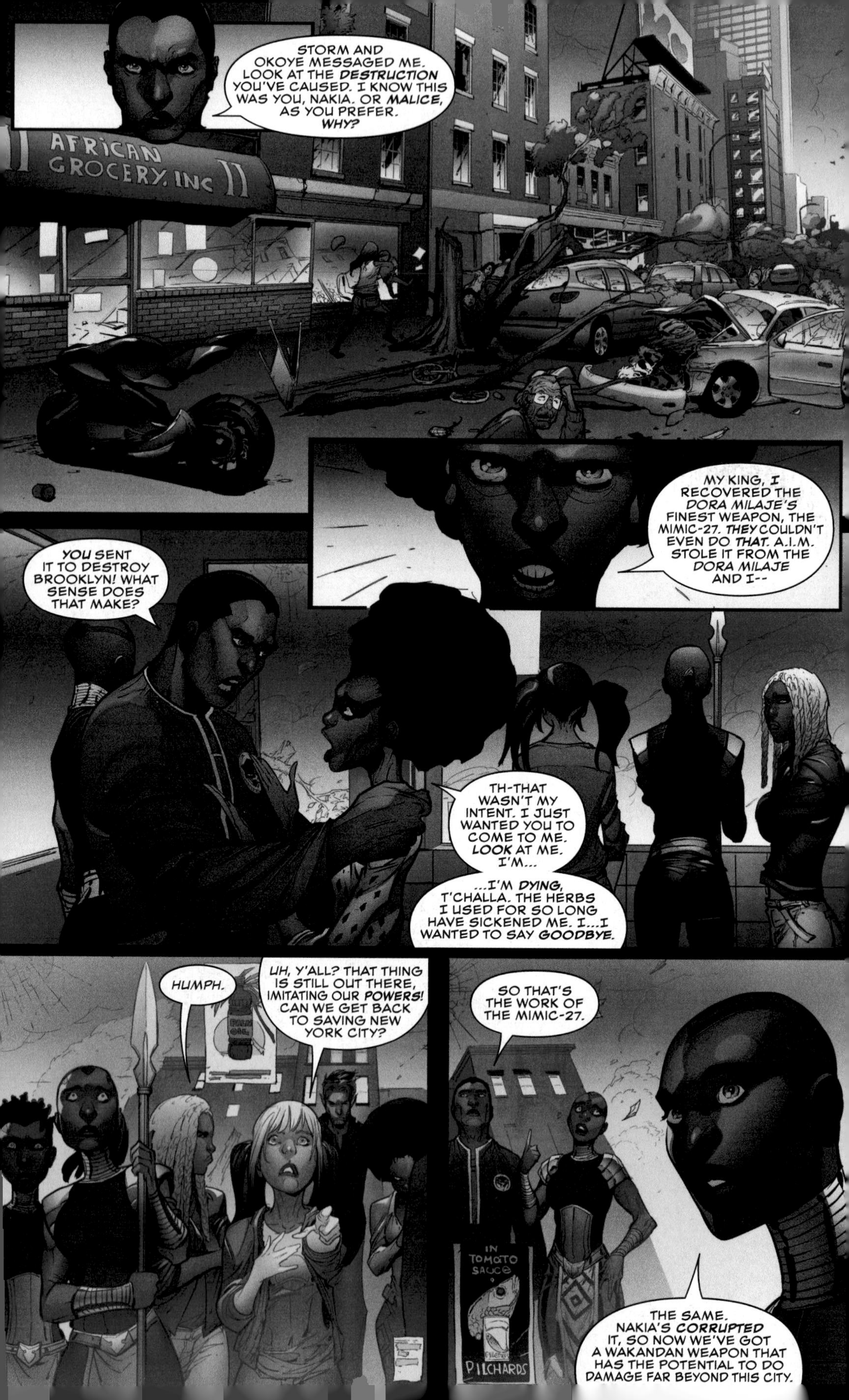

STORM AND OKOYE MESSAGED ME. LOOK AT THE DESTRUCTION YOU'VE CAUSED. I KNOW THIS WAS YOU, NAKIA. OR MALICE, AS YOU PREFER. WHY?
AFRICAN GROCERY, INC II
MY KING, I RECOVERED THE DORA MILAJE'S FINEST WEAPON, THE MIMIC-27. THEY COULDN'T EVEN DO THAT. A.I.M. STOLE IT FROM THE DORA MILAJE AND I--
YOU SENT IT TO DESTROY BROOKLYN! WHAT SENSE DOES THAT MAKE?
TH-THAT WASN'T MY INTENT. I JUST WANTED YOU TO COME TO ME. LOOK AT ME. I'M...
...I'M DYING, T'CHALLA. THE HERBS I USED FOR SO LONG HAVE SICKENED ME. I...I WANTED TO SAY GOODBYE.
HUMPH.
UH, Y'ALL? THAT THING IS STILL OUT THERE, IMITATING OUR POWERS! CAN WE GET BACK TO SAVING NEW YORK CITY?
SO THAT'S THE WORK OF THE MIMIC-27.
IN TOMATO SAUCE
PILCHARDS
THE SAME. NAKIA'S CORRUPTED IT, SO NOW WE'VE GOT A WAKANDAN WEAPON THAT HAS THE POTENTIAL TO DO DAMAGE FAR BEYOND THIS CITY.

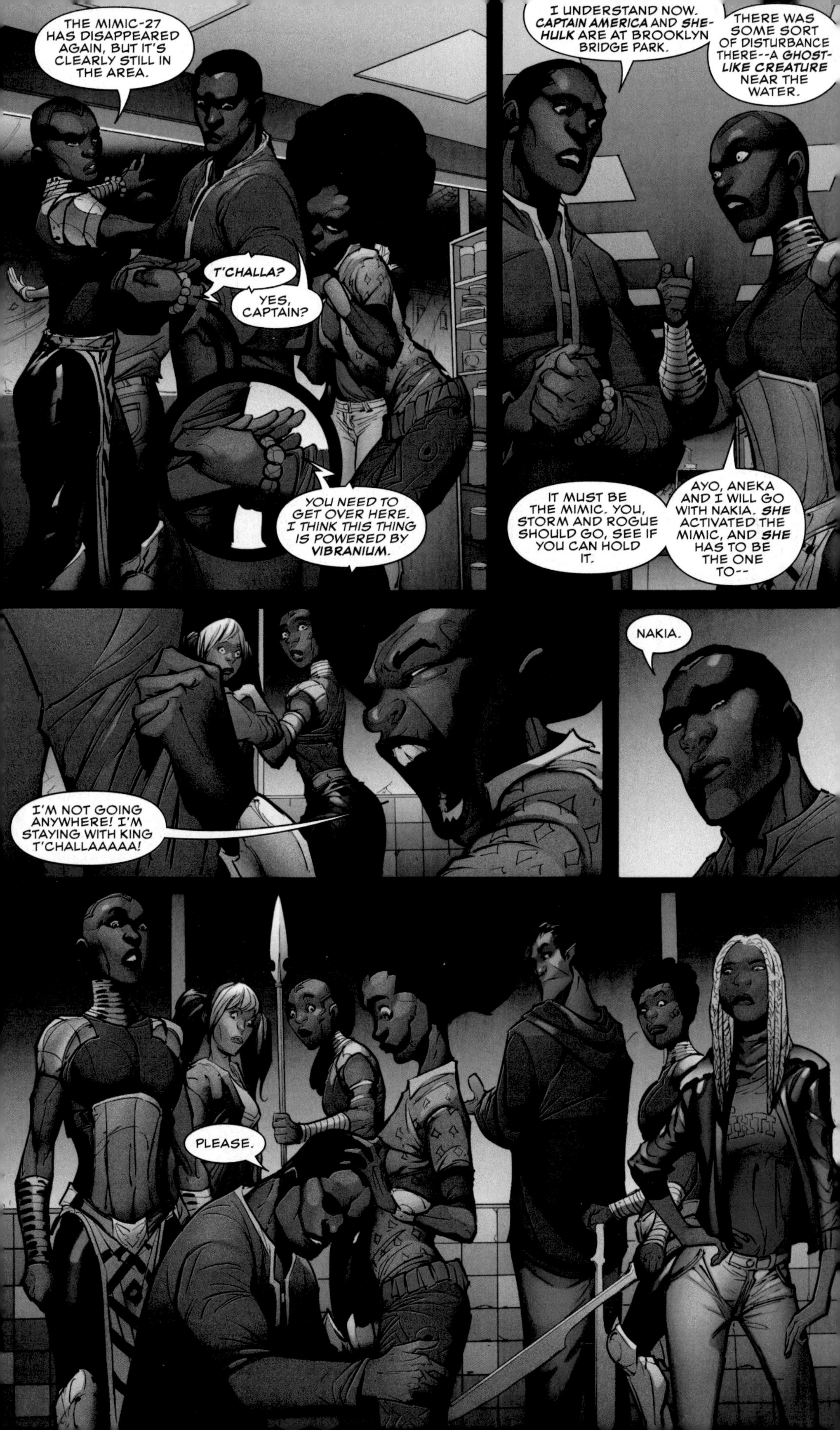
THE MIMIC-27 HAS DISAPPEARED AGAIN, BUT IT'S CLEARLY STILL IN THE AREA.
T'CHALLA?
YES, CAPTAIN?
YOU NEED TO GET OVER HERE. I THINK THIS THING IS POWERED BY VIBRANIUM.
I UNDERSTAND NOW. CAPTAIN AMERICA AND SHE-HULK ARE AT BROOKLYN BRIDGE PARK.
THERE WAS SOME SORT OF DISTURBANCE THERE--A GHOST-LIKE CREATURE NEAR THE WATER.
IT MUST BE THE MIMIC. YOU, STORM AND ROGUE SHOULD GO, SEE IF YOU CAN HOLD IT.
AYO, ANEKA AND I WILL GO WITH NAKIA. SHE ACTIVATED THE MIMIC, AND SHE HAS TO BE THE ONE TO--
I'M NOT GOING ANYWHERE! I'M STAYING WITH KING T'CHALLAAAAA!
NAKIA.
PLEASE.

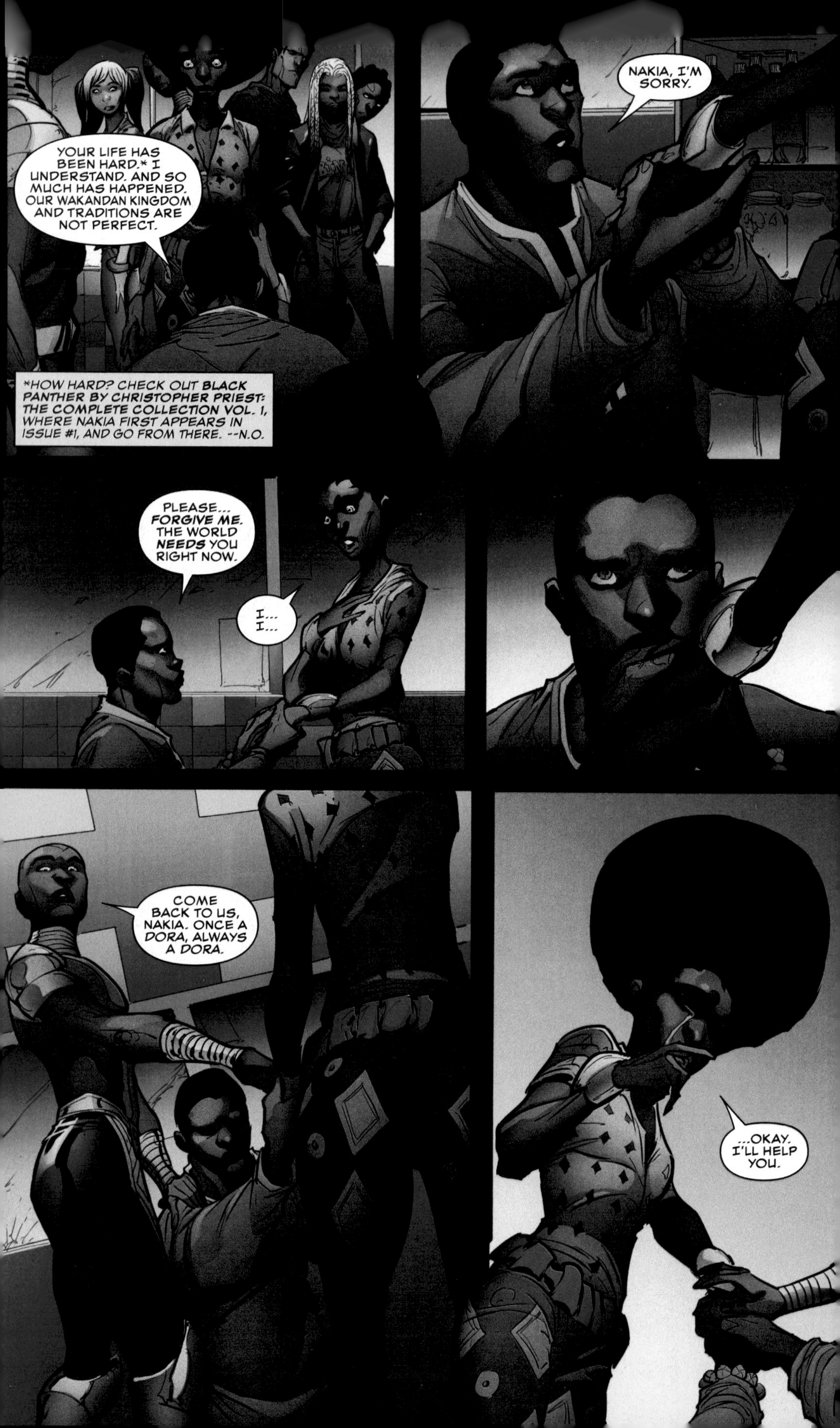
YOUR LIFE HAS BEEN HARD.* I UNDERSTAND. AND SO MUCH HAS HAPPENED. OUR WAKANDAN KINGDOM AND TRADITIONS ARE NOT PERFECT.
*HOW HARD? CHECK OUT BLACK PANTHER BY CHRISTOPHER PRIEST: THE COMPLETE COLLECTION VOL. 1, WHERE NAKIA FIRST APPEARS IN ISSUE #1, AND GO FROM THERE. --N.O.
NAKIA, I'M SORRY.
PLEASE... FORGIVE ME. THE WORLD NEEDS YOU RIGHT NOW.
I... I...
COME BACK TO US, NAKIA. ONCE A DORA, ALWAYS A DORA.
...OKAY. I'LL HELP YOU.

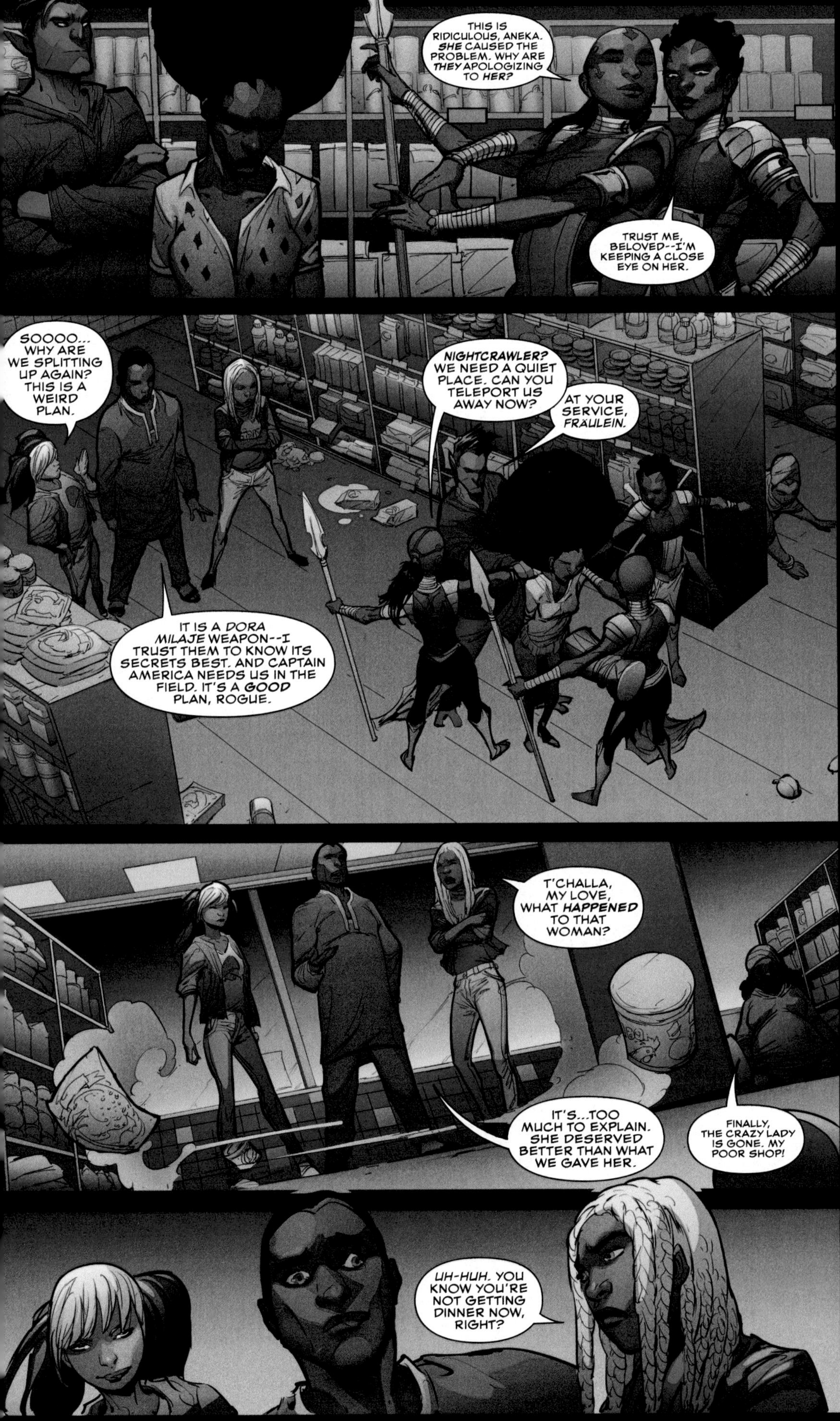
THIS IS RIDICULOUS, ANEKA. SHE CAUSED THE PROBLEM. WHY ARE THEY APOLOGIZING TO HER?
TRUST ME, BELOVED--I'M KEEPING A CLOSE EYE ON HER.
SOOOO... WHY ARE WE SPLITTING UP AGAIN? THIS IS A WEIRD PLAN.
NIGHTCRAWLER? WE NEED A QUIET PLACE. CAN YOU TELEPORT US AWAY NOW?
AT YOUR SERVICE, FRÄULEIN.
IT IS A DORA MILAJE WEAPON--I TRUST THEM TO KNOW ITS SECRETS BEST. AND CAPTAIN AMERICA NEEDS US IN THE FIELD. IT'S A GOOD PLAN, ROGUE.
T'CHALLA, MY LOVE, WHAT HAPPENED TO THAT WOMAN?
IT'S...TOO MUCH TO EXPLAIN. SHE DESERVED BETTER THAN WHAT WE GAVE HER.
FINALLY, THE CRAZY LADY IS GONE. MY POOR SHOP!
UH-HUH. YOU KNOW YOU'RE NOT GETTING DINNER NOW, RIGHT?

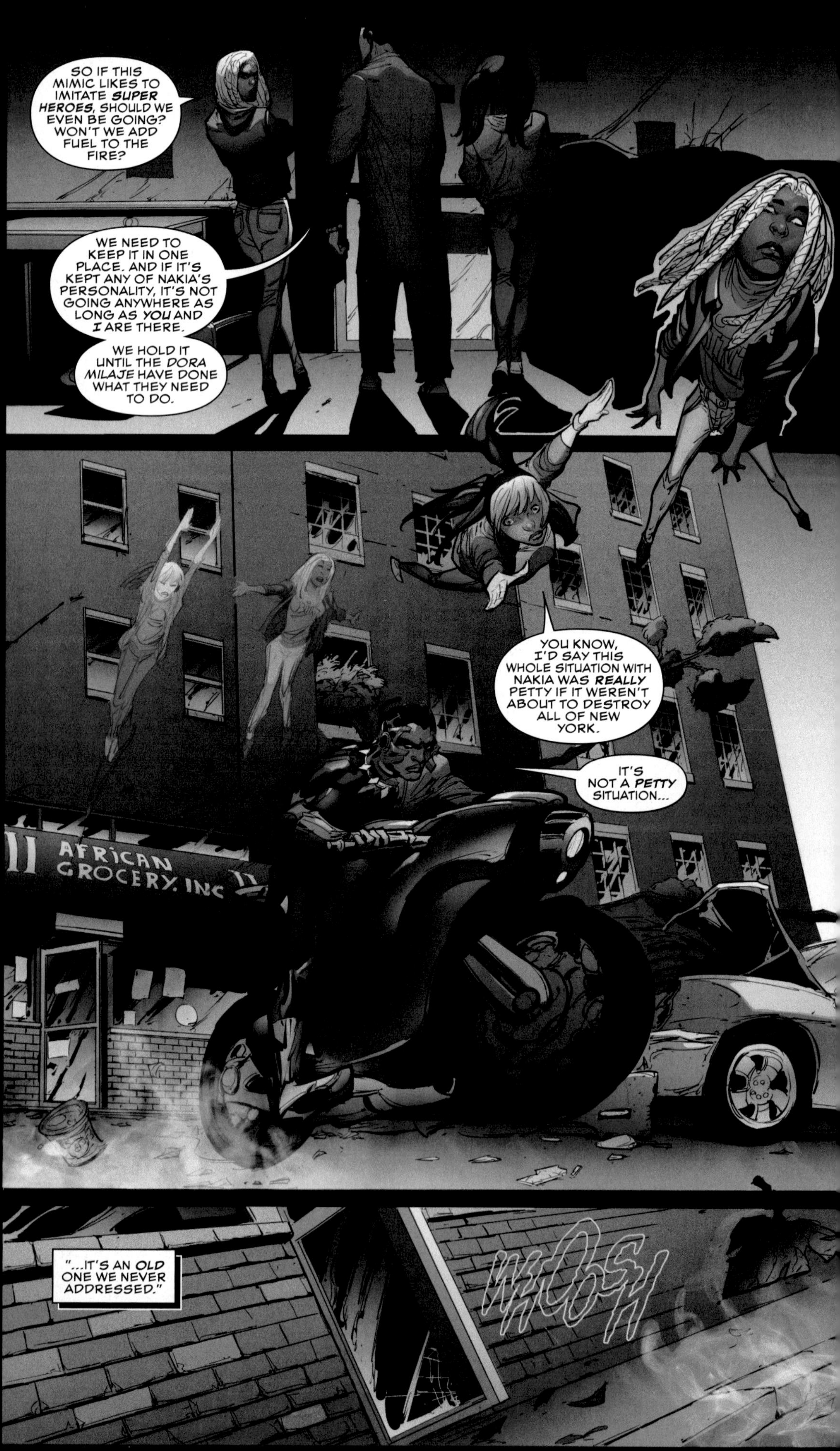

SO IF THIS MIMIC LIKES TO IMITATE SUPER HEROES, SHOULD WE EVEN BE GOING? WON'T WE ADD FUEL TO THE FIRE?
WE NEED TO KEEP IT IN ONE PLACE. AND IF IT'S KEPT ANY OF NAKIA'S PERSONALITY, IT'S NOT GOING ANYWHERE AS LONG AS YOU AND I ARE THERE.
WE HOLD IT UNTIL THE DORA MILAJE HAVE DONE WHAT THEY NEED TO DO.
YOU KNOW, I'D SAY THIS WHOLE SITUATION WITH NAKIA WAS REALLY PETTY IF IT WEREN'T ABOUT TO DESTROY ALL OF NEW YORK.
IT'S NOT A PETTY SITUATION...
AFRICAN GROCERY, INC
"...IT'S AN OLD ONE WE NEVER ADDRESSED."
WHOOSH

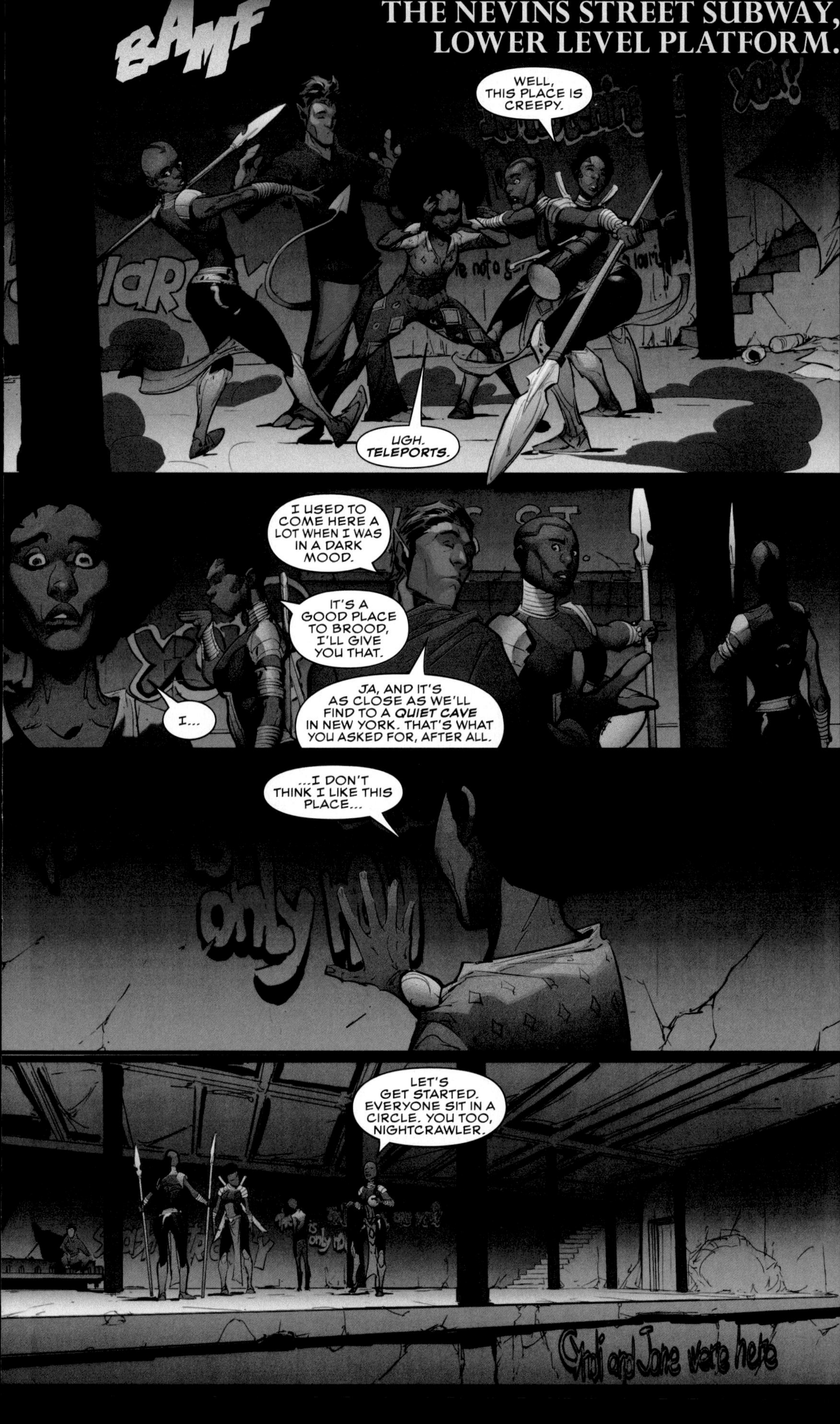
BAMF
THE NEVINS STREET SUBWAY, LOWER LEVEL PLATFORM.
WELL, THIS PLACE IS CREEPY.
UGH. TELEPORTS.
I USED TO COME HERE A LOT WHEN I WAS IN A DARK MOOD.
IT'S A GOOD PLACE TO BROOD, I'LL GIVE YOU THAT.
I...
JA, AND IT'S AS CLOSE AS WE'LL FIND TO A QUIET CAVE IN NEW YORK. THAT'S WHAT YOU ASKED FOR, AFTER ALL.
...I DON'T THINK I LIKE THIS PLACE...
LET'S GET STARTED. EVERYONE SIT IN A CIRCLE. YOU TOO, NIGHTCRAWLER.
Cyndi and Jane were here

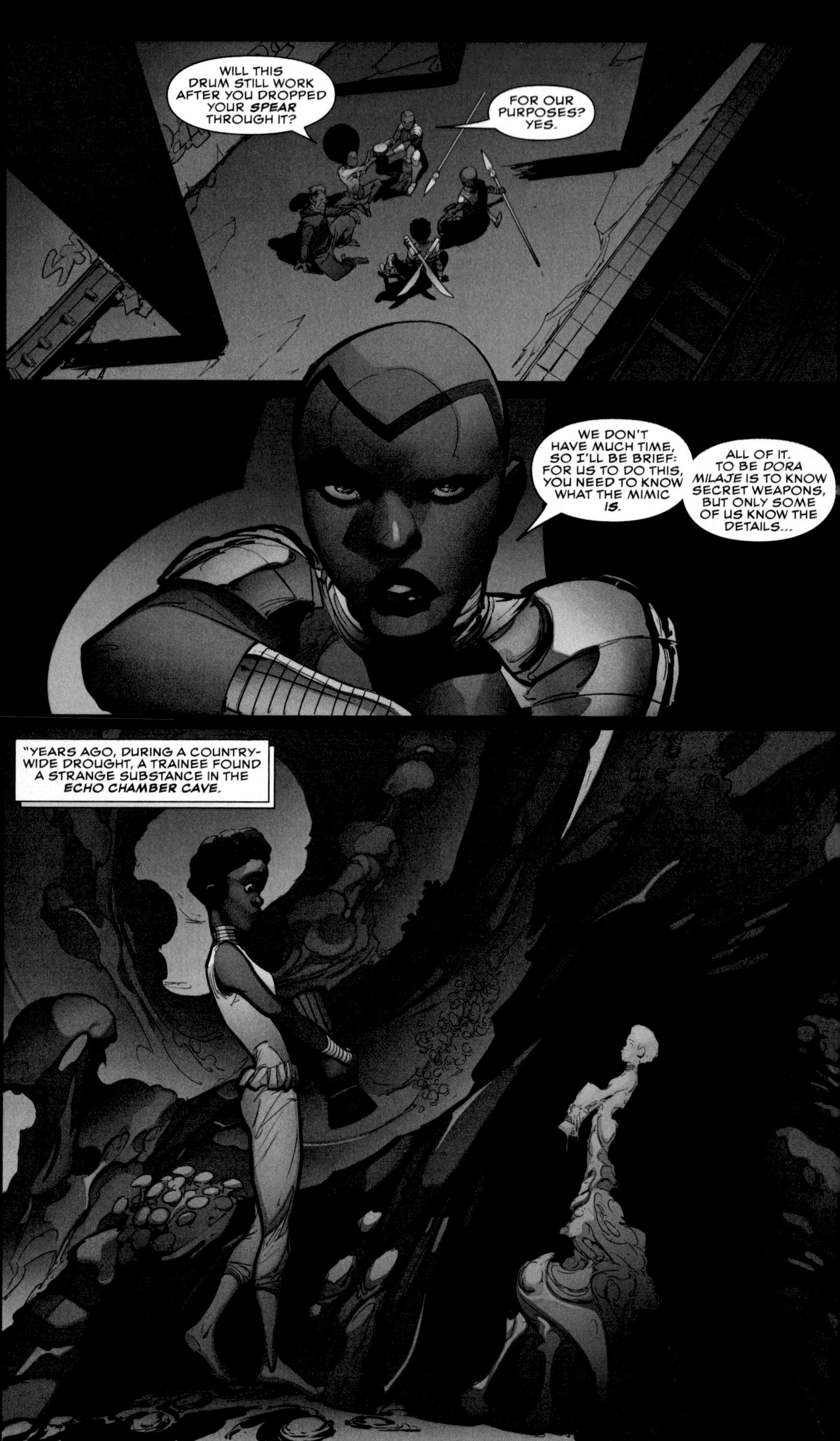
WILL THIS DRUM STILL WORK AFTER YOU DROPPED YOUR SPEAR THROUGH IT?
FOR OUR PURPOSES? YES.
WE DON'T HAVE MUCH TIME, SO I'LL BE BRIEF: FOR US TO DO THIS, YOU NEED TO KNOW WHAT THE MIMIC IS.
ALL OF IT. TO BE DORA MILAJE IS TO KNOW SECRET WEAPONS, BUT ONLY SOME OF US KNOW THE DETAILS...
"YEARS AGO, DURING A COUNTRY-WIDE DROUGHT, A TRAINEE FOUND A STRANGE SUBSTANCE IN THE ECHO CHAMBER CAVE.

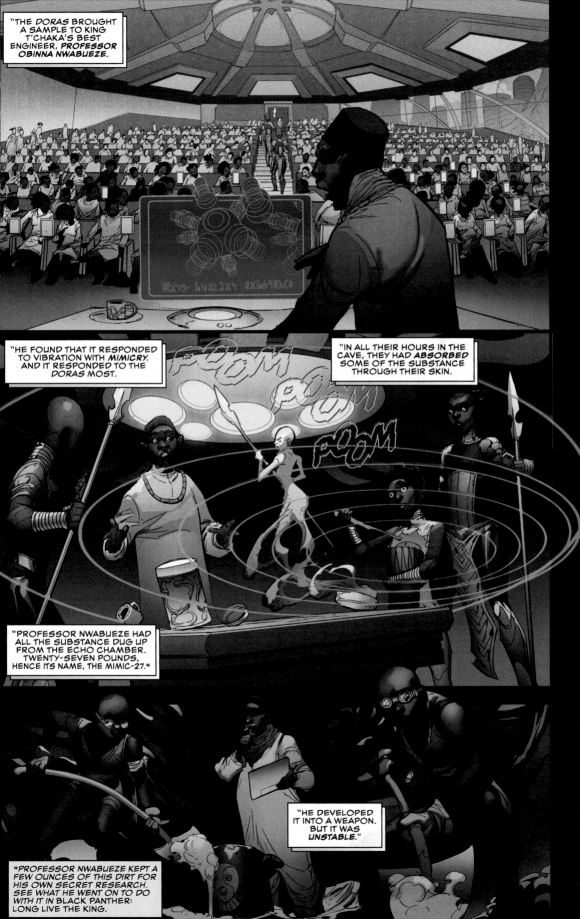

"THE DORAS BROUGHT A SAMPLE TO KING T'CHAKA'S BEST ENGINEER, PROFESSOR OBINNA NWABUEZE.

"HE FOUND THAT IT RESPONDED TO VIBRATION WITH *MIMICRY.* AND IT RESPONDED TO THE DORAS MOST.

"IN ALL THEIR HOURS IN THE CAVE, THEY HAD *ABSORBED* SOME OF THE SUBSTANCE THROUGH THEIR SKIN.

POOM
POOM
POOM

"PROFESSOR NWABUEZE HAD ALL THE SUBSTANCE DUG UP FROM THE ECHO CHAMBER. TWENTY-SEVEN POUNDS, HENCE ITS NAME, THE MIMIC-27.*

"HE DEVELOPED IT INTO A WEAPON. BUT IT WAS *UNSTABLE.*"

*PROFESSOR NWABUEZE KEPT A FEW OUNCES OF THIS DIRT FOR HIS OWN SECRET RESEARCH. SEE WHAT HE WENT ON TO DO WITH IT IN BLACK PANTHER: LONG LIVE THE KING.

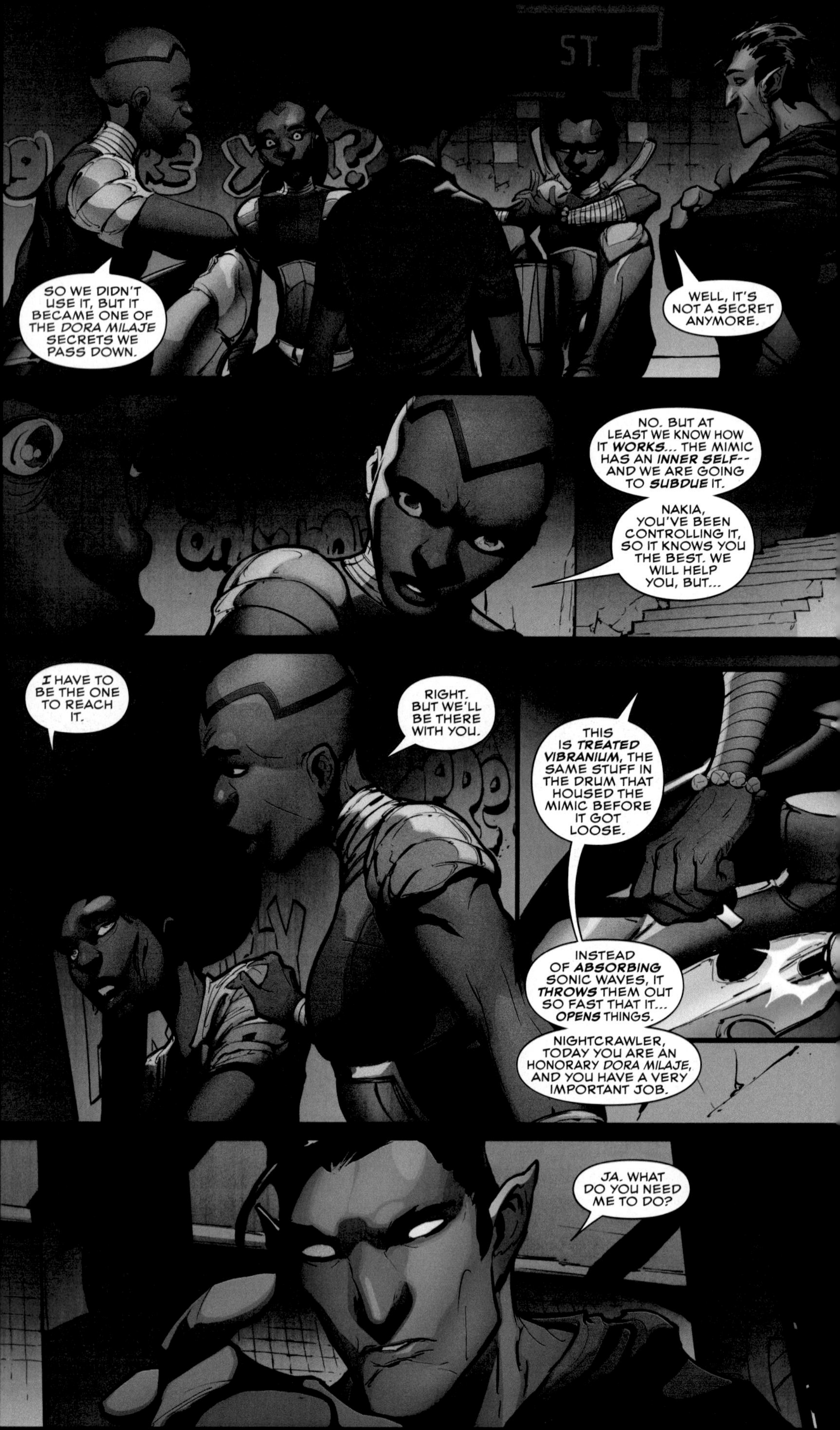
ST.
SO WE DIDN'T USE IT, BUT IT BECAME ONE OF THE *DORA MILAJE* SECRETS WE PASS DOWN.
WELL, IT'S NOT A SECRET ANYMORE.
NO. BUT AT LEAST WE KNOW HOW IT **WORKS**... THE MIMIC HAS AN **INNER SELF**-- AND WE ARE GOING TO **SUBDUE** IT.
NAKIA, YOU'VE BEEN CONTROLLING IT, SO IT KNOWS YOU THE BEST. WE WILL HELP YOU, BUT...
I HAVE TO BE THE ONE TO REACH IT.
RIGHT. BUT WE'LL BE THERE WITH YOU.
THIS IS ***TREATED VIBRANIUM***, THE SAME STUFF IN THE DRUM THAT HOUSED THE MIMIC BEFORE IT GOT LOOSE.
INSTEAD OF **ABSORBING** SONIC WAVES, IT **THROWS** THEM OUT SO FAST THAT IT... **OPENS** THINGS.
NIGHTCRAWLER, TODAY YOU ARE AN HONORARY *DORA MILAJE*, AND YOU HAVE A VERY IMPORTANT JOB.
JA. WHAT DO YOU NEED ME TO DO?

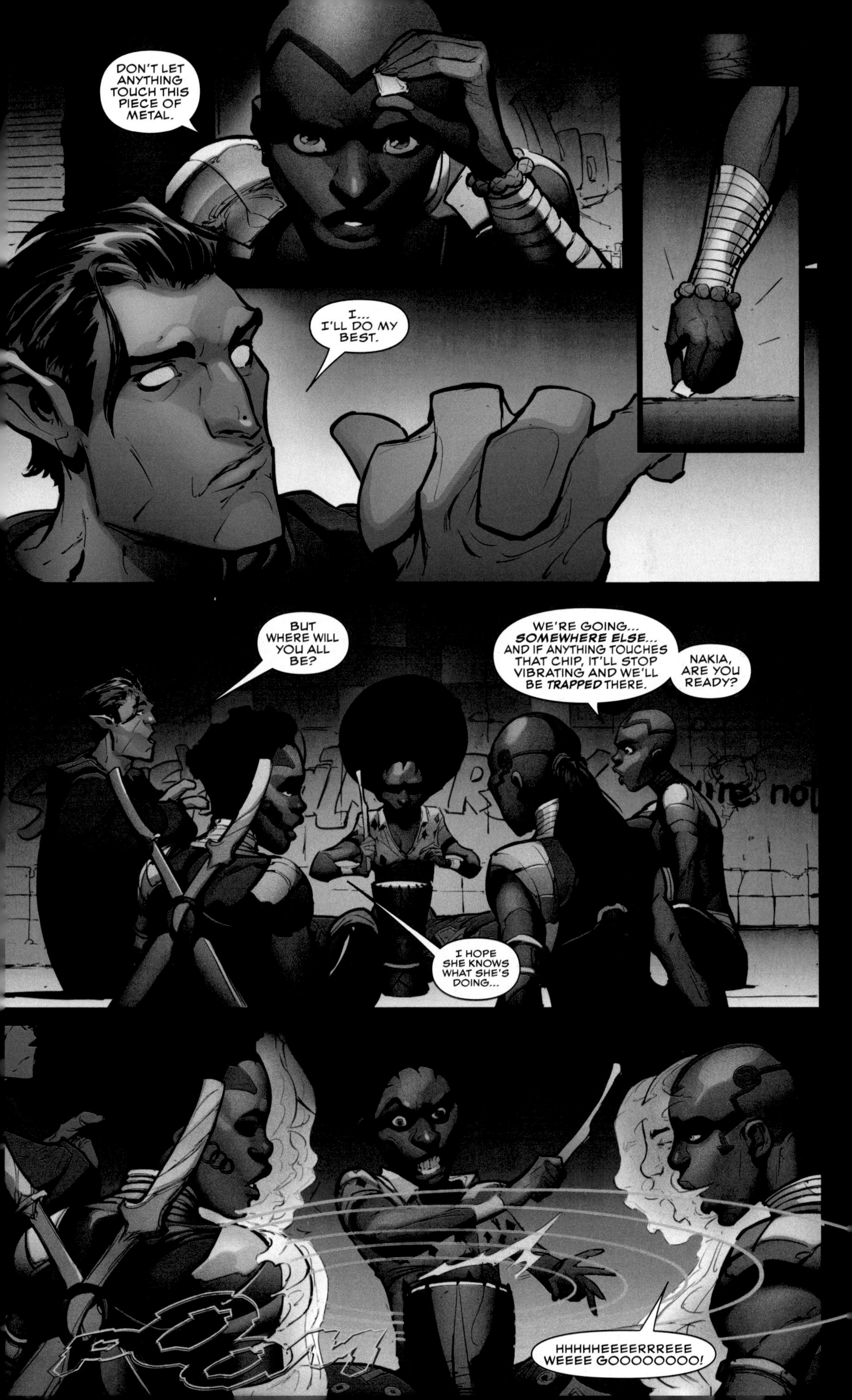
DON'T LET ANYTHING TOUCH THIS PIECE OF METAL.
I... I'LL DO MY BEST.
BUT WHERE WILL YOU ALL BE?
WE'RE GOING... SOMEWHERE ELSE... AND IF ANYTHING TOUCHES THAT CHIP, IT'LL STOP VIBRATING AND WE'LL BE TRAPPED THERE.
NAKIA, ARE YOU READY?
I HOPE SHE KNOWS WHAT SHE'S DOING...
HHHHHEEEERRREEE WEEEE GOOOOOOOO!

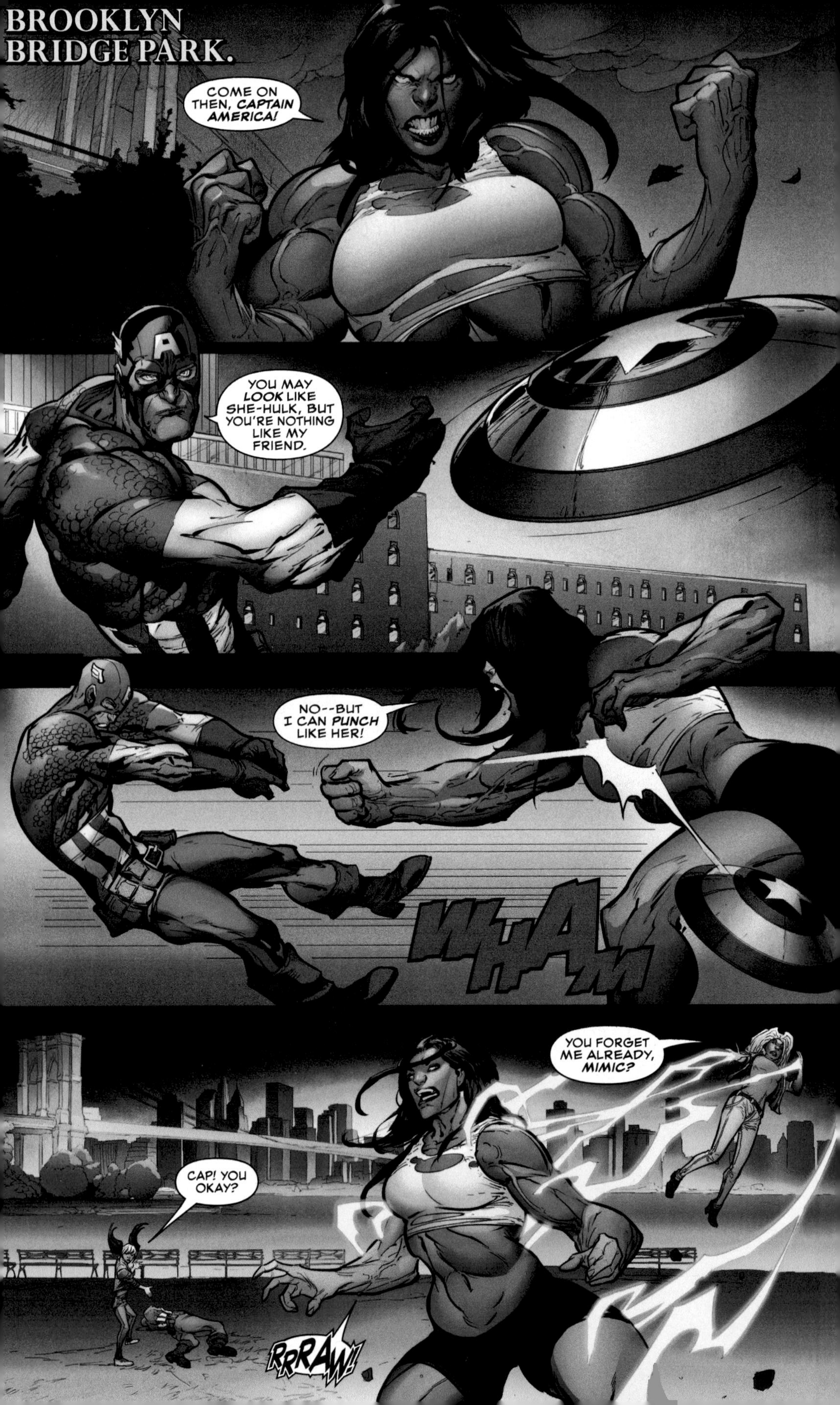
BROOKLYN BRIDGE PARK.
COME ON THEN, CAPTAIN AMERICA!
YOU MAY LOOK LIKE SHE-HULK, BUT YOU'RE NOTHING LIKE MY FRIEND.
NO--BUT I CAN PUNCH LIKE HER!
WHAM
YOU FORGET ME ALREADY, MIMIC?
CAP! YOU OKAY?
RRRAW!

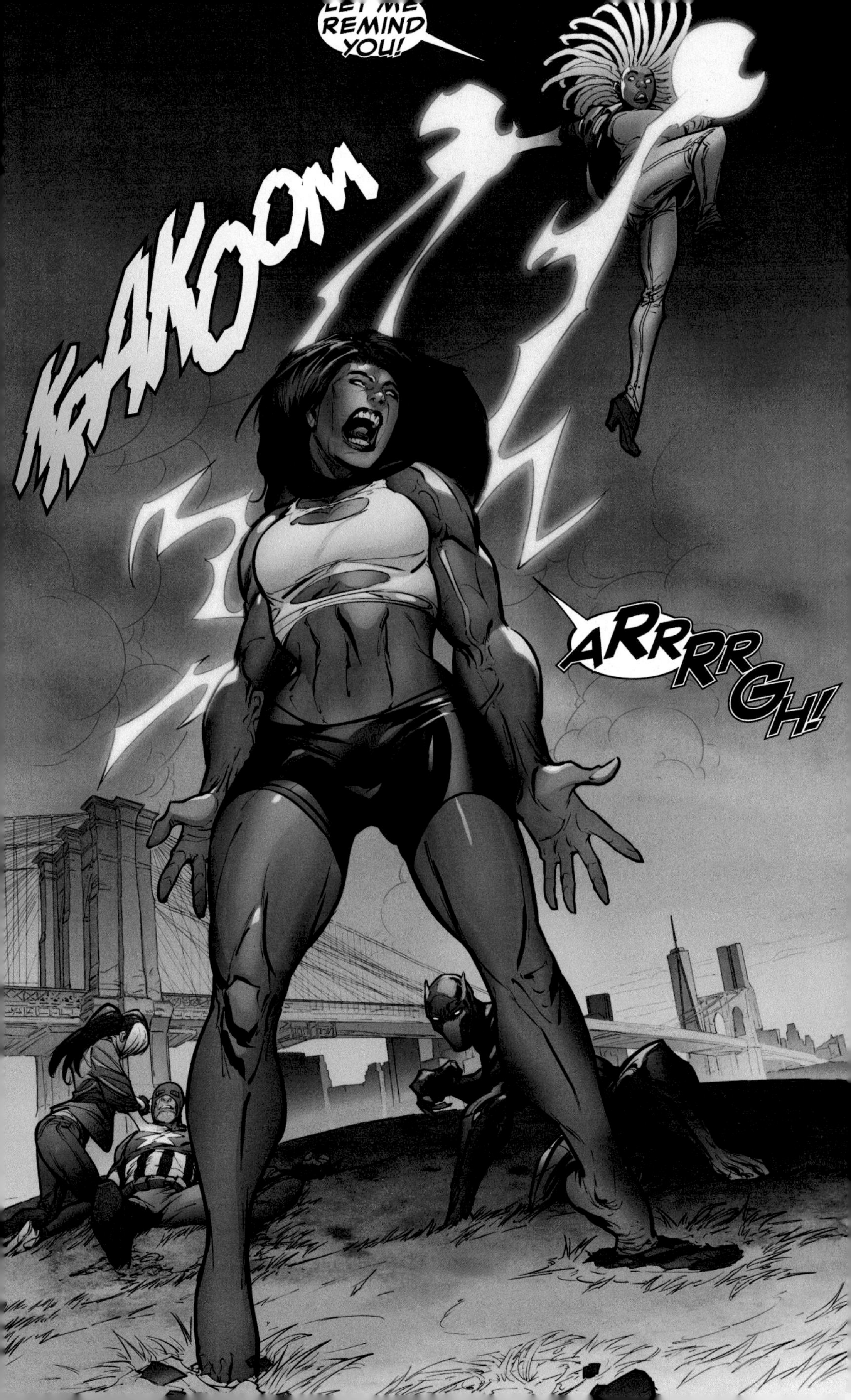
REMIND YOU!
KRAKOOM
ARRRRGH!

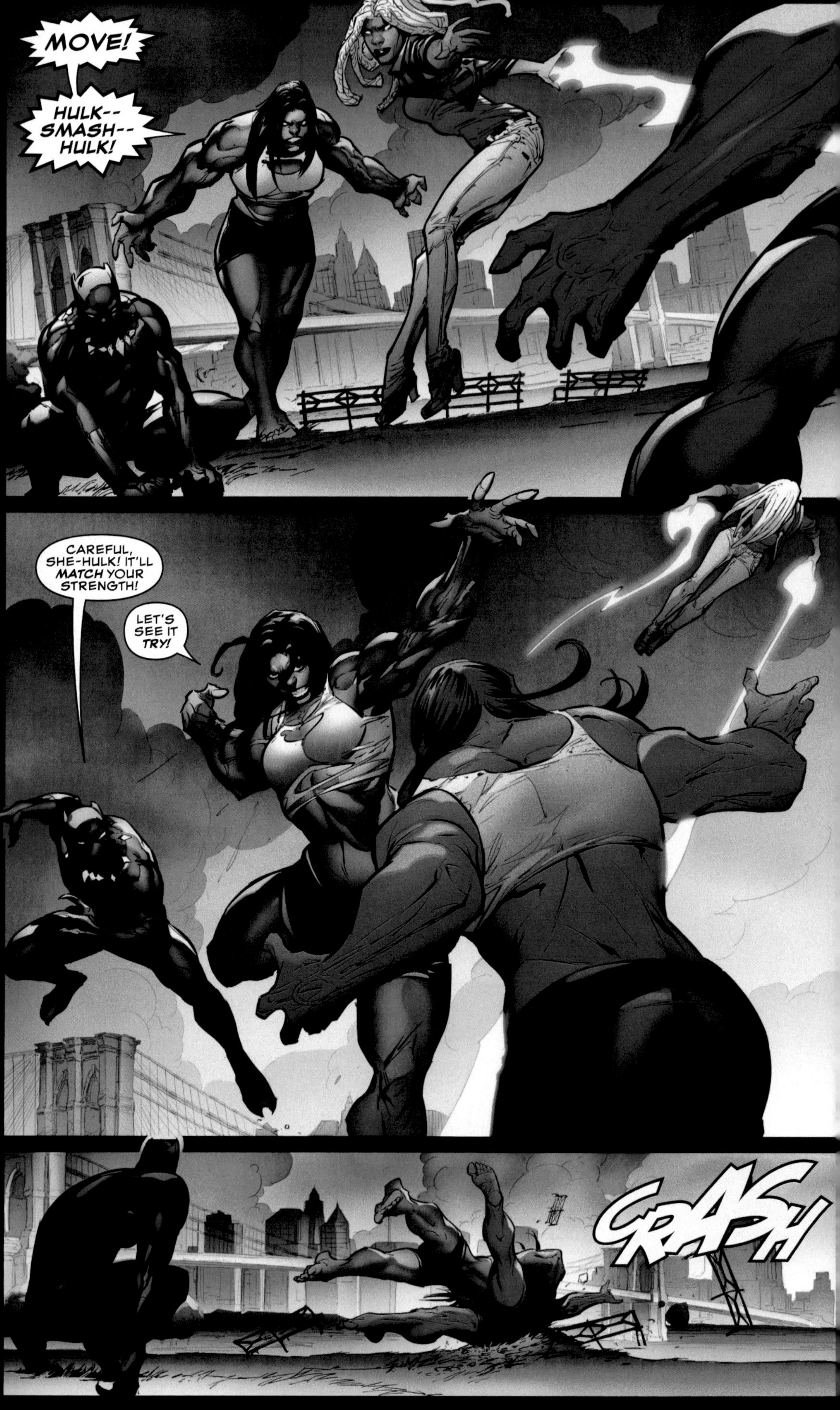
MOVE!
HULK-- SMASH-- HULK!
CAREFUL, SHE-HULK! IT'LL MATCH YOUR STRENGTH!
LET'S SEE IT TRY!
CRASH

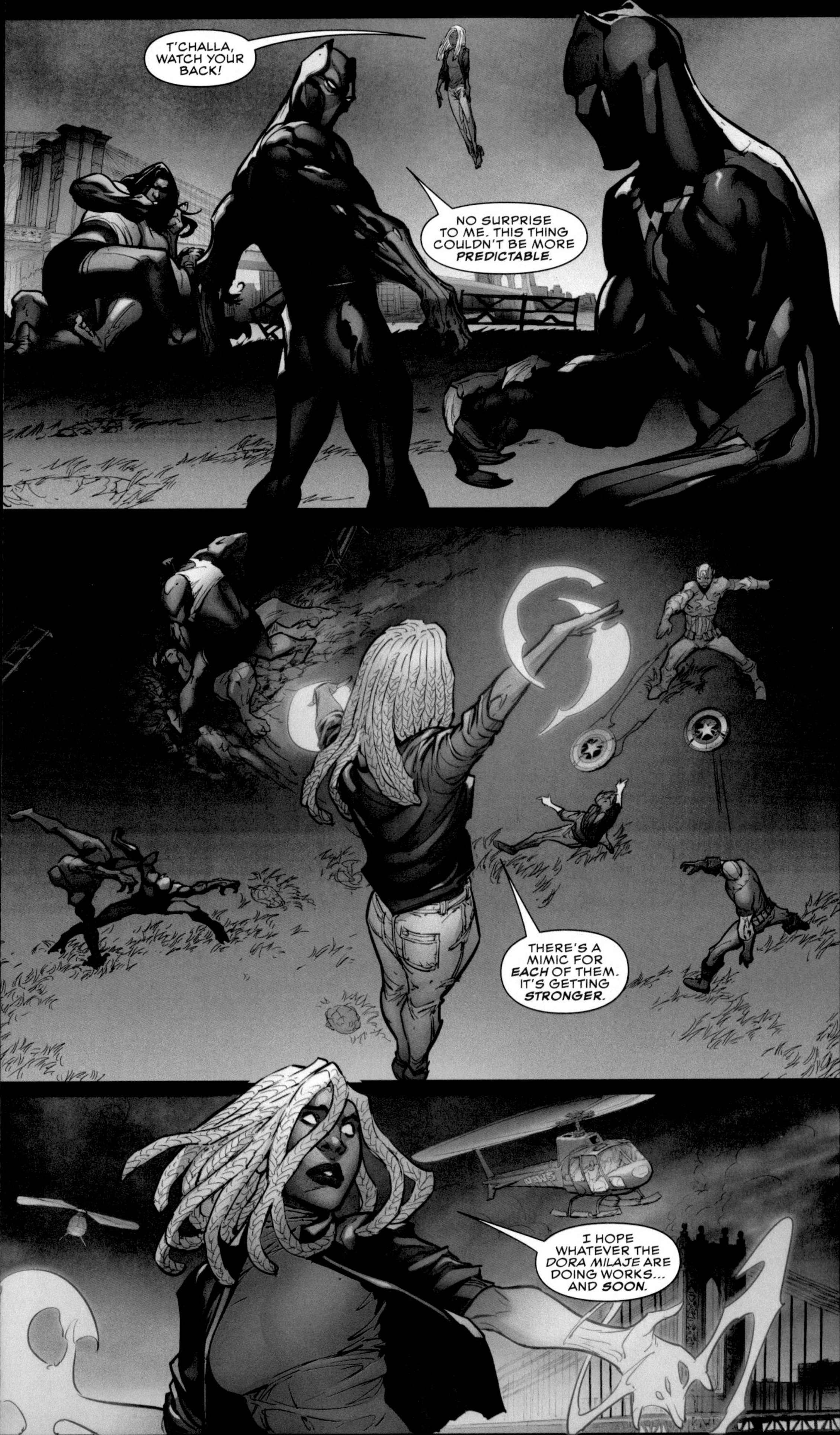
T'CHALLA, WATCH YOUR BACK!
NO SURPRISE TO ME. THIS THING COULDN'T BE MORE *PREDICTABLE*.
THERE'S A MIMIC FOR *EACH* OF THEM. IT'S GETTING *STRONGER*.
I HOPE WHATEVER THE *DORA MILAJE* ARE DOING WORKS... AND *SOON*.

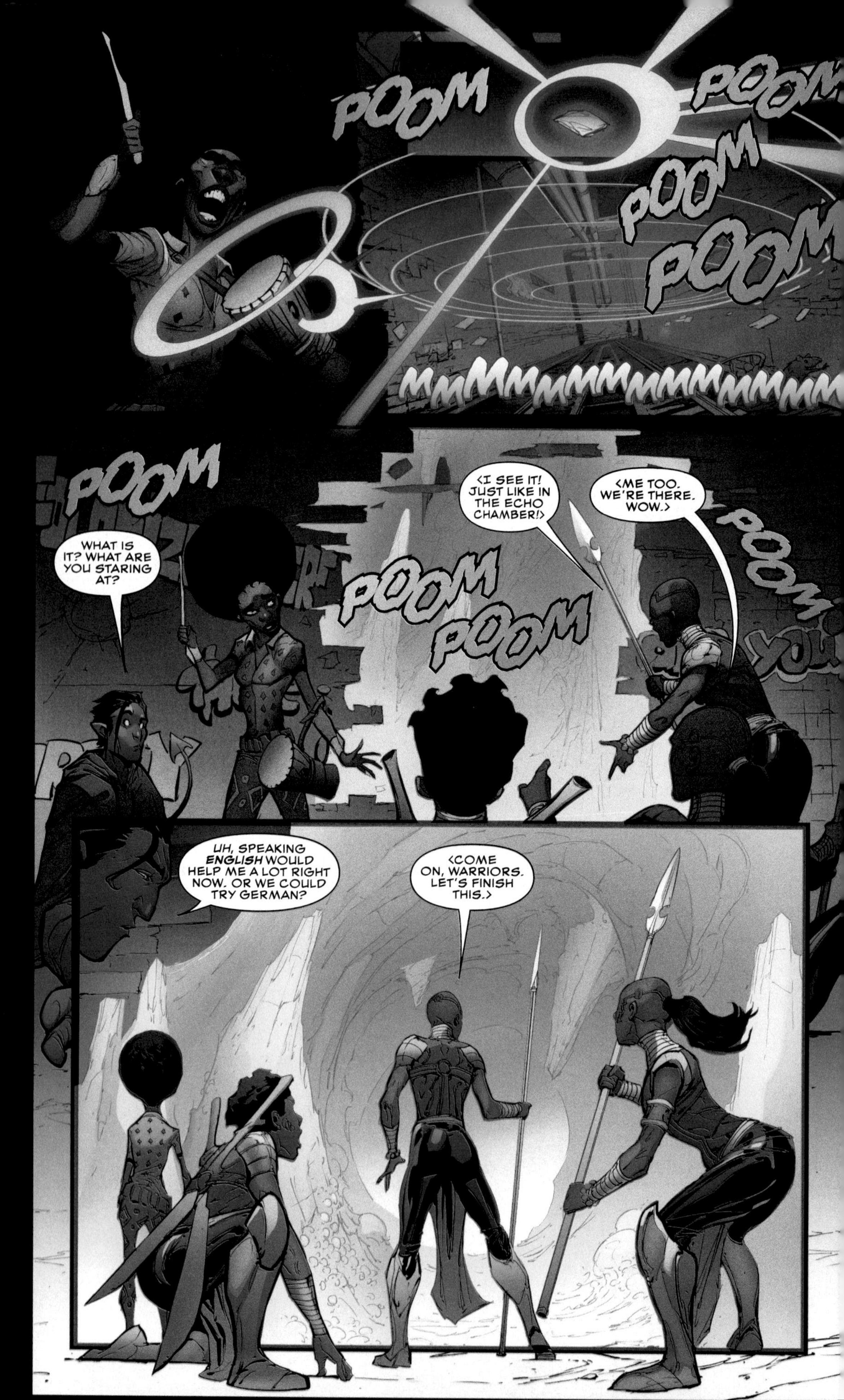
POOM
POOM
POOM
POOM
MMMMMMMMMMMMMMMMMMMM
POOM
WHAT IS IT? WHAT ARE YOU STARING AT?
POOM
POOM
<I SEE IT! JUST LIKE IN THE ECHO CHAMBER!>
<ME TOO. WE'RE THERE. WOW.>
POOM
UH, SPEAKING *ENGLISH* WOULD HELP ME A LOT RIGHT NOW. OR WE COULD TRY GERMAN?
<COME ON, WARRIORS. LET'S FINISH THIS.>

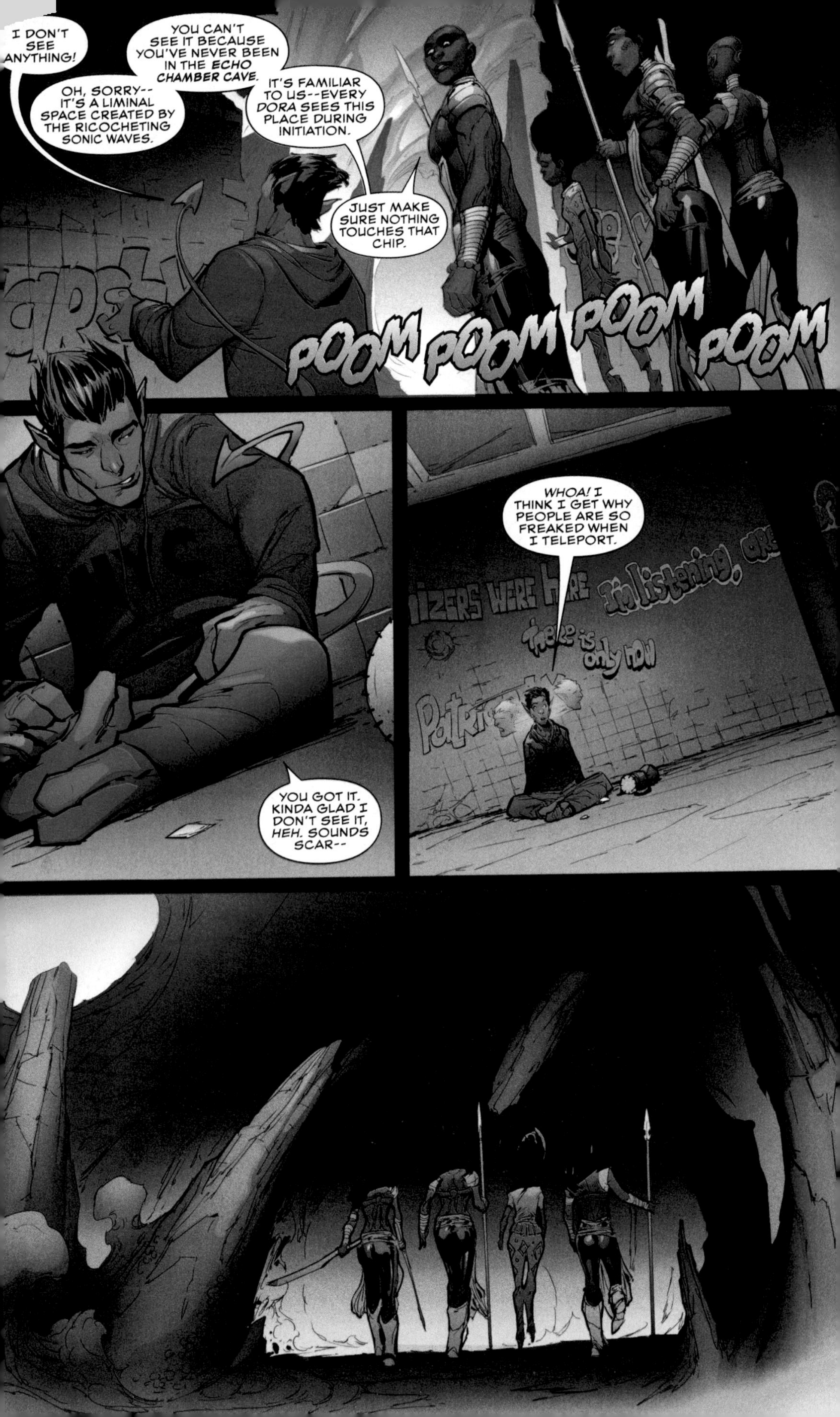
I DON'T SEE ANYTHING!
YOU CAN'T SEE IT BECAUSE YOU'VE NEVER BEEN IN THE *ECHO CHAMBER CAVE*.
OH, SORRY-- IT'S A LIMINAL SPACE CREATED BY THE RICOCHETING SONIC WAVES.
IT'S FAMILIAR TO US--EVERY *DORA* SEES THIS PLACE DURING INITIATION.
JUST MAKE SURE NOTHING TOUCHES THAT CHIP.
POOM POOM POOM POOM
YOU GOT IT. KINDA GLAD I DON'T SEE IT, *HEH*. SOUNDS SCAR--
WHOA! I THINK I GET WHY PEOPLE ARE SO FREAKED WHEN I TELEPORT.
IZERS WERE HERE
I'm listening.
there is only now

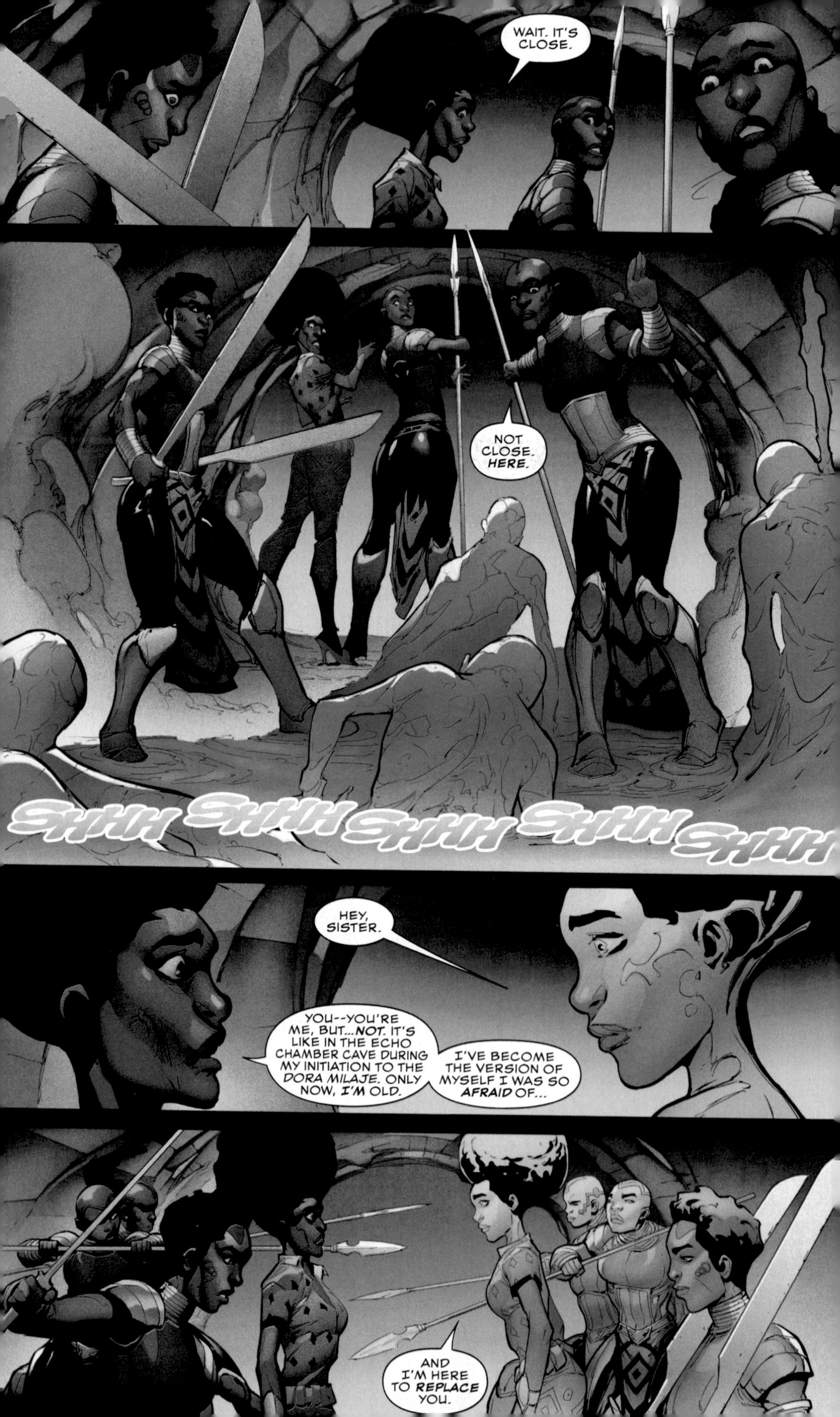
WAIT. IT'S CLOSE.
NOT CLOSE. HERE.
SHHH SHHH SHHH SHHH SHHH
HEY, SISTER.
YOU--YOU'RE ME, BUT...NOT. IT'S LIKE IN THE ECHO CHAMBER CAVE DURING MY INITIATION TO THE DORA MILAJE. ONLY NOW, I'M OLD.
I'VE BECOME THE VERSION OF MYSELF I WAS SO AFRAID OF...
AND I'M HERE TO REPLACE YOU.

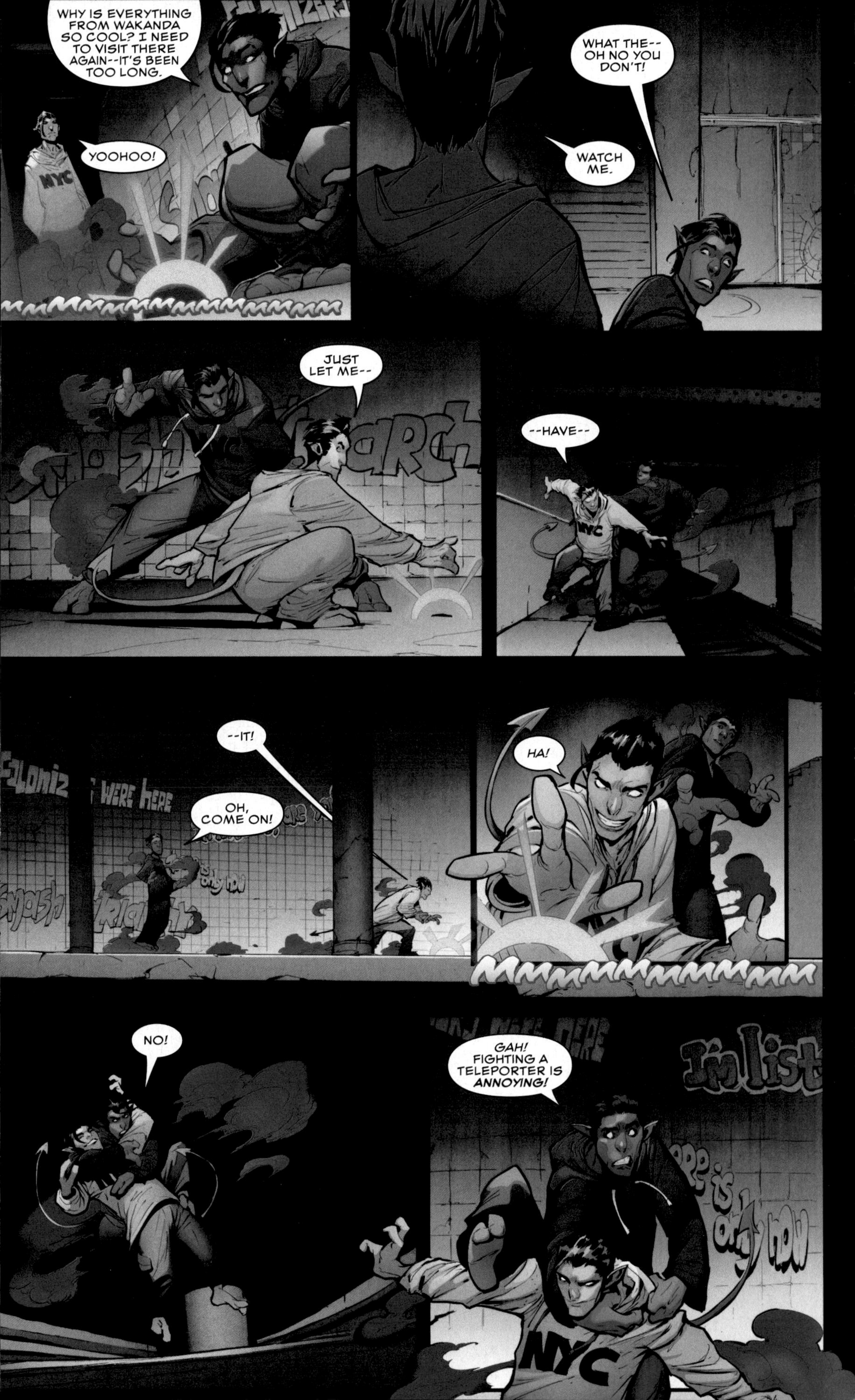
WHY IS EVERYTHING FROM WAKANDA SO COOL? I NEED TO VISIT THERE AGAIN--IT'S BEEN TOO LONG.
YOOHOO!
MMMMMMMMMMMMMMM
WHAT THE-- OH NO YOU DON'T!
WATCH ME.
JUST LET ME--
--HAVE--
--IT!
OH, COME ON!
HA!
MMMMMMMMMMMMM
NO!
GAH! FIGHTING A TELEPORTER IS ANNOYING!

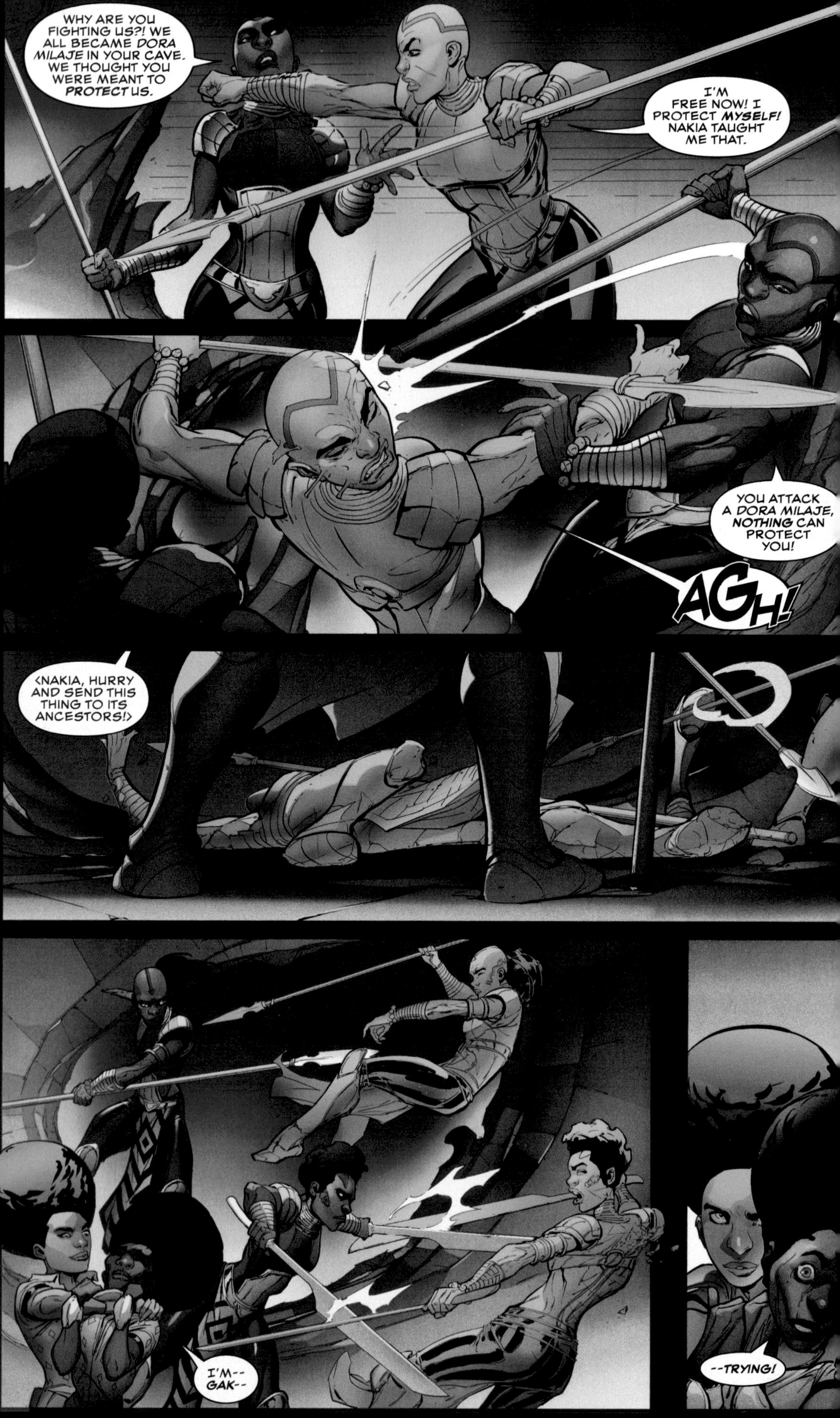

WHY ARE YOU FIGHTING US?! WE ALL BECAME *DORA MILAJE* IN YOUR CAVE. WE THOUGHT YOU WERE MEANT TO *PROTECT* US.
I'M FREE NOW! I PROTECT **MYSELF!** NAKIA TAUGHT ME THAT.
YOU ATTACK A *DORA MILAJE*, **NOTHING** CAN PROTECT YOU!
AGH!
<NAKIA, HURRY AND SEND THIS THING TO ITS ANCESTORS!>
I'M-- GAK--
--TRYING!

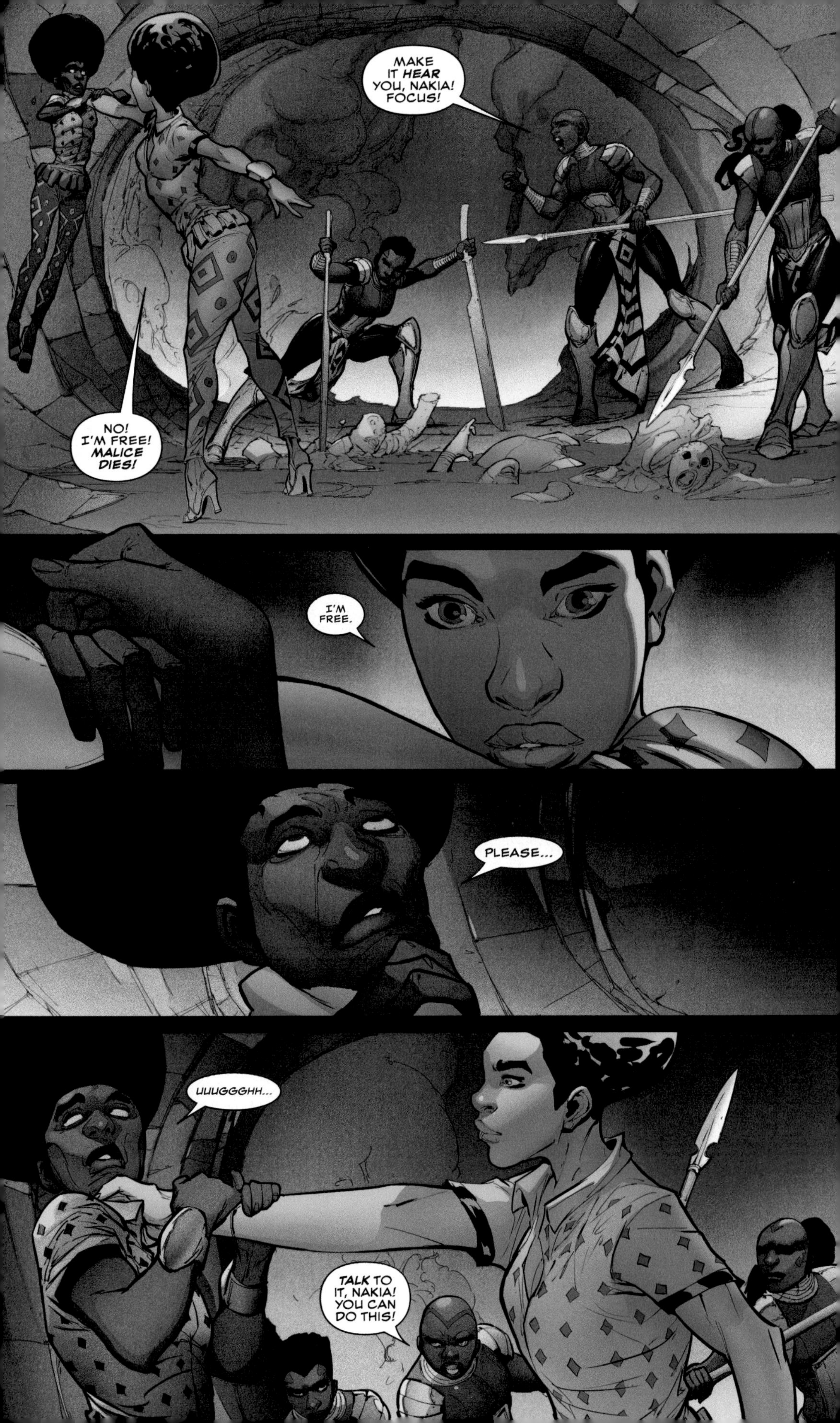
MAKE IT HEAR YOU, NAKIA! FOCUS!
NO! I'M FREE! MALICE DIES!
I'M FREE.
PLEASE...
UUUGGGHH...
TALK TO IT, NAKIA! YOU CAN DO THIS!

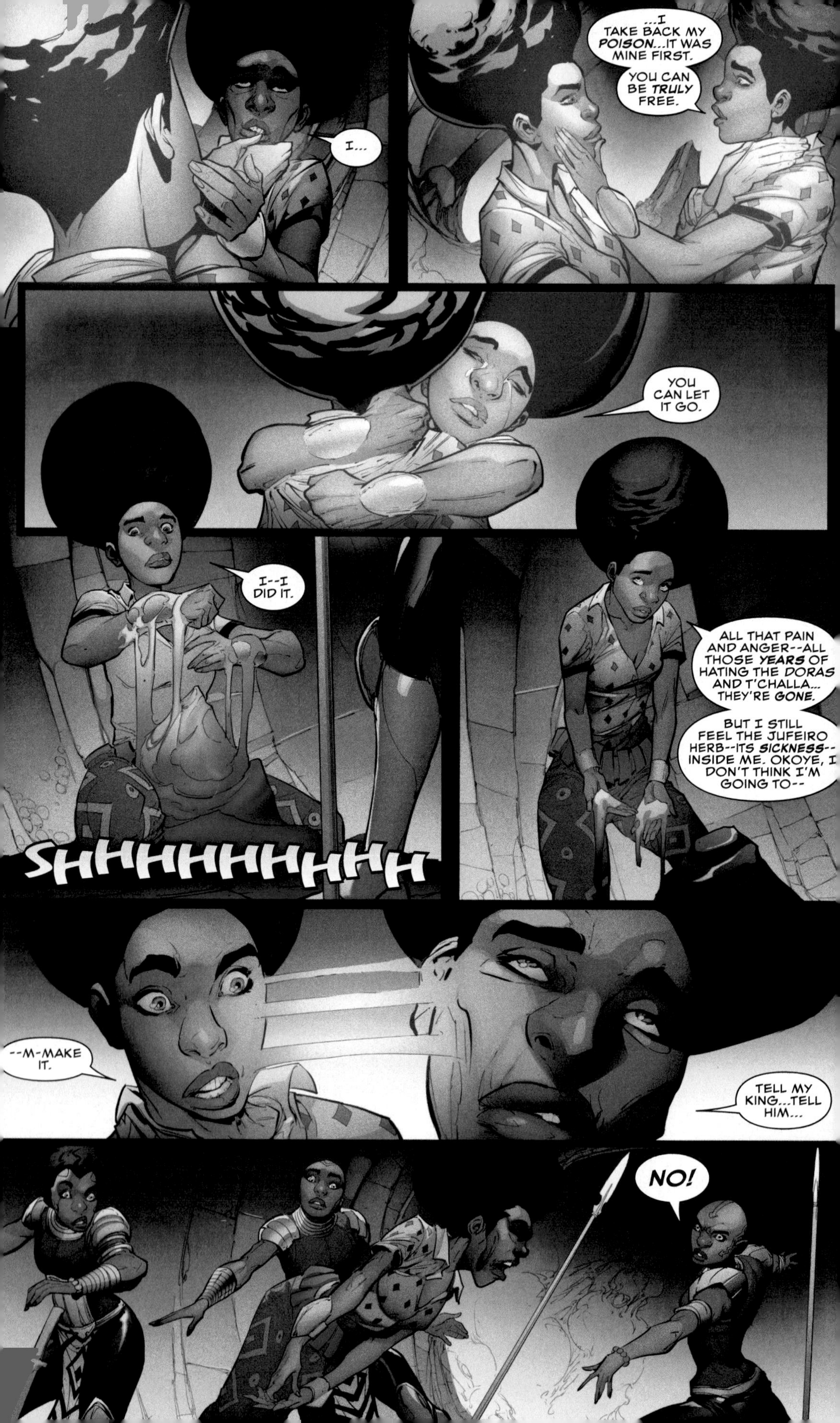

I...
...I TAKE BACK MY POISON...IT WAS MINE FIRST.
YOU CAN BE TRULY FREE.
YOU CAN LET IT GO.
I--I DID IT.
SHHHHHHHHHH
ALL THAT PAIN AND ANGER--ALL THOSE YEARS OF HATING THE DORAS AND T'CHALLA... THEY'RE GONE.
BUT I STILL FEEL THE JUFEIRO HERB--ITS SICKNESS--INSIDE ME. OKOYE, I DON'T THINK I'M GOING TO--
--M-MAKE IT.
TELL MY KING...TELL HIM...
NO!

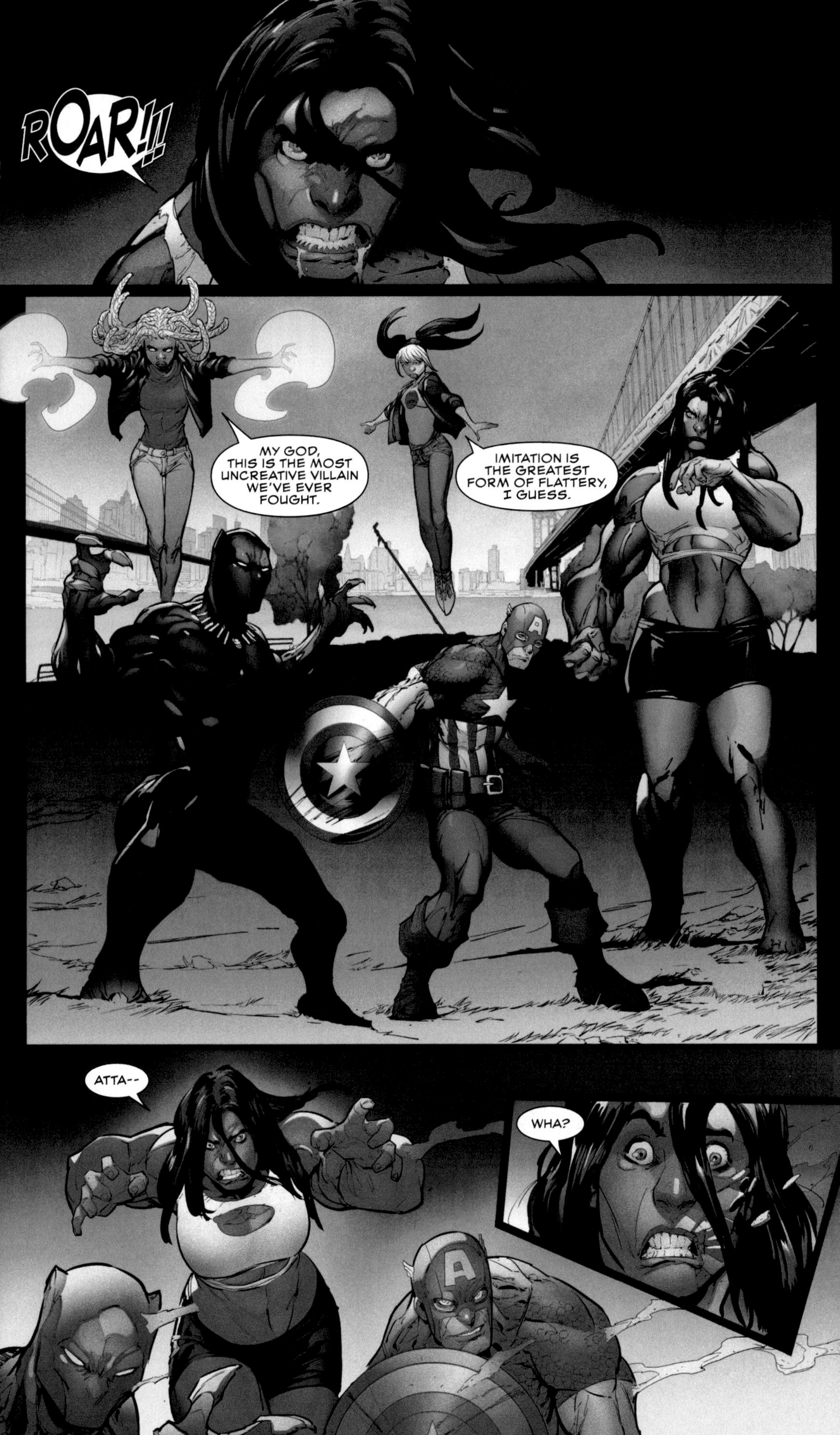
ROAR!!!
MY GOD, THIS IS THE MOST UNCREATIVE VILLAIN WE'VE EVER FOUGHT.
IMITATION IS THE GREATEST FORM OF FLATTERY, I GUESS.
ATTA--
WHA?

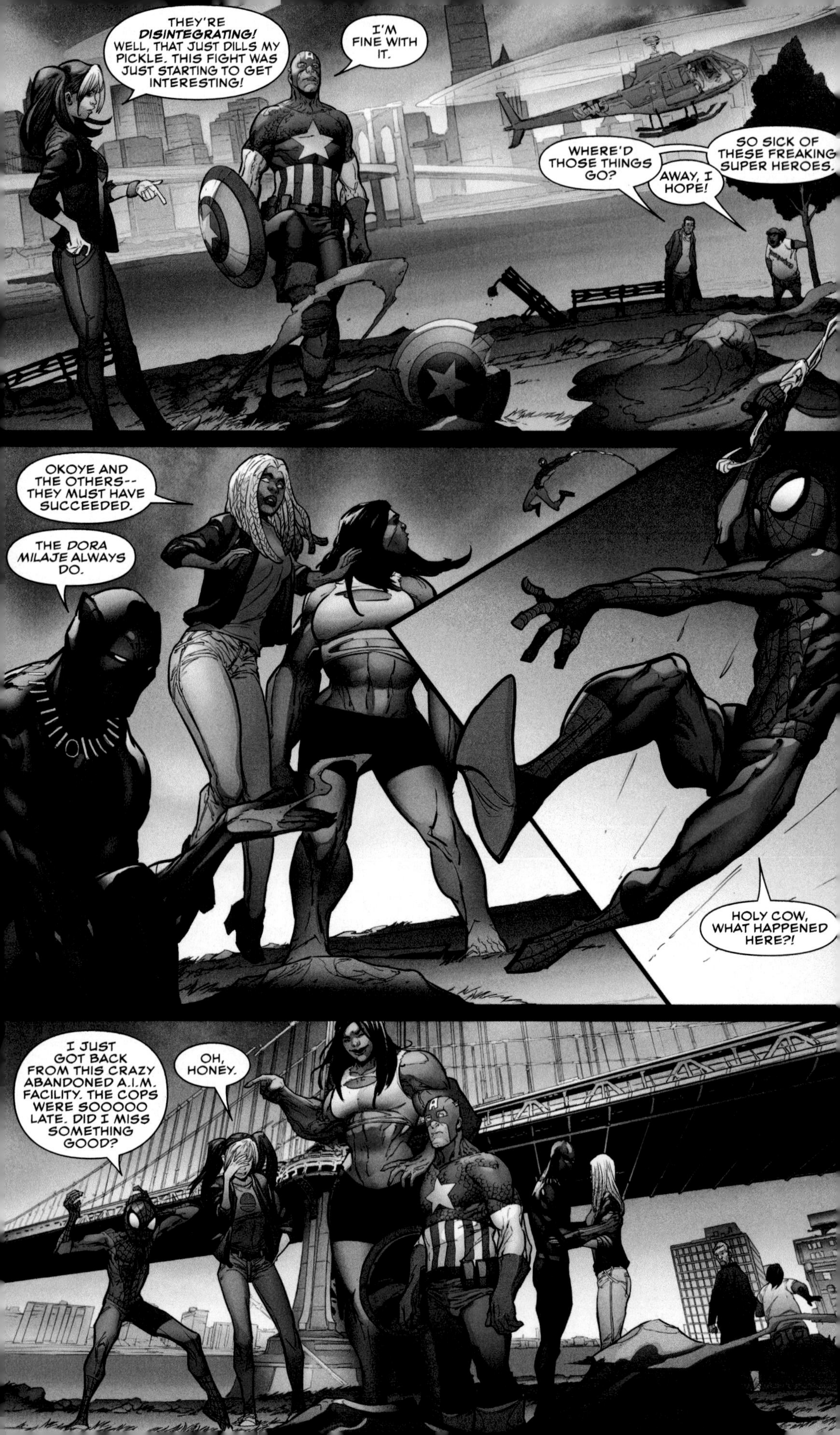
THEY'RE DISINTEGRATING! WELL, THAT JUST DILLS MY PICKLE. THIS FIGHT WAS JUST STARTING TO GET INTERESTING!
I'M FINE WITH IT.
WHERE'D THOSE THINGS GO?
SO SICK OF THESE FREAKING SUPER HEROES.
AWAY, I HOPE!
OKOYE AND THE OTHERS-- THEY MUST HAVE SUCCEEDED.
THE DORA MILAJE ALWAYS DO.
HOLY COW, WHAT HAPPENED HERE?!
I JUST GOT BACK FROM THIS CRAZY ABANDONED A.I.M. FACILITY. THE COPS WERE SOOOOO LATE. DID I MISS SOMETHING GOOD?
OH, HONEY.

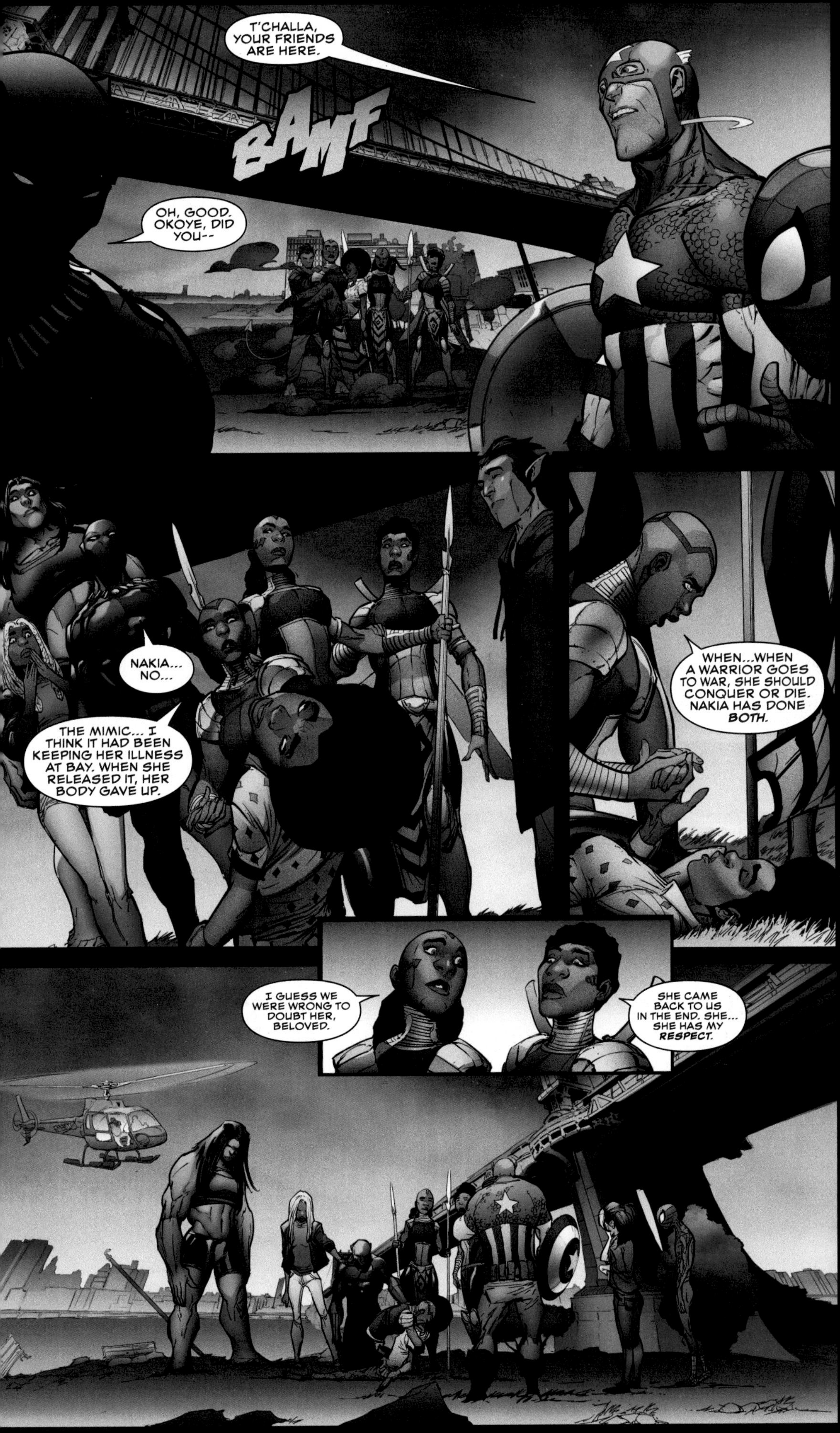
T'CHALLA, YOUR FRIENDS ARE HERE.
BAMF
OH, GOOD. OKOYE, DID YOU--
NAKIA... NO...
THE MIMIC... I THINK IT HAD BEEN KEEPING HER ILLNESS AT BAY. WHEN SHE RELEASED IT, HER BODY GAVE UP.
WHEN...WHEN A WARRIOR GOES TO WAR, SHE SHOULD CONQUER OR DIE. NAKIA HAS DONE BOTH.
I GUESS WE WERE WRONG TO DOUBT HER, BELOVED.
SHE CAME BACK TO US IN THE END. SHE... SHE HAS MY RESPECT.

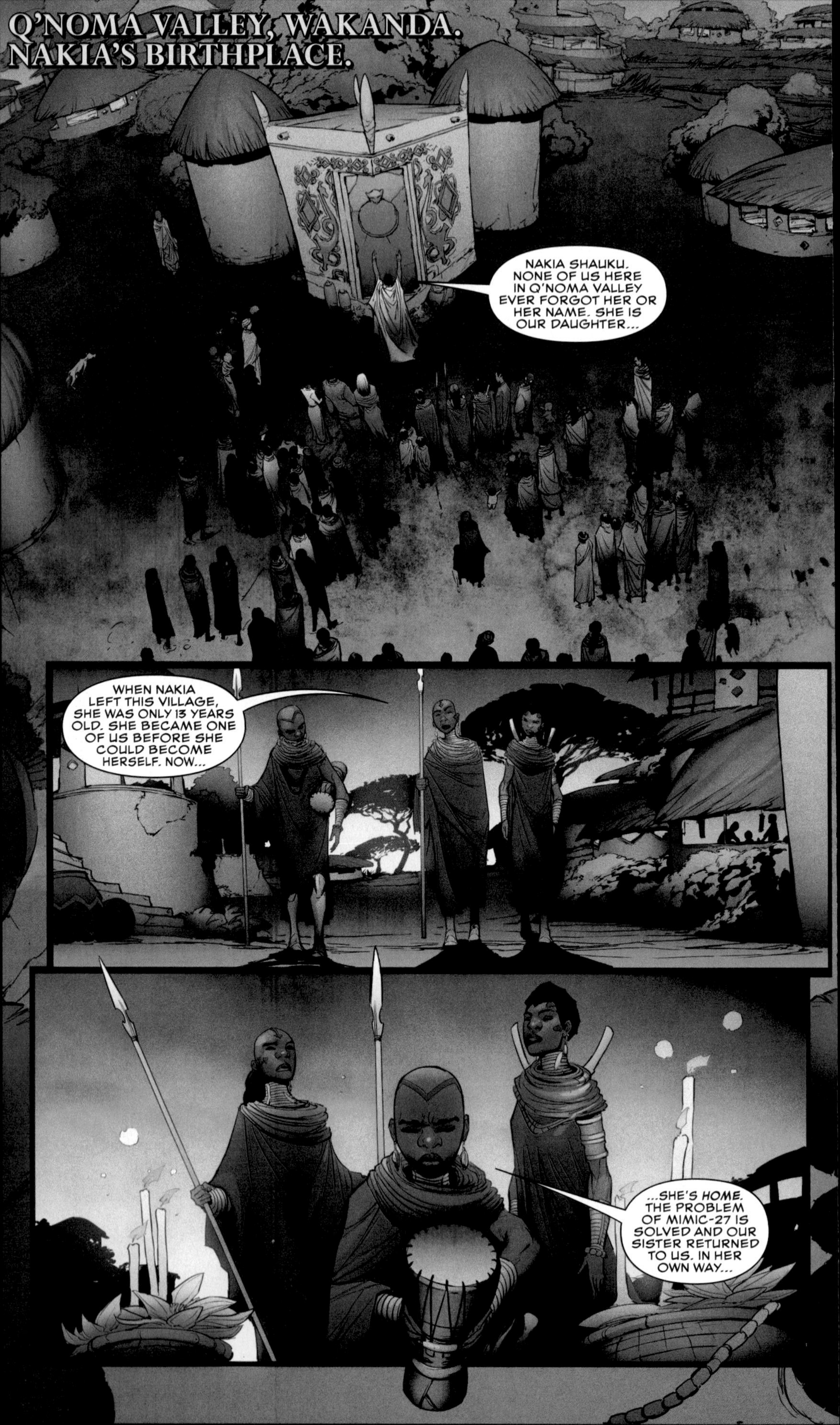
Q'NOMA VALLEY, WAKANDA. NAKIA'S BIRTHPLACE.
NAKIA SHAUKU. NONE OF US HERE IN Q'NOMA VALLEY EVER FORGOT HER OR HER NAME. SHE IS OUR DAUGHTER...
WHEN NAKIA LEFT THIS VILLAGE, SHE WAS ONLY 13 YEARS OLD. SHE BECAME ONE OF US BEFORE SHE COULD BECOME HERSELF. NOW...
...SHE'S *HOME*. THE PROBLEM OF MIMIC-27 IS SOLVED AND OUR SISTER RETURNED TO US. IN HER OWN WAY...

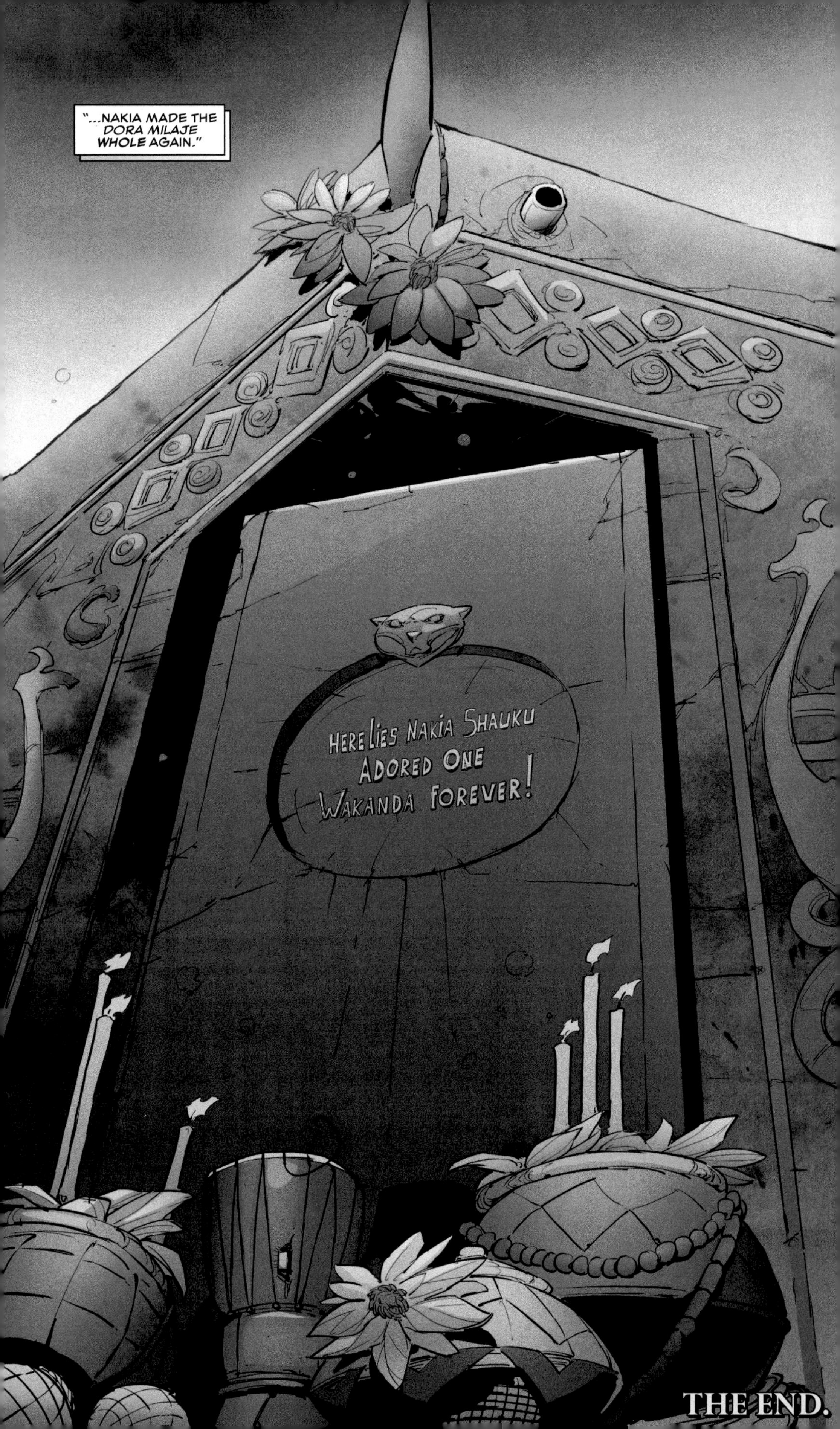
"...NAKIA MADE THE DORA MILAJE WHOLE AGAIN."
HERE LIES NAKIA SHAUKU
ADORED ONE
WAKANDA FOREVER!
THE END.

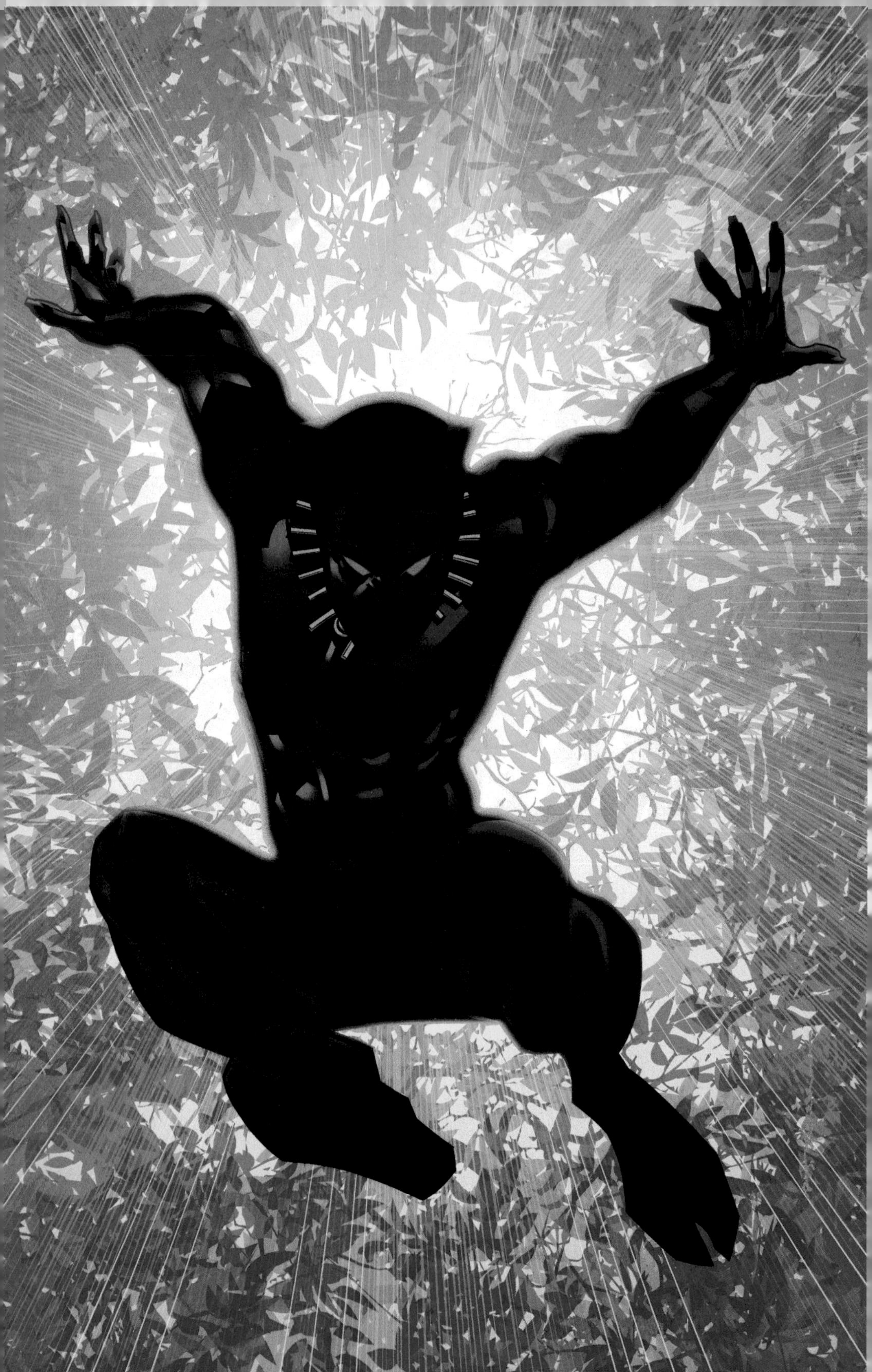

BLACK PANTHER ANNUAL #1 VARIANT BY **BRIAN STELFREEZE**

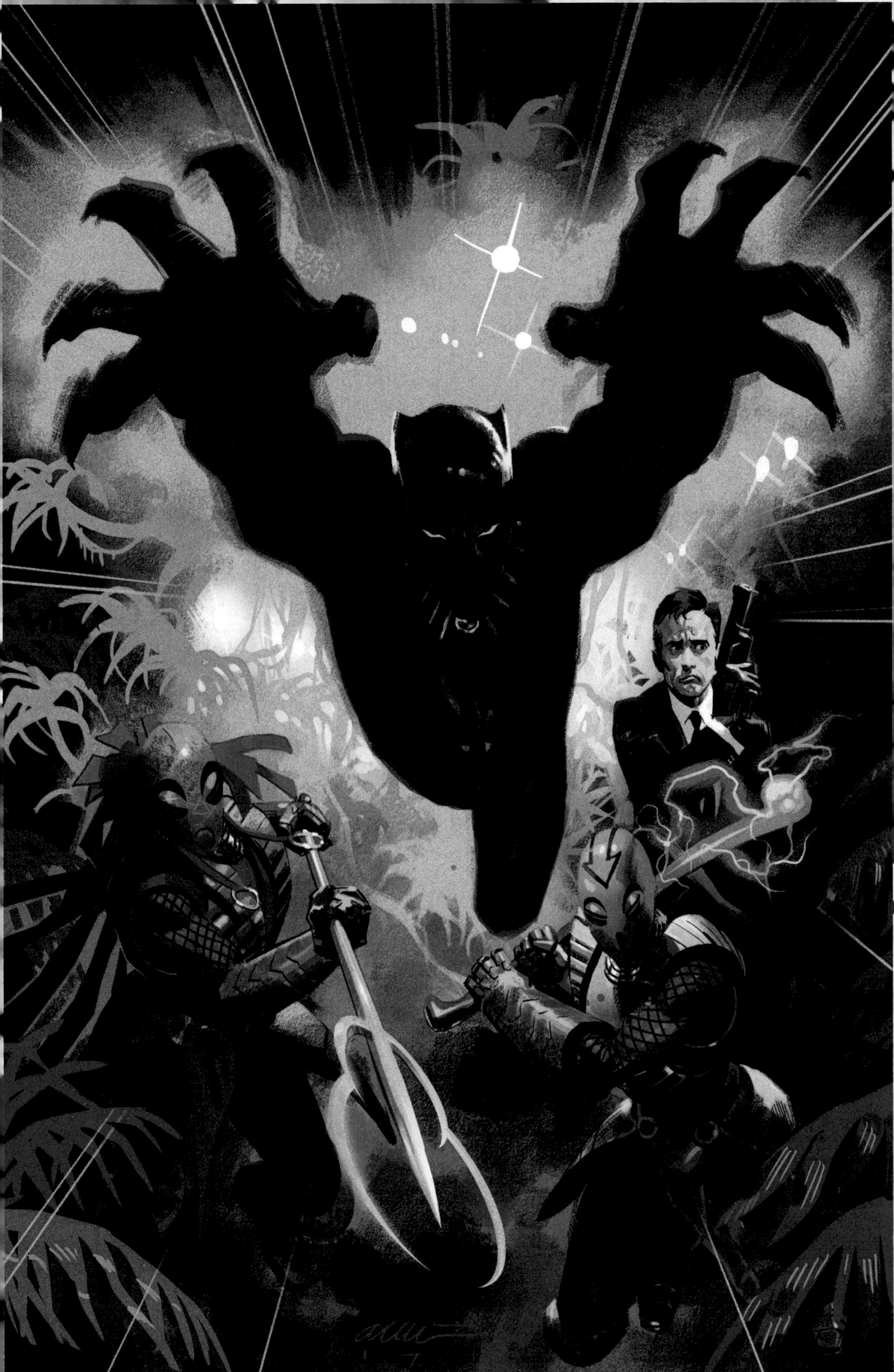

BLACK PANTHER ANNUAL 1

A CELEBRATION OF THREE LEGENDARY ERAS OF BLACK PANTHER COMIC BOO[K]

A BLACK PANTHER STORY SET IN THE PRESENT...

"BACK IN BLACK"

writer **PRIEST**   artist **MIKE PERKINS**   color artist **ANDY TRO**

ONCE, ON A DIPLOMATIC MISSION TO THE UNITED STATES, TH[E] BLACK PANTHER FOUND AN UNEXPECTED ALLY IN EVERETT K. ROSS[,] AN EMPLOYEE OF THE U.S. STATE DEPARTMENT. BUT IT HAS BEEN [A] WHILE SINCE THEY LAST SAW EACH OTHER.

RECENTLY THERE HAS BEEN GREAT POLITICAL UPHEAVA[L] IN WAKANDA, RESULTING IN THE COUNTRY BECOMING [A] CONSTITUTIONAL MONARCHY. SO WHILE T'CHALLA IS STIL[L] KING, THE PEOPLE OF WAKANDA NOW HAVE A SAY IN HOW TH[E] COUNTRY IS RUN.

A BLACK PANTHER STORY SET IN AN ALTERNATE PAST...

"PANTHER'S HEART"

writer **DON McGREGOR**   artist **DANIEL ACUÑA**

NOT LONG AFTER HE FIRST BECAME THE BLACK PANTHE[R,] T'CHALLA FELL IN LOVE WITH AN AMERICAN NAMED MONIC[A] LYNNE. THEY EVENTUALLY BROKE UP, BUT T'CHALLA NEVE[R] STOPPED CARING FOR HER.

A BLACK PANTHER STORY SET IN AN ALTERNATE FUTURE...

"BLACK TO THE FUTURE PART II"

writer **REGGIE HUDLIN**   artist **KEN LASHLEY**   color artist **MATT MILL[A]**

STORM OF THE X-MEN AND THE BLACK PANTHER WERE ONC[E] MARRIED, AND IN AN ALTERNATE TIMELINE, THEIR UNIO[N] RESULTED IN A DYNASTY THAT — FOLLOWING A WAR WITH TH[E] UNITED STATES — SAW WAKANDA BECOME THE RULING POWE[R] OF THE ENTIRE WORLD.

letterer **VC's JOE SABINO**
design **MANNY MEDEROS**
logo **RIAN HUGHES**
cover by **DANIEL ACUÑA**
variant cover by **BRIAN STELFREEZE**

associate editor **SARAH BRUNSTA[D]**
editor **WIL MOS[S]**
executive editor **TOM BREVOOR[T]**
editor in chief **C.B. CEBULS[KI]**
chief creative officer **JOE QUESAD[A]**
president **DAN BUCKLE[Y]**
executive producer **ALAN FIN[E]**

BACK IN BLACK

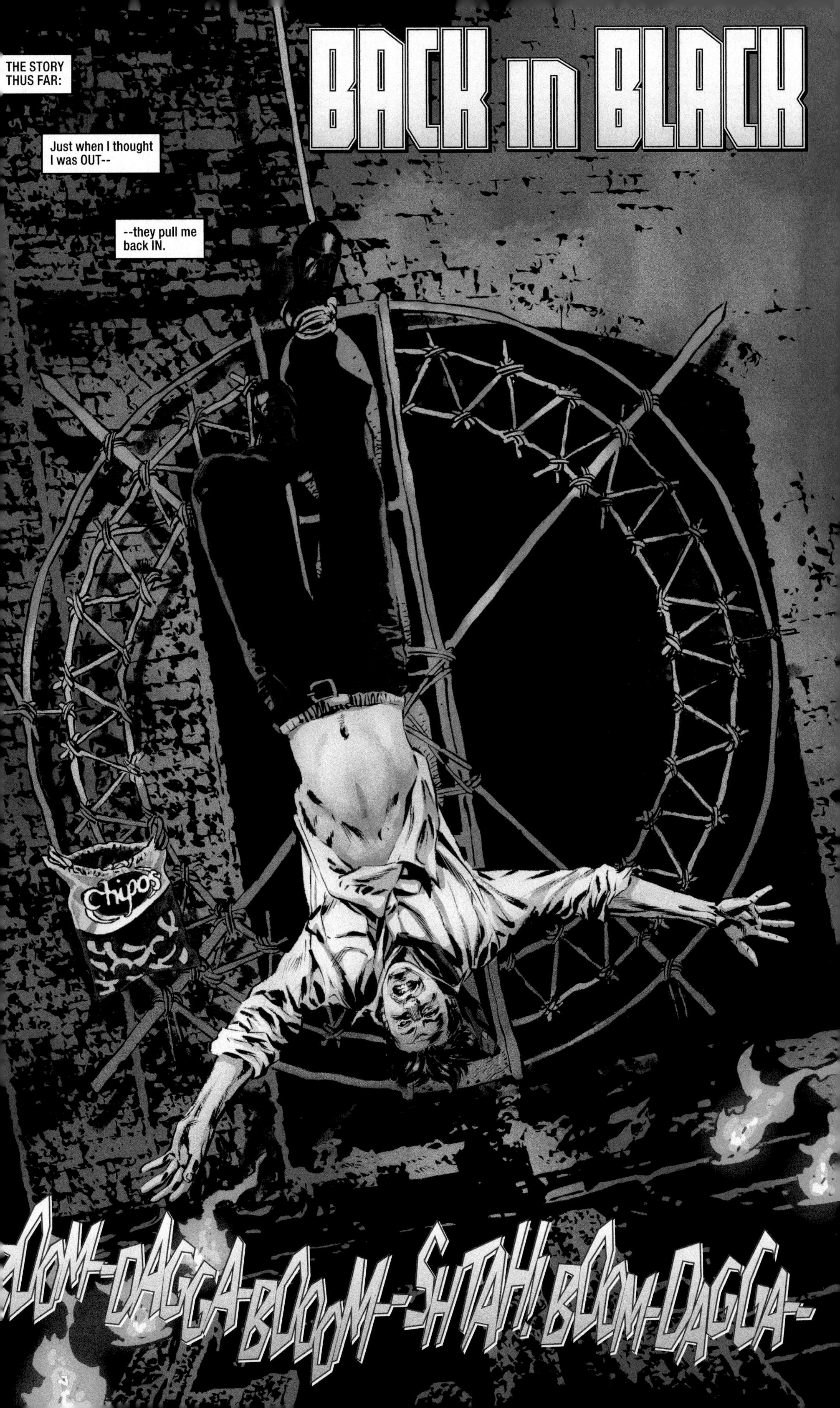

THE STORY THUS FAR:
Just when I thought I was OUT--
--they pull me back IN.
Chipos
OOM-DAGGA-BOOOM--SHTAH! BOOM-DAGGA-

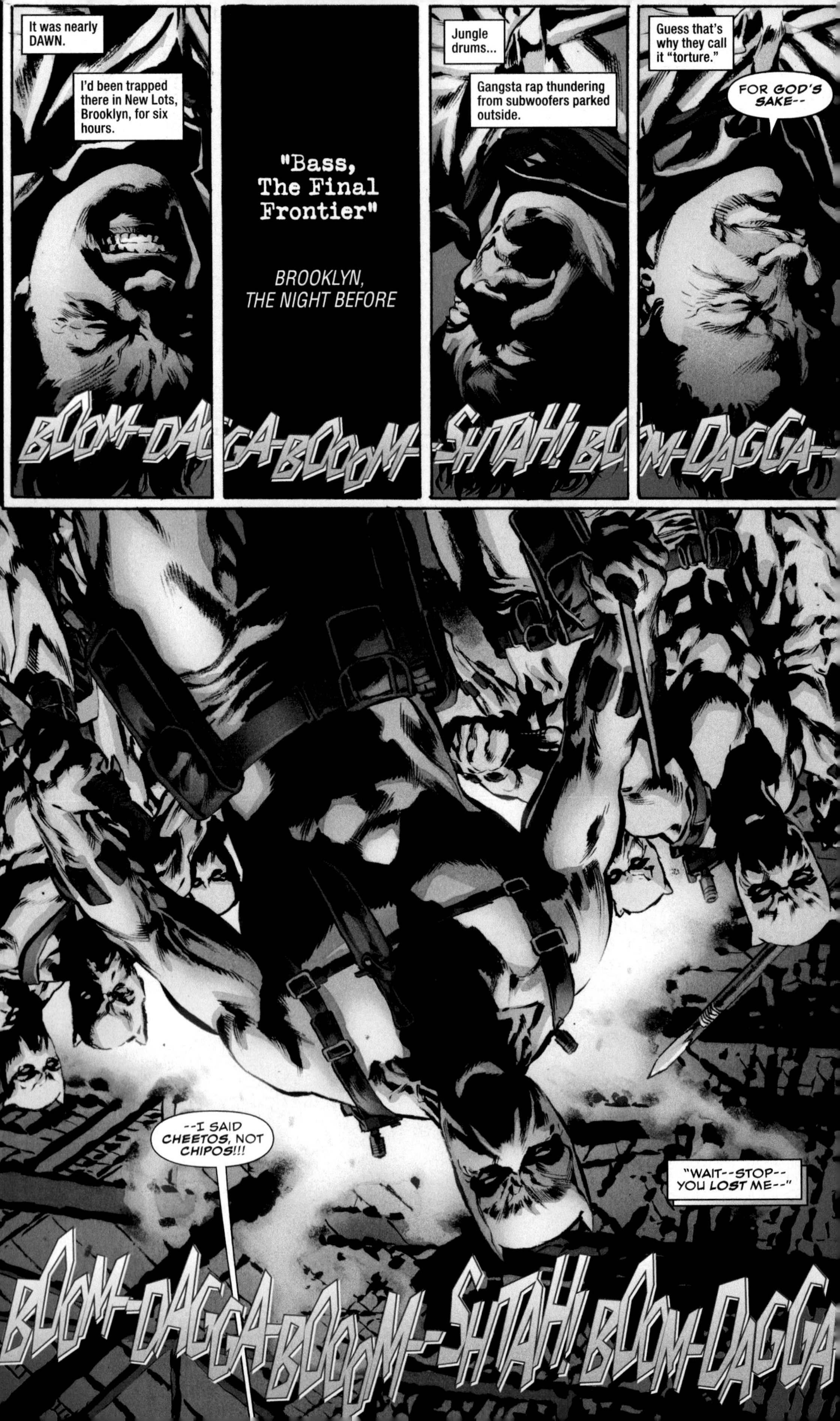

It was nearly DAWN.
I'd been trapped there in New Lots, Brooklyn, for six hours.
BOOM-DAGGA-BOOOM--SHTAH! BOOM-DAGGA--
"Bass, The Final Frontier"
BROOKLYN, THE NIGHT BEFORE
Jungle drums...
Gangsta rap thundering from subwoofers parked outside.
Guess that's why they call it "torture."
FOR GOD'S SAKE--
--I SAID CHEETOS, NOT CHIPOS!!!
"WAIT--STOP--YOU LOST ME--"
BOOM-DAGGA-BOOOM--SHTAH! BOOM-DAGGA

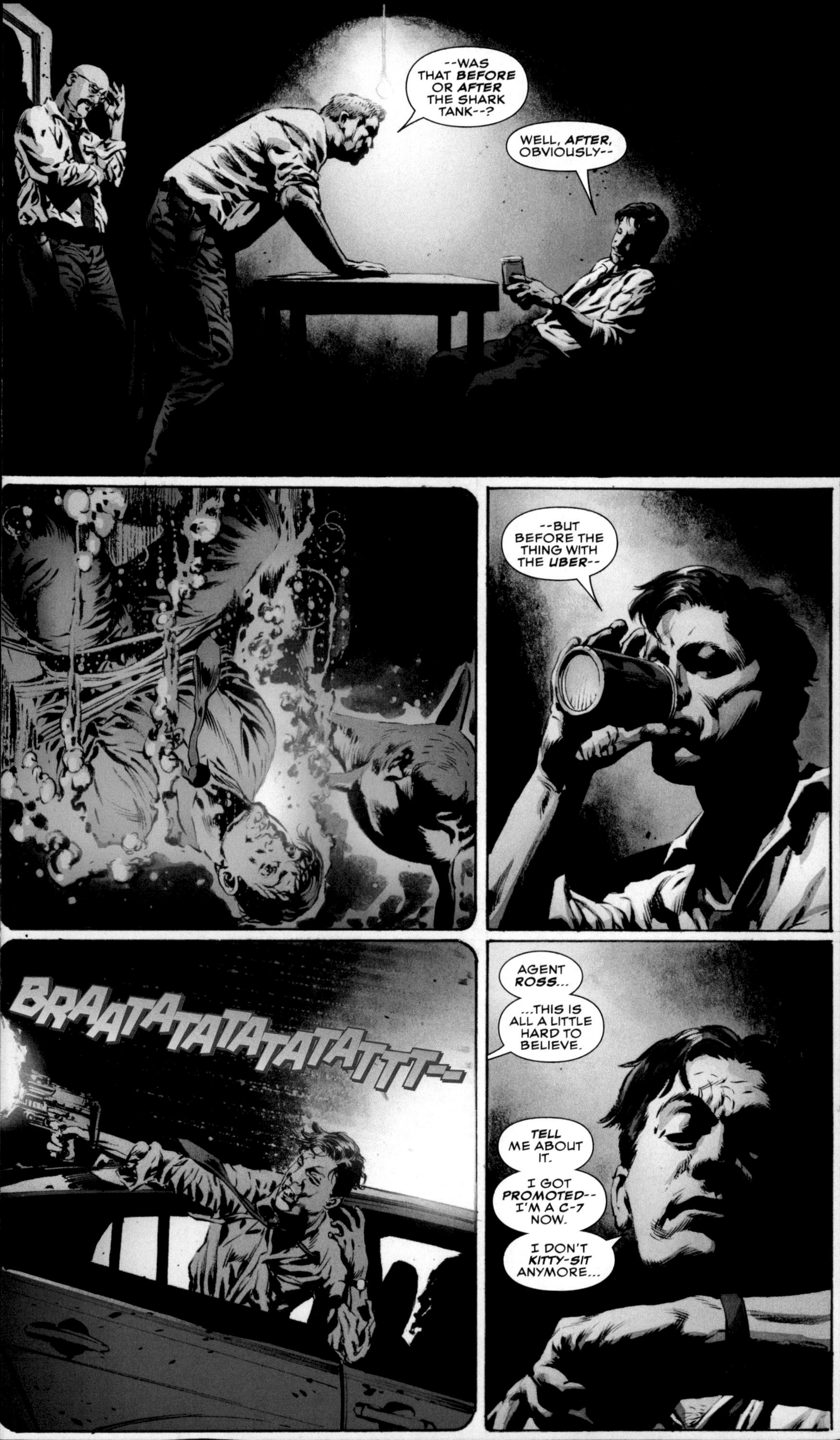
--WAS THAT BEFORE OR AFTER THE SHARK TANK--?
WELL, AFTER, OBVIOUSLY--
--BUT BEFORE THE THING WITH THE UBER--
BRAATATATATATATATTTT--
AGENT ROSS...
...THIS IS ALL A LITTLE HARD TO BELIEVE.
TELL ME ABOUT IT.
I GOT PROMOTED--I'M A C-7 NOW.
I DON'T KITTY-SIT ANYMORE...

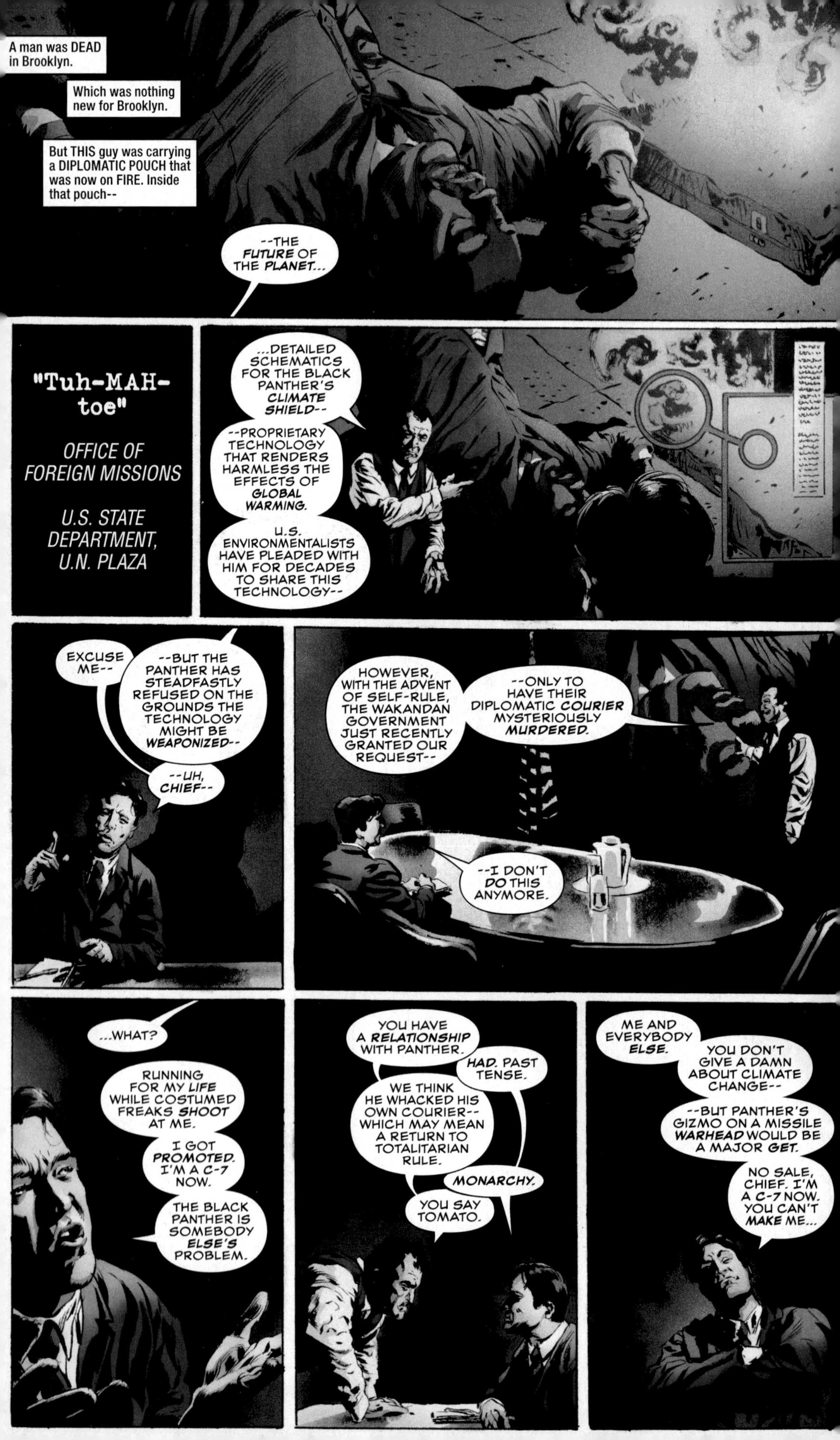

A man was DEAD in Brooklyn.
Which was nothing new for Brooklyn.
But THIS guy was carrying a DIPLOMATIC POUCH that was now on FIRE. Inside that pouch--
--THE FUTURE OF THE PLANET...
"Tuh-MAH-toe"
OFFICE OF FOREIGN MISSIONS
U.S. STATE DEPARTMENT, U.N. PLAZA
...DETAILED SCHEMATICS FOR THE BLACK PANTHER'S CLIMATE SHIELD--
--PROPRIETARY TECHNOLOGY THAT RENDERS HARMLESS THE EFFECTS OF GLOBAL WARMING.
U.S. ENVIRONMENTALISTS HAVE PLEADED WITH HIM FOR DECADES TO SHARE THIS TECHNOLOGY--
EXCUSE ME--
--BUT THE PANTHER HAS STEADFASTLY REFUSED ON THE GROUNDS THE TECHNOLOGY MIGHT BE WEAPONIZED--
--UH, CHIEF--
HOWEVER, WITH THE ADVENT OF SELF-RULE, THE WAKANDAN GOVERNMENT JUST RECENTLY GRANTED OUR REQUEST--
--ONLY TO HAVE THEIR DIPLOMATIC COURIER MYSTERIOUSLY MURDERED.
--I DON'T DO THIS ANYMORE.
...WHAT?
RUNNING FOR MY LIFE WHILE COSTUMED FREAKS SHOOT AT ME.
I GOT PROMOTED. I'M A C-7 NOW.
THE BLACK PANTHER IS SOMEBODY ELSE'S PROBLEM.
YOU HAVE A RELATIONSHIP WITH PANTHER.
HAD. PAST TENSE.
WE THINK HE WHACKED HIS OWN COURIER-- WHICH MAY MEAN A RETURN TO TOTALITARIAN RULE.
MONARCHY.
YOU SAY TOMATO.
ME AND EVERYBODY ELSE.
YOU DON'T GIVE A DAMN ABOUT CLIMATE CHANGE--
--BUT PANTHER'S GIZMO ON A MISSILE WARHEAD WOULD BE A MAJOR GET.
NO SALE, CHIEF. I'M A C-7 NOW. YOU CAN'T MAKE ME...

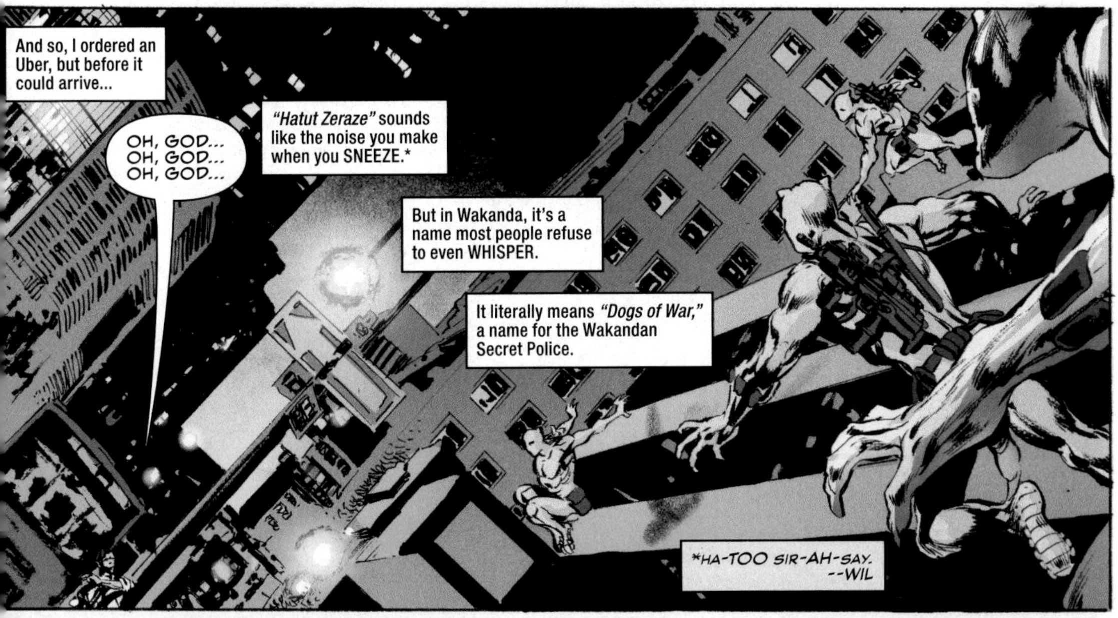
And so, I ordered an Uber, but before it could arrive...
OH, GOD... OH, GOD... OH, GOD...
"Hatut Zeraze" sounds like the noise you make when you SNEEZE.*
But in Wakanda, it's a name most people refuse to even WHISPER.
It literally means "Dogs of War," a name for the Wakandan Secret Police.
*HA-TOO SIR-AH-SAY. --WIL

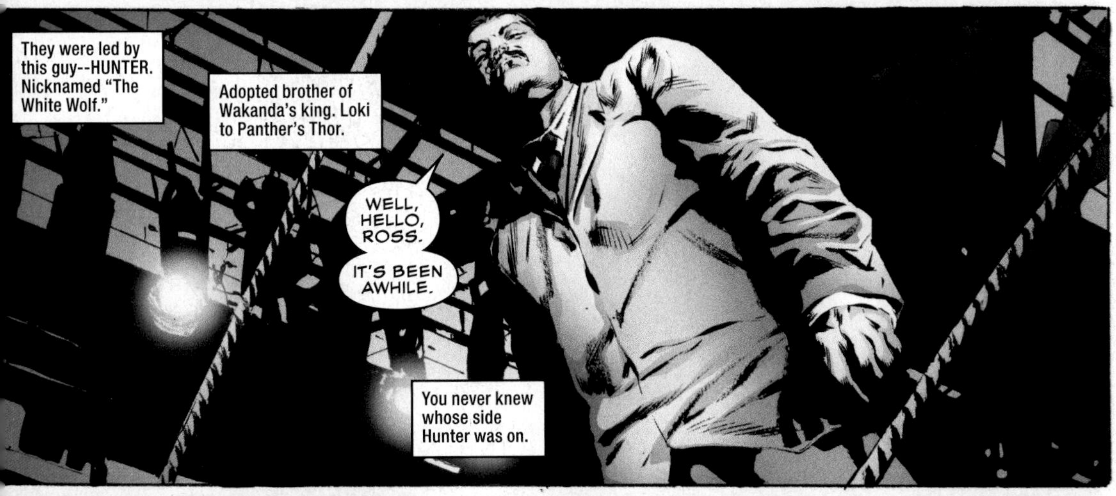
They were led by this guy--HUNTER. Nicknamed "The White Wolf."
Adopted brother of Wakanda's king. Loki to Panther's Thor.
WELL, HELLO, ROSS.
IT'S BEEN AWHILE.
You never knew whose side Hunter was on.

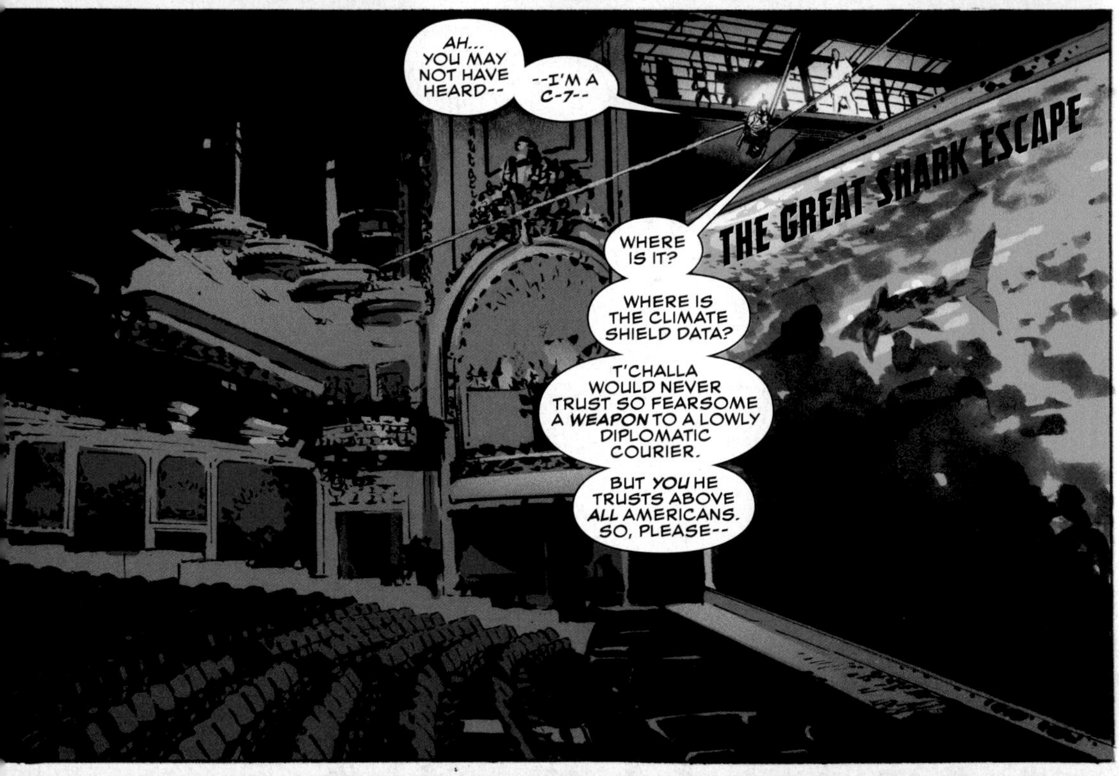
AH... YOU MAY NOT HAVE HEARD--
--I'M A C-7--
THE GREAT SHARK ESCAPE
WHERE IS IT?
WHERE IS THE CLIMATE SHIELD DATA?
T'CHALLA WOULD NEVER TRUST SO FEARSOME A WEAPON TO A LOWLY DIPLOMATIC COURIER.
BUT YOU HE TRUSTS ABOVE ALL AMERICANS. SO, PLEASE--

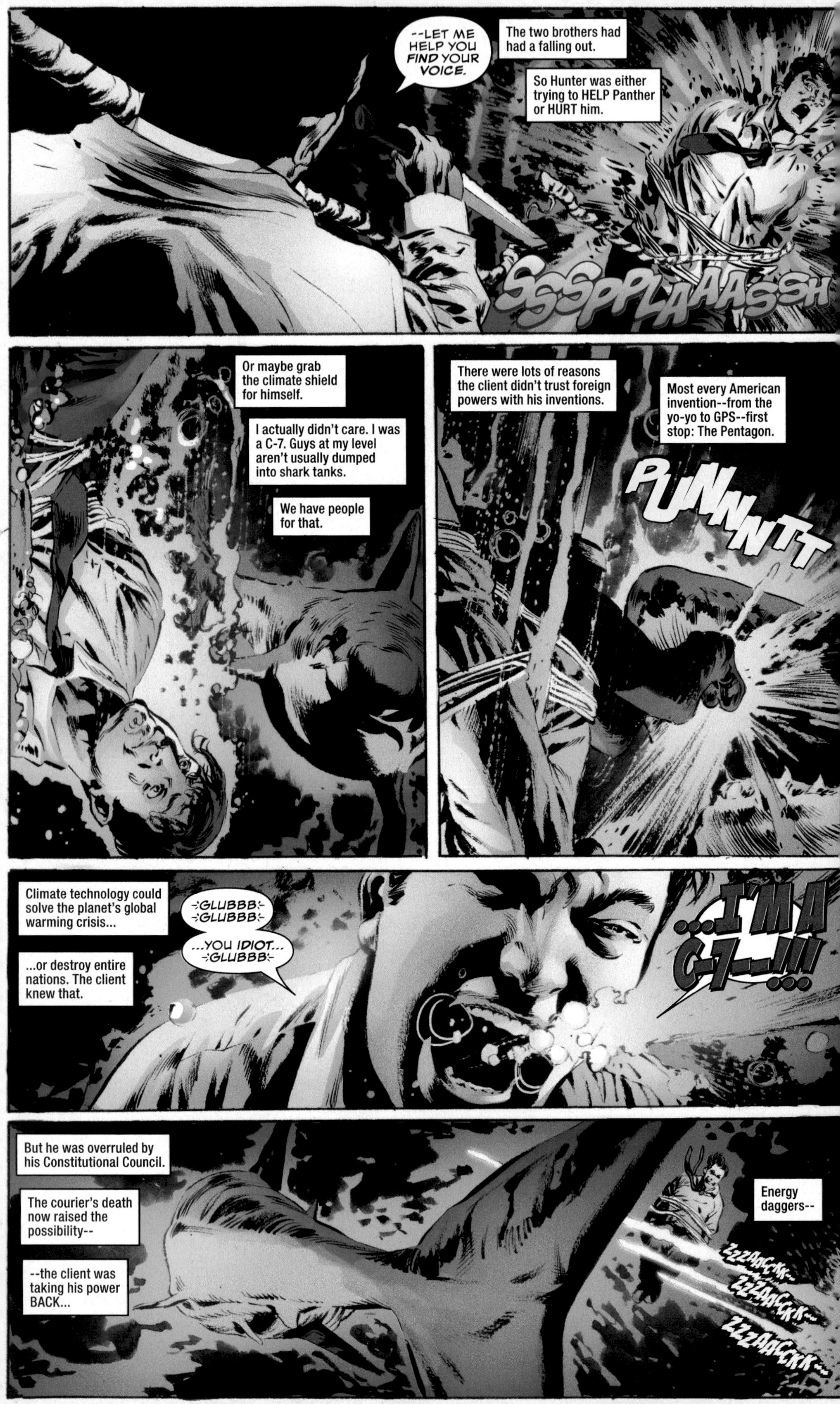
--LET ME HELP YOU FIND YOUR VOICE.
The two brothers had had a falling out.
So Hunter was either trying to HELP Panther or HURT him.
SSSSPPLAAASSSH
Or maybe grab the climate shield for himself.
I actually didn't care. I was a C-7. Guys at my level aren't usually dumped into shark tanks.
We have people for that.
There were lots of reasons the client didn't trust foreign powers with his inventions.
Most every American invention--from the yo-yo to GPS--first stop: The Pentagon.
PUNNNNTT
Climate technology could solve the planet's global warming crisis...
...or destroy entire nations. The client knew that.
GLUBBB GLUBBB
...YOU IDIOT... GLUBBB
...I'M A C-7--!!!...
But he was overruled by his Constitutional Council.
The courier's death now raised the possibility--
--the client was taking his power BACK...
Energy daggers--
ZZZAACCKK--
ZZZAACCKK--
ZZZAACCKK--

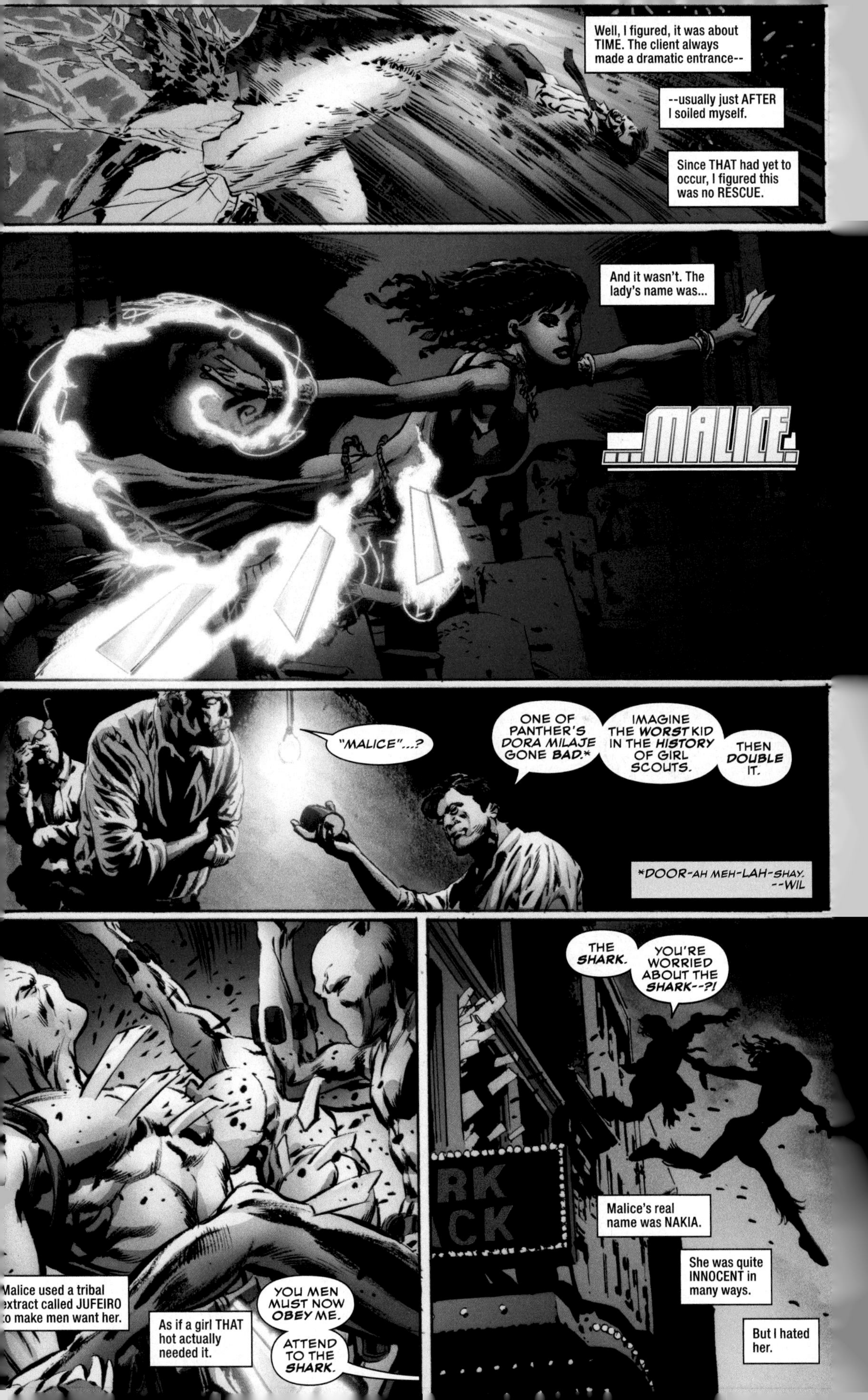
Well, I figured, it was about TIME. The client always made a dramatic entrance--
--usually just AFTER I soiled myself.
Since THAT had yet to occur, I figured this was no RESCUE.
And it wasn't. The lady's name was...
...MALICE.
"MALICE"...?
ONE OF PANTHER'S DORA MILAJE GONE BAD.*
IMAGINE THE WORST KID IN THE HISTORY OF GIRL SCOUTS.
THEN DOUBLE IT.
*DOOR-AH MEH-LAH-SHAY. --WIL
Malice used a tribal extract called JUFEIRO to make men want her.
As if a girl THAT hot actually needed it.
YOU MEN MUST NOW OBEY ME.
ATTEND TO THE SHARK.
THE SHARK.
YOU'RE WORRIED ABOUT THE SHARK--?!
Malice's real name was NAKIA.
She was quite INNOCENT in many ways.
But I hated her.

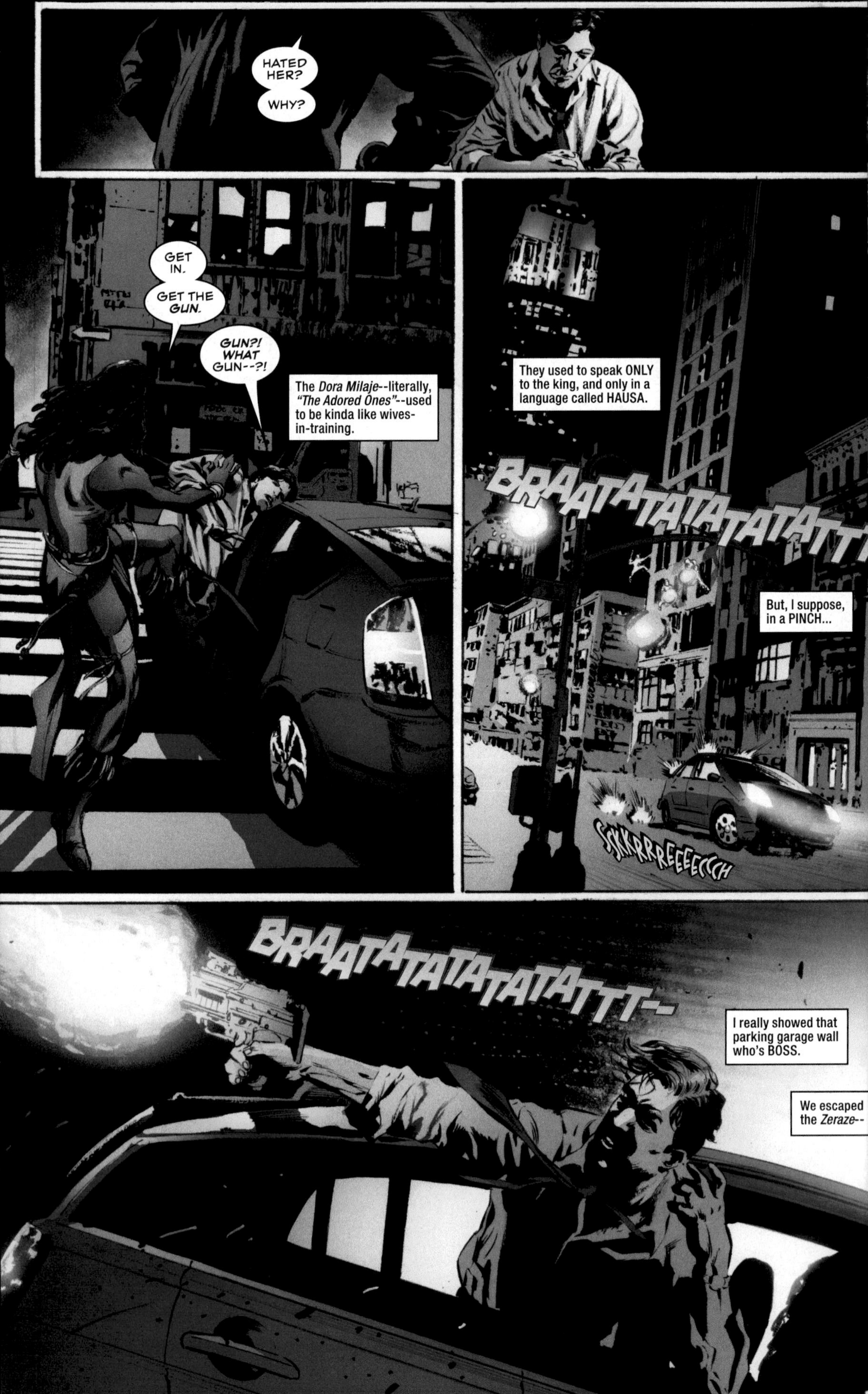
HATED HER?
WHY?
GET IN.
GET THE GUN.
GUN?! WHAT GUN--?!
The *Dora Milaje*--literally, *"The Adored Ones"*--used to be kinda like wives-in-training.
They used to speak ONLY to the king, and only in a language called HAUSA.
BRAATATATATATATATT
But, I suppose, in a PINCH...
SSKKRRRREEEECCCH
BRAATATATATATATATTT--
I really showed that parking garage wall who's BOSS.
We escaped the *Zeraze*--

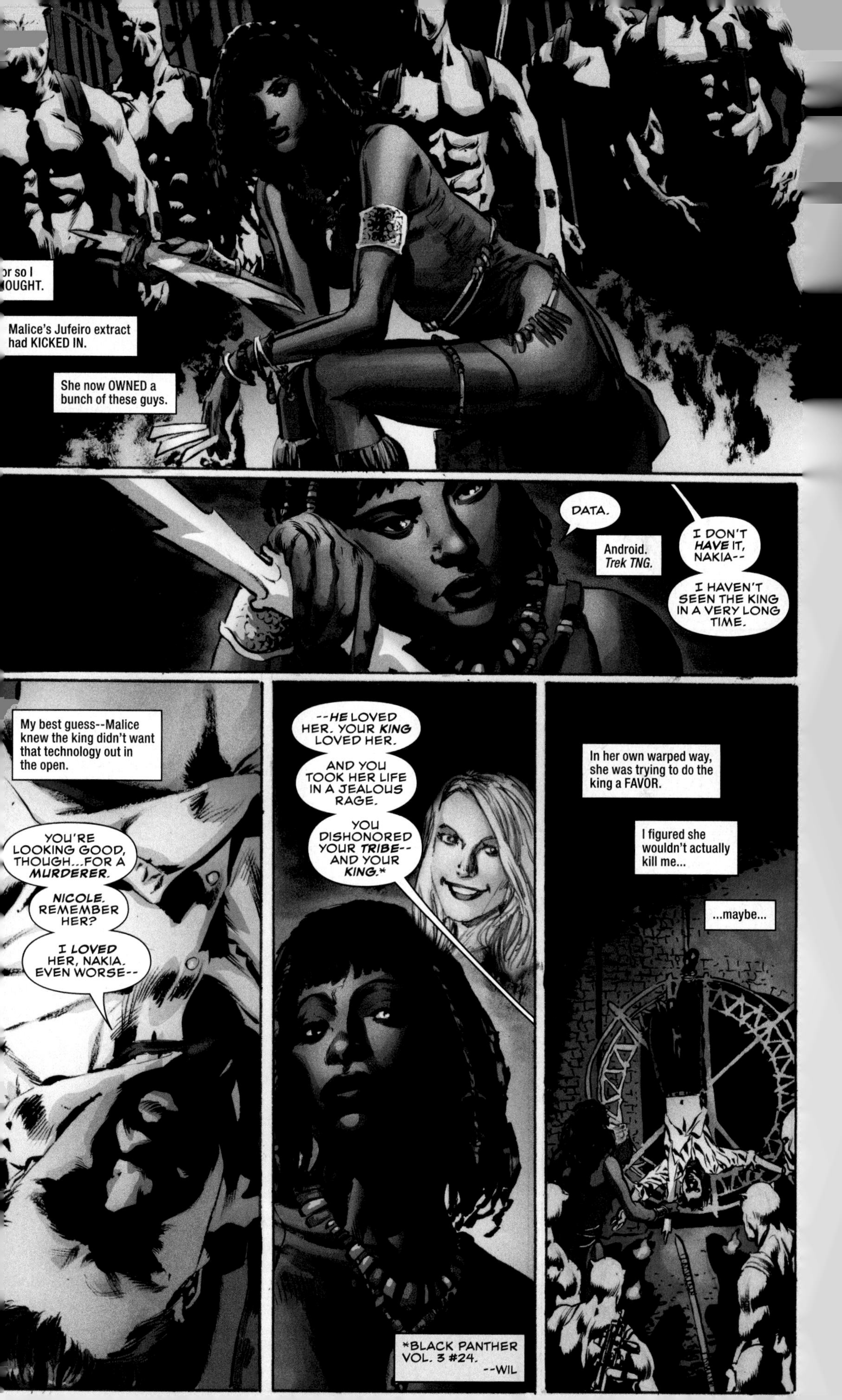

or so I
OUGHT.
Malice's Jufeiro extract had KICKED IN.
She now OWNED a bunch of these guys.
DATA.
Android. Trek TNG.
I DON'T HAVE IT, NAKIA--
I HAVEN'T SEEN THE KING IN A VERY LONG TIME.
My best guess--Malice knew the king didn't want that technology out in the open.
YOU'RE LOOKING GOOD, THOUGH...FOR A MURDERER.
NICOLE. REMEMBER HER?
I LOVED HER, NAKIA. EVEN WORSE--
--HE LOVED HER. YOUR KING LOVED HER.
AND YOU TOOK HER LIFE IN A JEALOUS RAGE.
YOU DISHONORED YOUR TRIBE--AND YOUR KING.*
*BLACK PANTHER VOL. 3 #24. --WIL
In her own warped way, she was trying to do the king a FAVOR.
I figured she wouldn't actually kill me...
...maybe...

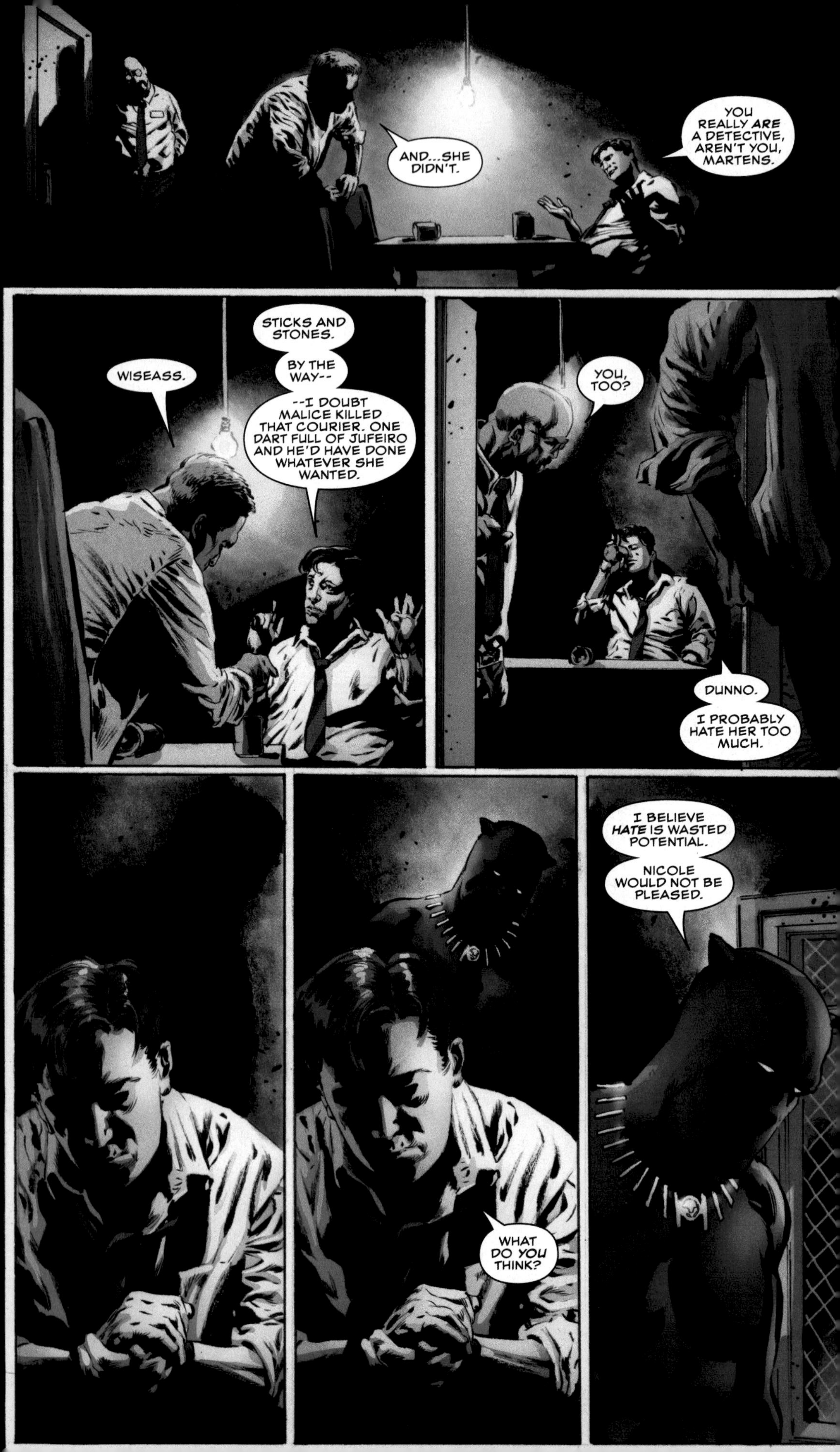
AND...SHE DIDN'T.
YOU REALLY ARE A DETECTIVE, AREN'T YOU, MARTENS.
WISEASS.
STICKS AND STONES.
BY THE WAY--
--I DOUBT MALICE KILLED THAT COURIER. ONE DART FULL OF JUFEIRO AND HE'D HAVE DONE WHATEVER SHE WANTED.
YOU, TOO?
DUNNO.
I PROBABLY HATE HER TOO MUCH.
WHAT DO YOU THINK?
I BELIEVE HATE IS WASTED POTENTIAL.
NICOLE WOULD NOT BE PLEASED.

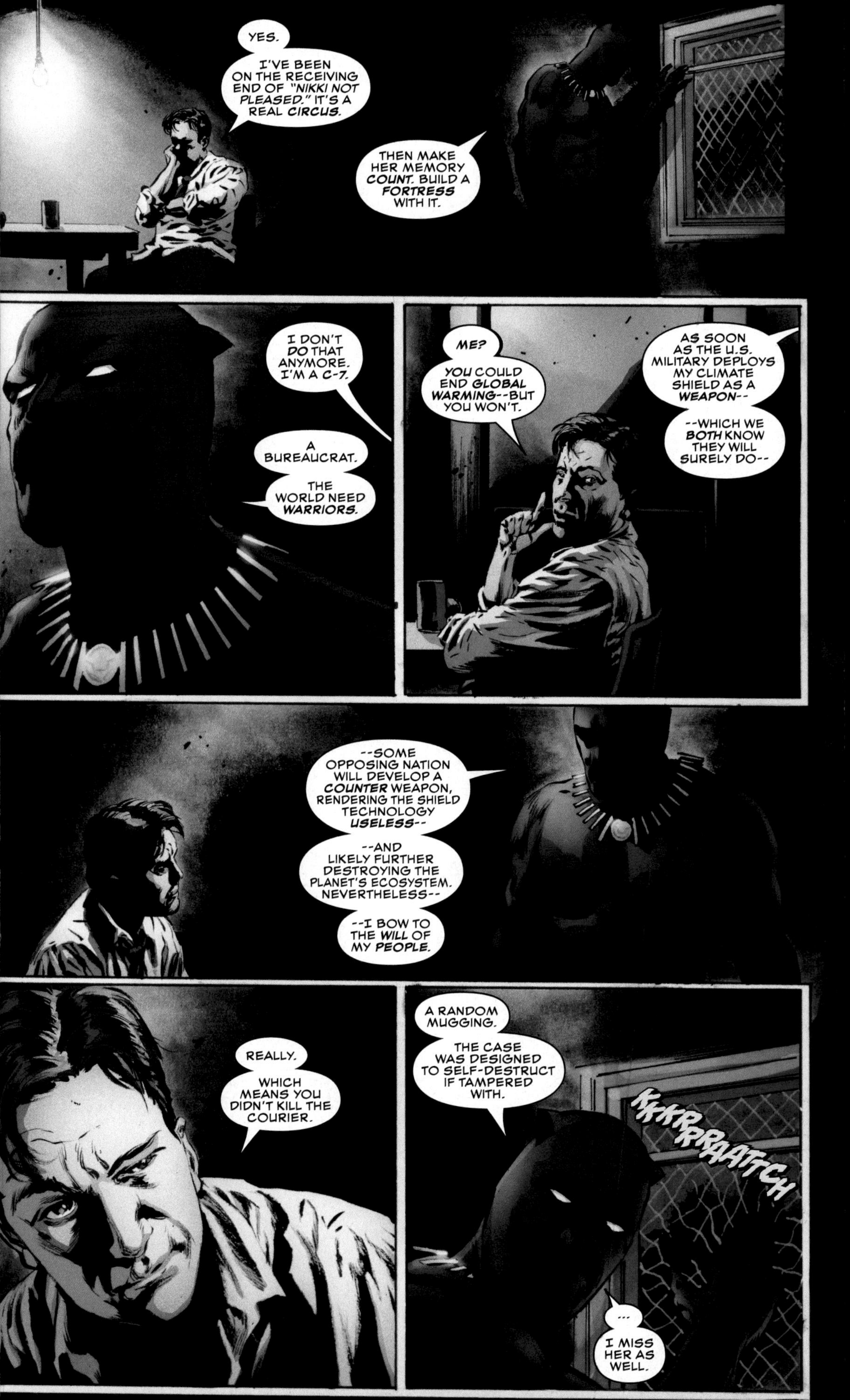
YES.
I'VE BEEN ON THE RECEIVING END OF "NIKKI NOT PLEASED." IT'S A REAL CIRCUS.
THEN MAKE HER MEMORY COUNT. BUILD A FORTRESS WITH IT.
I DON'T DO THAT ANYMORE. I'M A C-7.
A BUREAUCRAT.
THE WORLD NEED WARRIORS.
ME?
YOU COULD END GLOBAL WARMING--BUT YOU WON'T.
AS SOON AS THE U.S. MILITARY DEPLOYS MY CLIMATE SHIELD AS A WEAPON--
--WHICH WE BOTH KNOW THEY WILL SURELY DO--
--SOME OPPOSING NATION WILL DEVELOP A COUNTER WEAPON, RENDERING THE SHIELD TECHNOLOGY USELESS--
--AND LIKELY FURTHER DESTROYING THE PLANET'S ECOSYSTEM. NEVERTHELESS--
--I BOW TO THE WILL OF MY PEOPLE.
REALLY.
WHICH MEANS YOU DIDN'T KILL THE COURIER.
A RANDOM MUGGING.
THE CASE WAS DESIGNED TO SELF-DESTRUCT IF TAMPERED WITH.
KKKRRRAATTCH
...
I MISS HER AS WELL.

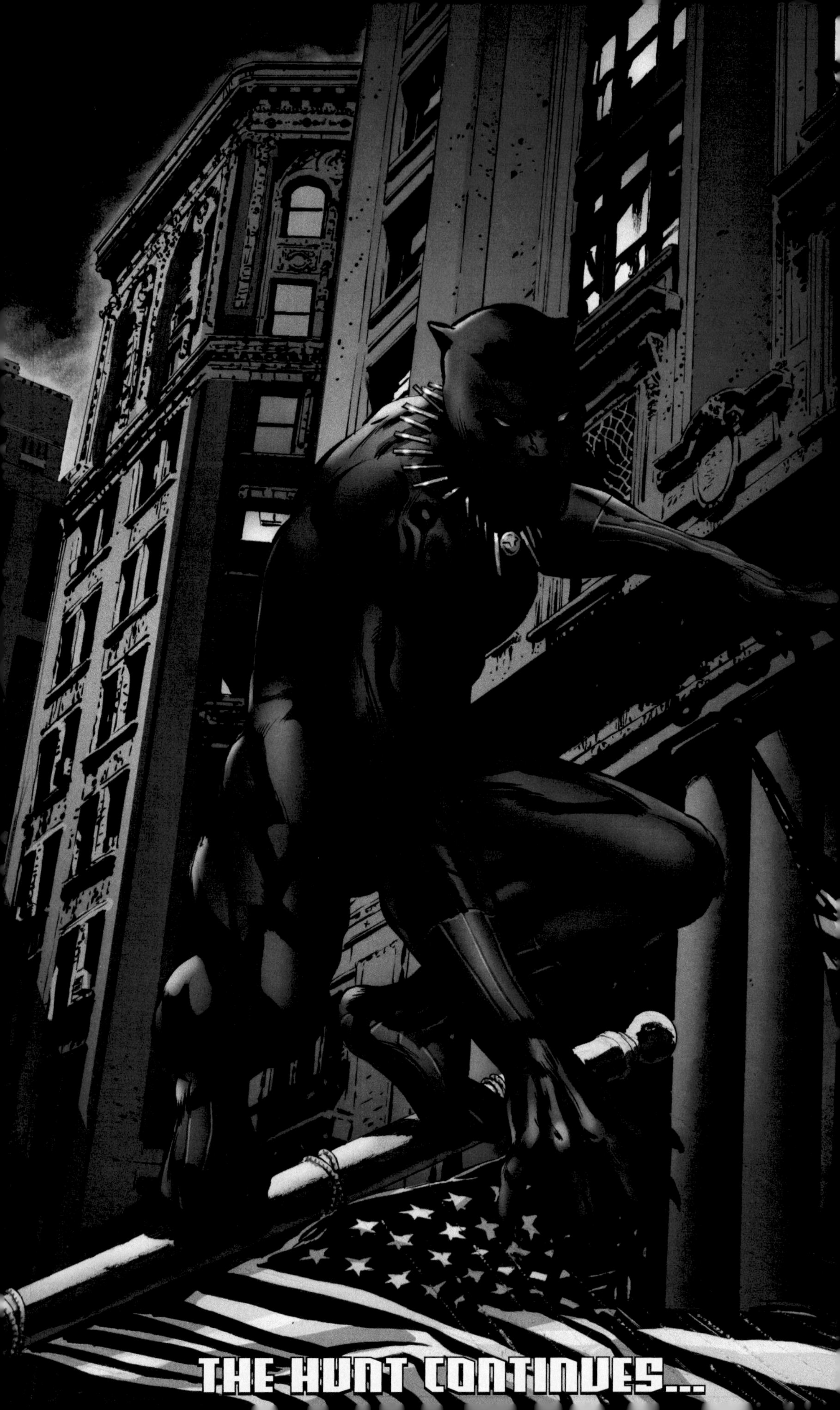
THE HUNT CONTINUES...

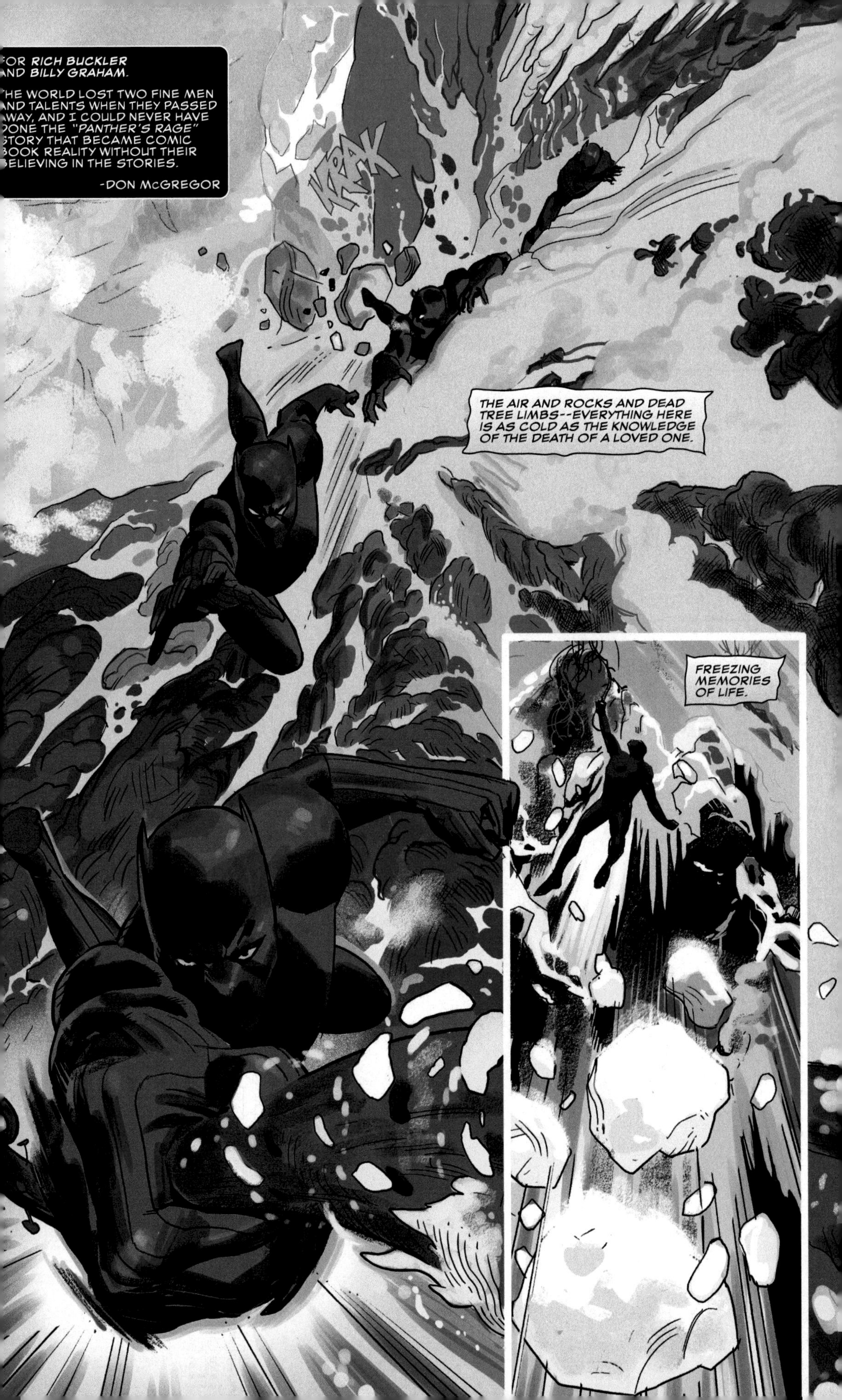
FOR RICH BUCKLER AND BILLY GRAHAM.
THE WORLD LOST TWO FINE MEN AND TALENTS WHEN THEY PASSED AWAY, AND I COULD NEVER HAVE DONE THE "PANTHER'S RAGE" STORY THAT BECAME COMIC BOOK REALITY WITHOUT THEIR BELIEVING IN THE STORIES.
-DON McGREGOR
KRAK
THE AIR AND ROCKS AND DEAD TREE LIMBS--EVERYTHING HERE IS AS COLD AS THE KNOWLEDGE OF THE DEATH OF A LOVED ONE.
FREEZING MEMORIES OF LIFE.

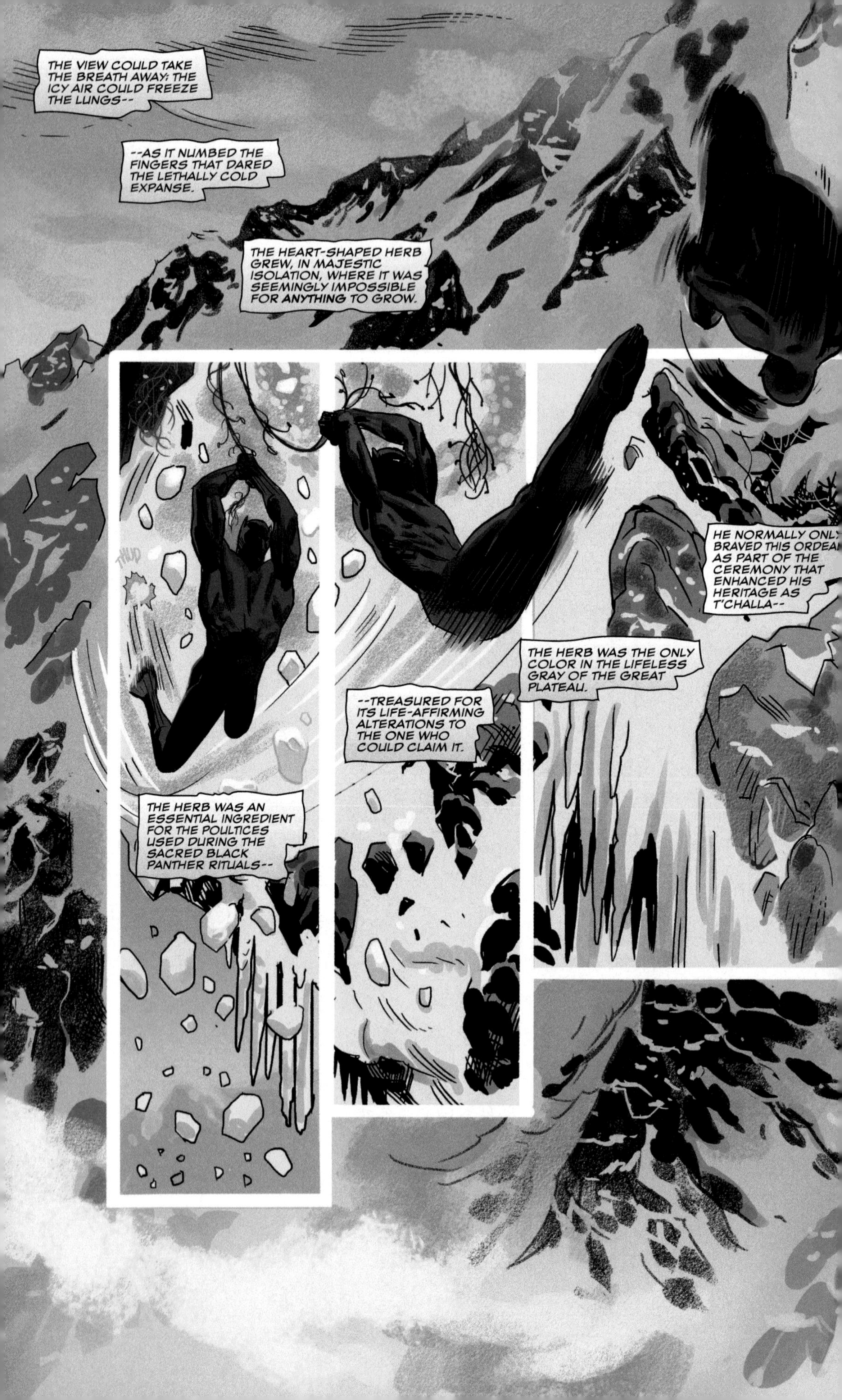
THE VIEW COULD TAKE THE BREATH AWAY; THE ICY AIR COULD FREEZE THE LUNGS--
--AS IT NUMBED THE FINGERS THAT DARED THE LETHALLY COLD EXPANSE.
THE HEART-SHAPED HERB GREW, IN MAJESTIC ISOLATION, WHERE IT WAS SEEMINGLY IMPOSSIBLE FOR ANYTHING TO GROW.
THUD
THE HERB WAS AN ESSENTIAL INGREDIENT FOR THE POULTICES USED DURING THE SACRED BLACK PANTHER RITUALS--
--TREASURED FOR ITS LIFE-AFFIRMING ALTERATIONS TO THE ONE WHO COULD CLAIM IT.
HE NORMALLY ONLY BRAVED THIS ORDEAL AS PART OF THE CEREMONY THAT ENHANCED HIS HERITAGE AS T'CHALLA--
THE HERB WAS THE ONLY COLOR IN THE LIFELESS GRAY OF THE GREAT PLATEAU.

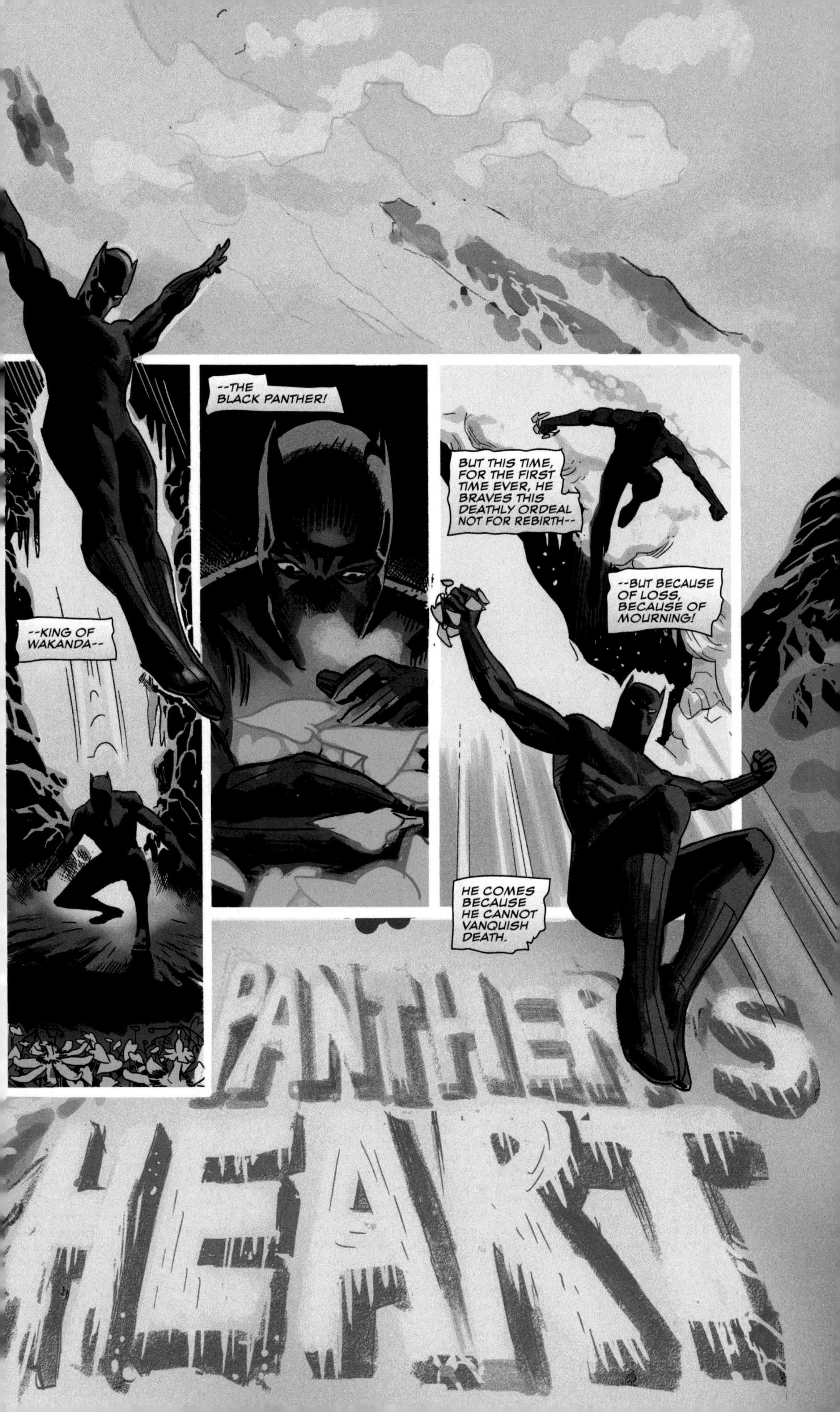
--KING OF WAKANDA--
--THE BLACK PANTHER!
BUT THIS TIME, FOR THE FIRST TIME EVER, HE BRAVES THIS DEATHLY ORDEAL NOT FOR REBIRTH--
--BUT BECAUSE OF LOSS, BECAUSE OF MOURNING!
HE COMES BECAUSE HE CANNOT VANQUISH DEATH.
PANTHER'S HEART

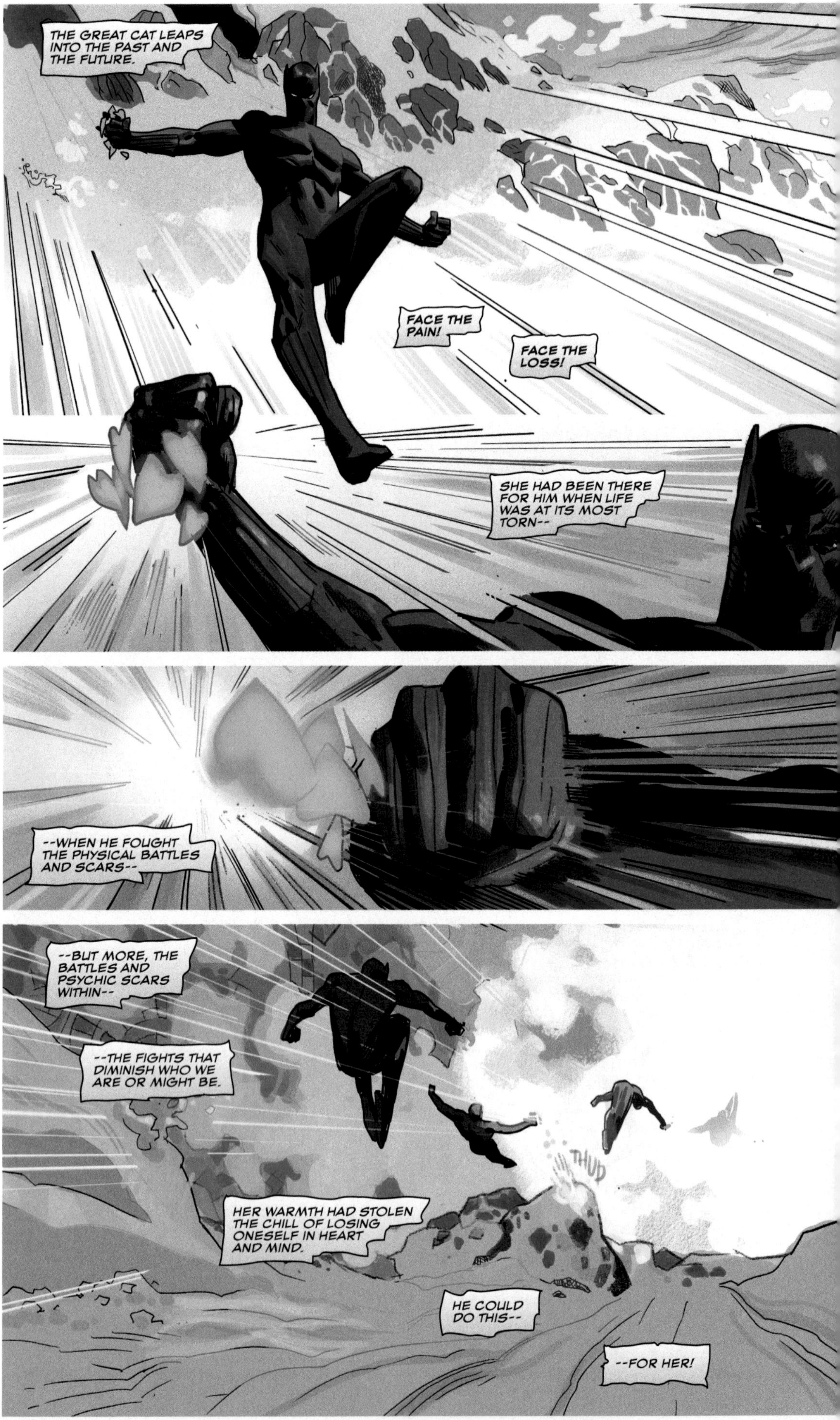
THE GREAT CAT LEAPS INTO THE PAST AND THE FUTURE.
FACE THE PAIN!
FACE THE LOSS!
SHE HAD BEEN THERE FOR HIM WHEN LIFE WAS AT ITS MOST TORN--
--WHEN HE FOUGHT THE PHYSICAL BATTLES AND SCARS--
--BUT MORE, THE BATTLES AND PSYCHIC SCARS WITHIN--
--THE FIGHTS THAT DIMINISH WHO WE ARE OR MIGHT BE.
THUD
HER WARMTH HAD STOLEN THE CHILL OF LOSING ONESELF IN HEART AND MIND.
HE COULD DO THIS--
--FOR HER!

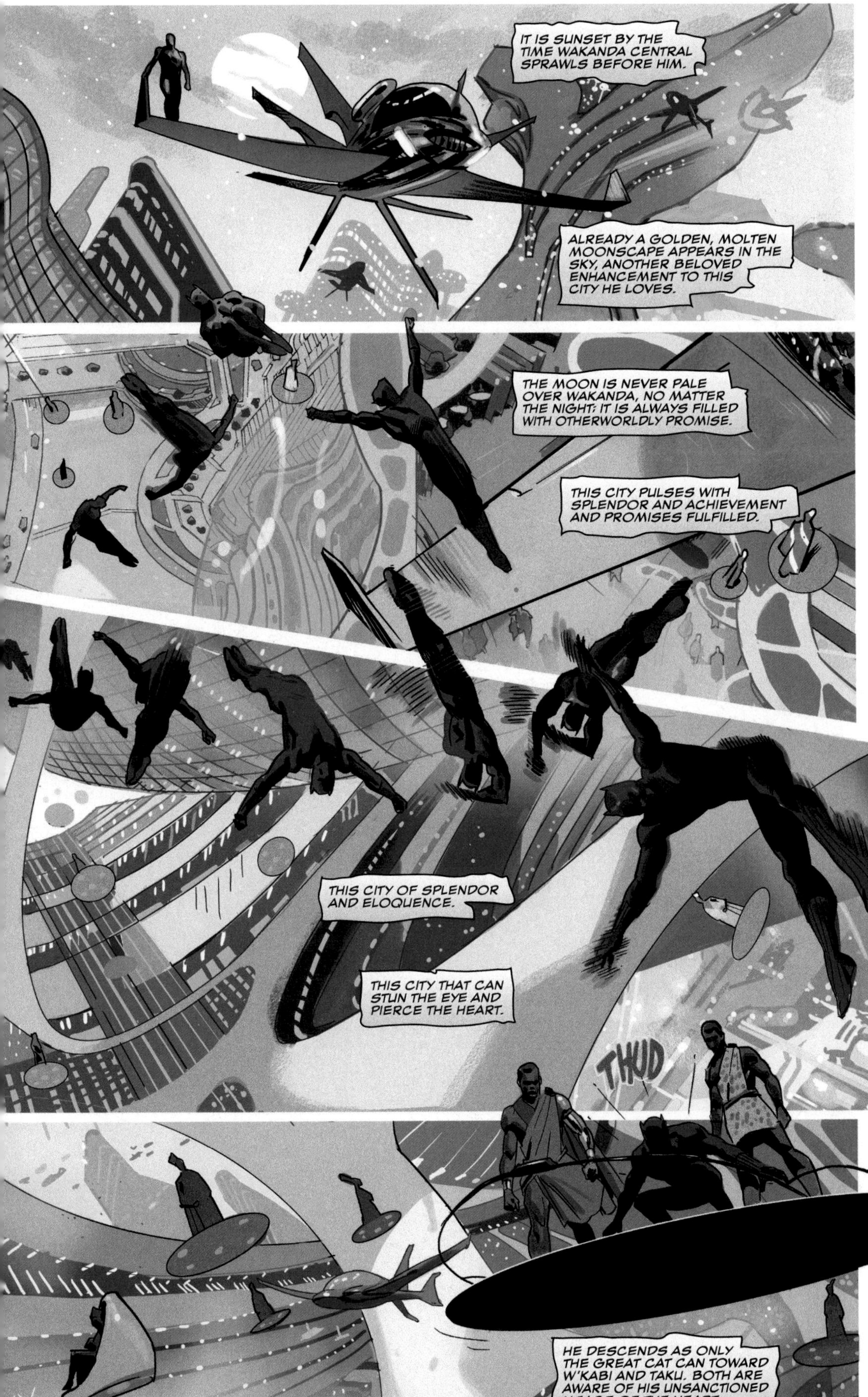
IT IS SUNSET BY THE TIME WAKANDA CENTRAL SPRAWLS BEFORE HIM.
ALREADY A GOLDEN, MOLTEN MOONSCAPE APPEARS IN THE SKY, ANOTHER BELOVED ENHANCEMENT TO THIS CITY HE LOVES.
THE MOON IS NEVER PALE OVER WAKANDA, NO MATTER THE NIGHT: IT IS ALWAYS FILLED WITH OTHERWORLDLY PROMISE.
THIS CITY PULSES WITH SPLENDOR AND ACHIEVEMENT AND PROMISES FULFILLED.
THIS CITY OF SPLENDOR AND ELOQUENCE.
THIS CITY THAT CAN STUN THE EYE AND PIERCE THE HEART.
THUD
HE DESCENDS AS ONLY THE GREAT CAT CAN TOWARD W'KABI AND TAKU. BOTH ARE AWARE OF HIS UNSANCTIONED USAGE OF THE HEART-SHAPED HERB.

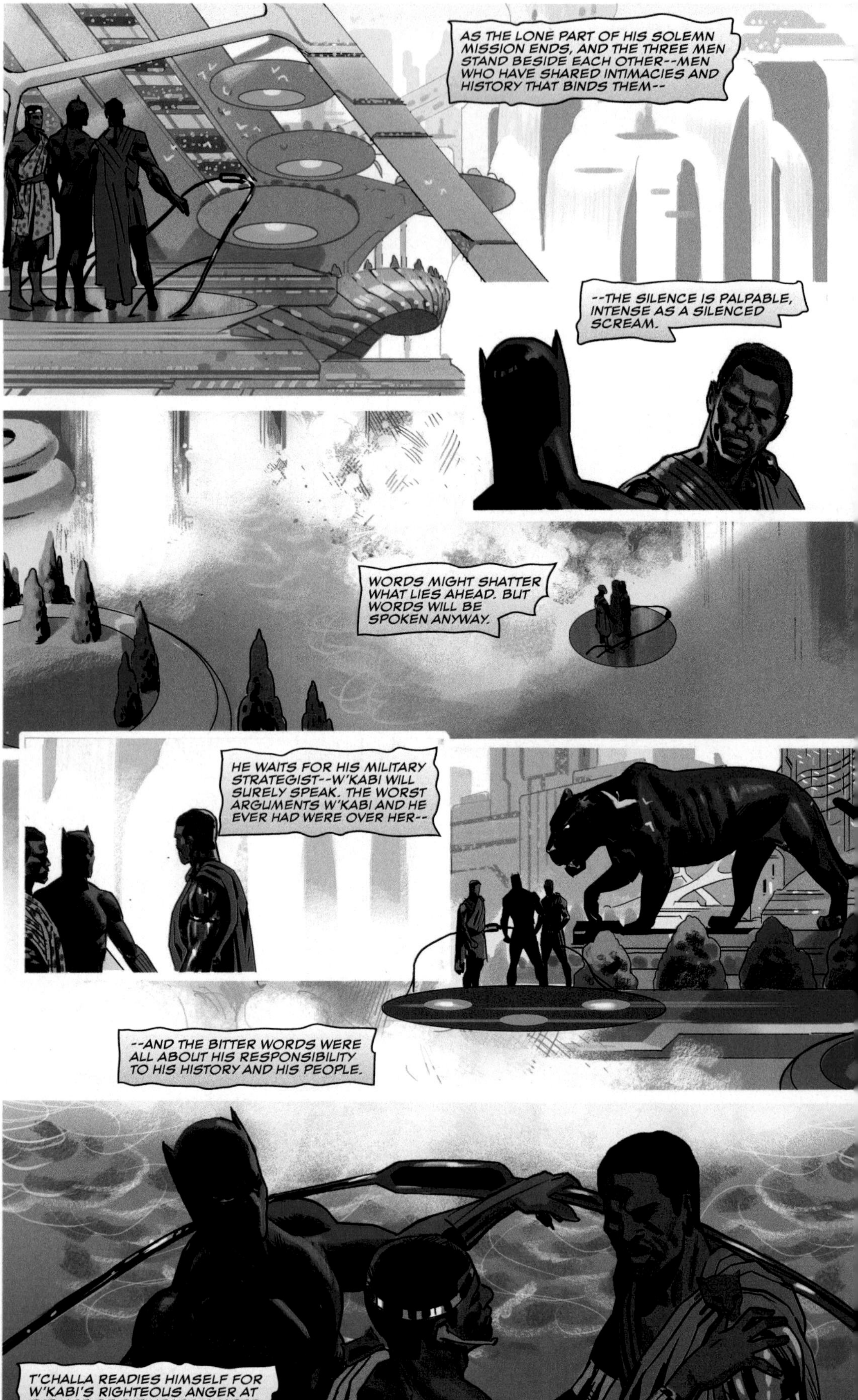
AS THE LONE PART OF HIS SOLEMN MISSION ENDS, AND THE THREE MEN STAND BESIDE EACH OTHER--MEN WHO HAVE SHARED INTIMACIES AND HISTORY THAT BINDS THEM--
--THE SILENCE IS PALPABLE, INTENSE AS A SILENCED SCREAM.
WORDS MIGHT SHATTER WHAT LIES AHEAD. BUT WORDS WILL BE SPOKEN ANYWAY.
HE WAITS FOR HIS MILITARY STRATEGIST--W'KABI WILL SURELY SPEAK. THE WORST ARGUMENTS W'KABI AND HE EVER HAD WERE OVER HER--
--AND THE BITTER WORDS WERE ALL ABOUT HIS RESPONSIBILITY TO HIS HISTORY AND HIS PEOPLE.
T'CHALLA READIES HIMSELF FOR W'KABI'S RIGHTEOUS ANGER AT THE USE OF THE HEART-SHAPED HERB IN SUCH A WAY AS THIS...

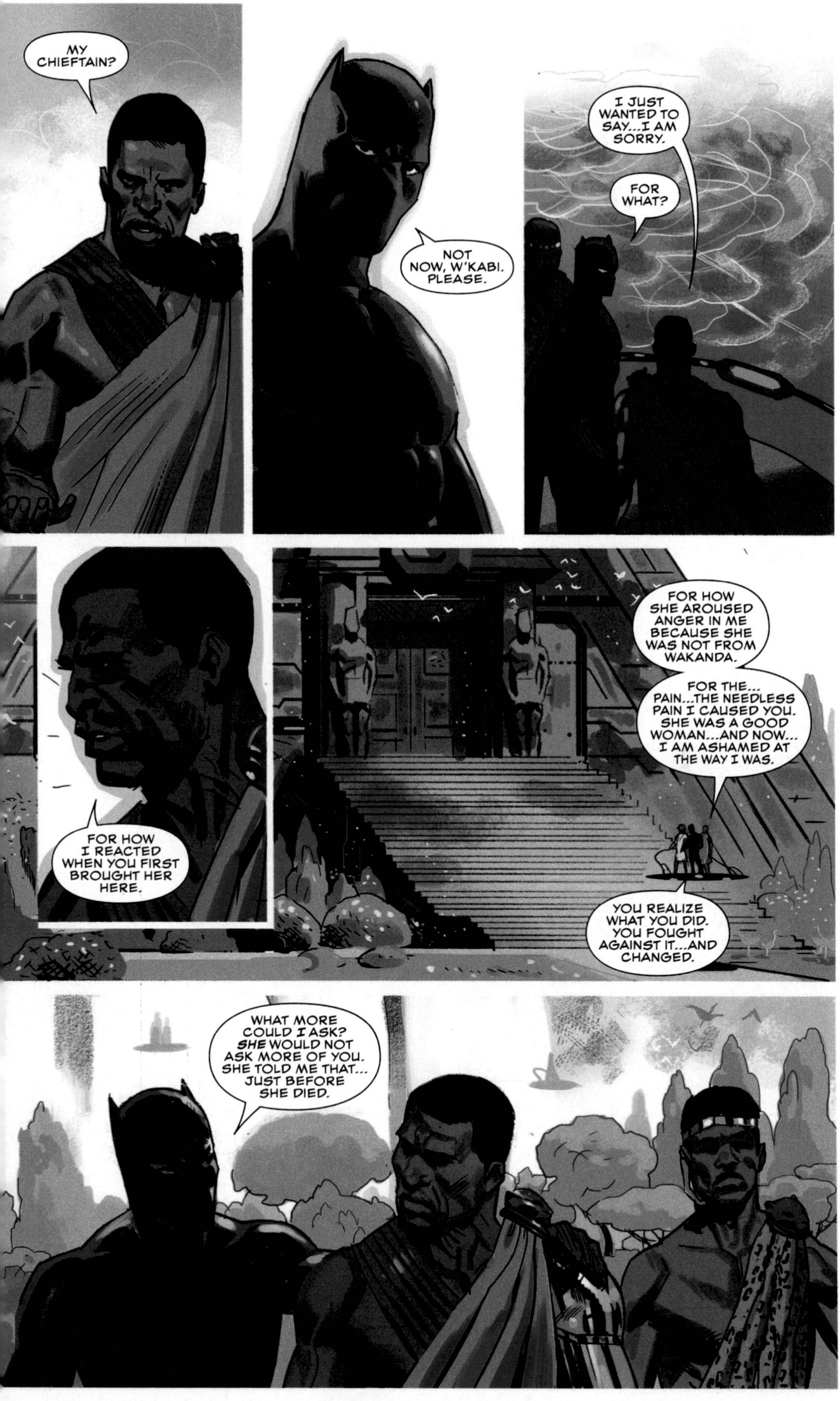
MY CHIEFTAIN?
NOT NOW, W'KABI. PLEASE.
I JUST WANTED TO SAY...I AM SORRY.
FOR WHAT?
FOR HOW I REACTED WHEN YOU FIRST BROUGHT HER HERE.
FOR HOW SHE AROUSED ANGER IN ME BECAUSE SHE WAS NOT FROM WAKANDA.
FOR THE... PAIN...THE NEEDLESS PAIN I CAUSED YOU. SHE WAS A GOOD WOMAN...AND NOW... I AM ASHAMED AT THE WAY I WAS.
YOU REALIZE WHAT YOU DID. YOU FOUGHT AGAINST IT...AND CHANGED.
WHAT MORE COULD I ASK? SHE WOULD NOT ASK MORE OF YOU. SHE TOLD ME THAT... JUST BEFORE SHE DIED.

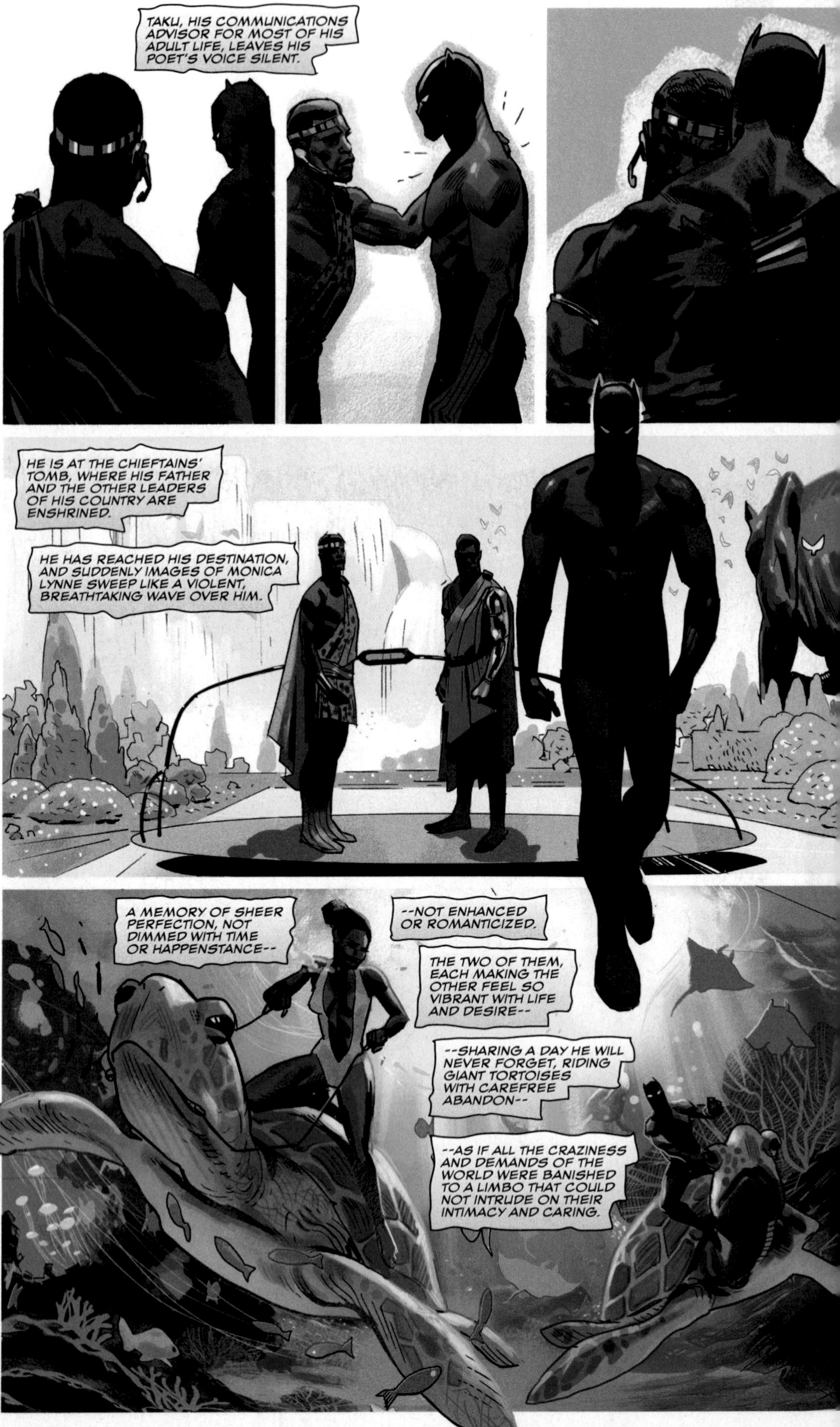
TAKU, HIS COMMUNICATIONS ADVISOR FOR MOST OF HIS ADULT LIFE, LEAVES HIS POET'S VOICE SILENT.
HE IS AT THE CHIEFTAINS' TOMB, WHERE HIS FATHER AND THE OTHER LEADERS OF HIS COUNTRY ARE ENSHRINED.
HE HAS REACHED HIS DESTINATION, AND SUDDENLY IMAGES OF MONICA LYNNE SWEEP LIKE A VIOLENT, BREATHTAKING WAVE OVER HIM.
A MEMORY OF SHEER PERFECTION, NOT DIMMED WITH TIME OR HAPPENSTANCE--
--NOT ENHANCED OR ROMANTICIZED.
THE TWO OF THEM, EACH MAKING THE OTHER FEEL SO VIBRANT WITH LIFE AND DESIRE--
--SHARING A DAY HE WILL NEVER FORGET, RIDING GIANT TORTOISES WITH CAREFREE ABANDON--
--AS IF ALL THE CRAZINESS AND DEMANDS OF THE WORLD WERE BANISHED TO A LIMBO THAT COULD NOT INTRUDE ON THEIR INTIMACY AND CARING.

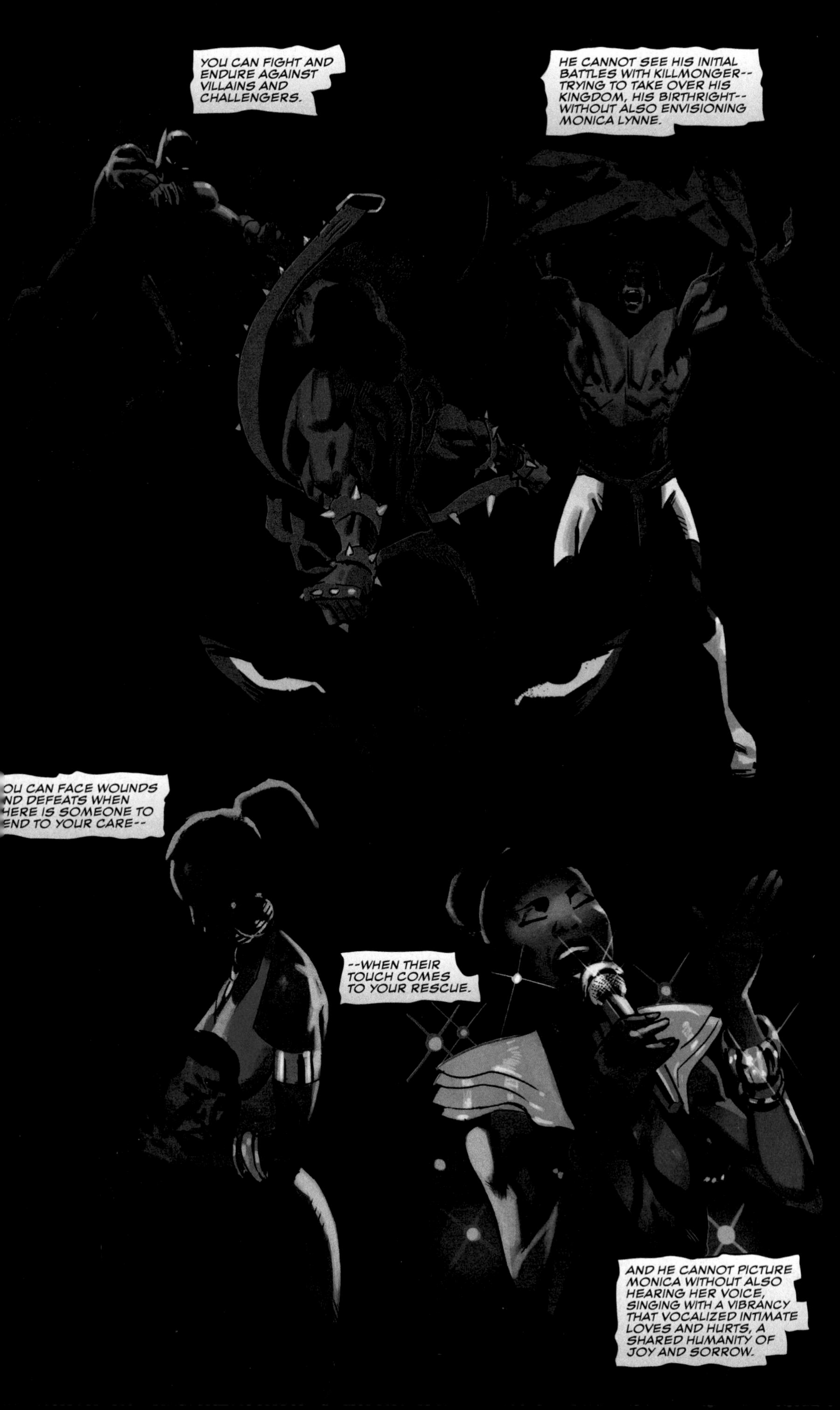
YOU CAN FIGHT AND ENDURE AGAINST VILLAINS AND CHALLENGERS.
HE CANNOT SEE HIS INITIAL BATTLES WITH KILLMONGER-- TRYING TO TAKE OVER HIS KINGDOM, HIS BIRTHRIGHT-- WITHOUT ALSO ENVISIONING MONICA LYNNE.
OU CAN FACE WOUNDS ND DEFEATS WHEN HERE IS SOMEONE TO END TO YOUR CARE--
--WHEN THEIR TOUCH COMES TO YOUR RESCUE.
AND HE CANNOT PICTURE MONICA WITHOUT ALSO HEARING HER VOICE, SINGING WITH A VIBRANCY THAT VOCALIZED INTIMATE LOVES AND HURTS, A SHARED HUMANITY OF JOY AND SORROW.

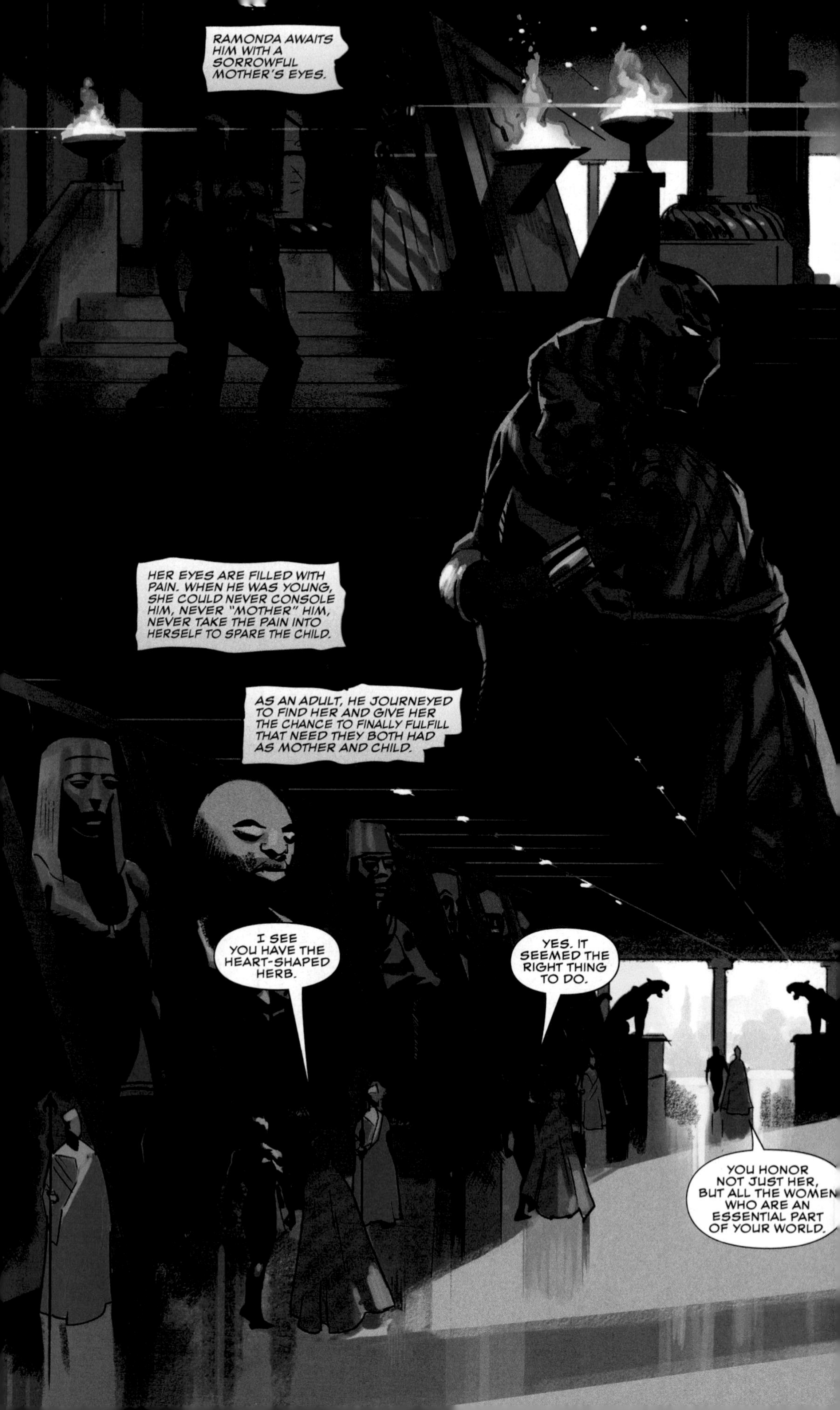

RAMONDA AWAITS HIM WITH A SORROWFUL MOTHER'S EYES.
HER EYES ARE FILLED WITH PAIN. WHEN HE WAS YOUNG, SHE COULD NEVER CONSOLE HIM, NEVER "MOTHER" HIM, NEVER TAKE THE PAIN INTO HERSELF TO SPARE THE CHILD.
AS AN ADULT, HE JOURNEYED TO FIND HER AND GIVE HER THE CHANCE TO FINALLY FULFILL THAT NEED THEY BOTH HAD AS MOTHER AND CHILD.
I SEE YOU HAVE THE HEART-SHAPED HERB.
YES. IT SEEMED THE RIGHT THING TO DO.
YOU HONOR NOT JUST HER, BUT ALL THE WOMEN WHO ARE AN ESSENTIAL PART OF YOUR WORLD.

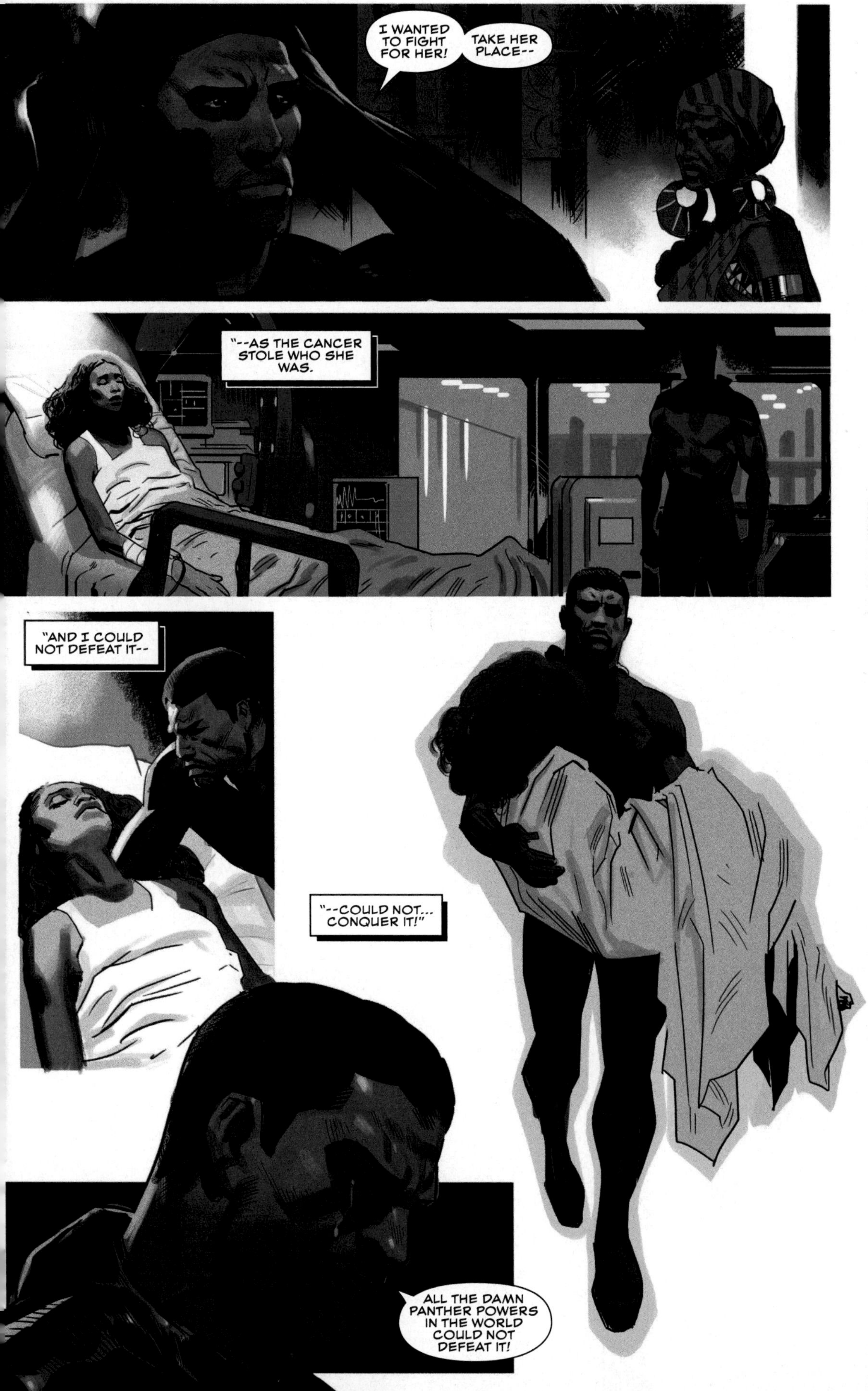
I WANTED TO FIGHT FOR HER!
TAKE HER PLACE--
"--AS THE CANCER STOLE WHO SHE WAS.
"AND I COULD NOT DEFEAT IT--
"--COULD NOT... CONQUER IT!"
ALL THE DAMN PANTHER POWERS IN THE WORLD COULD NOT DEFEAT IT!

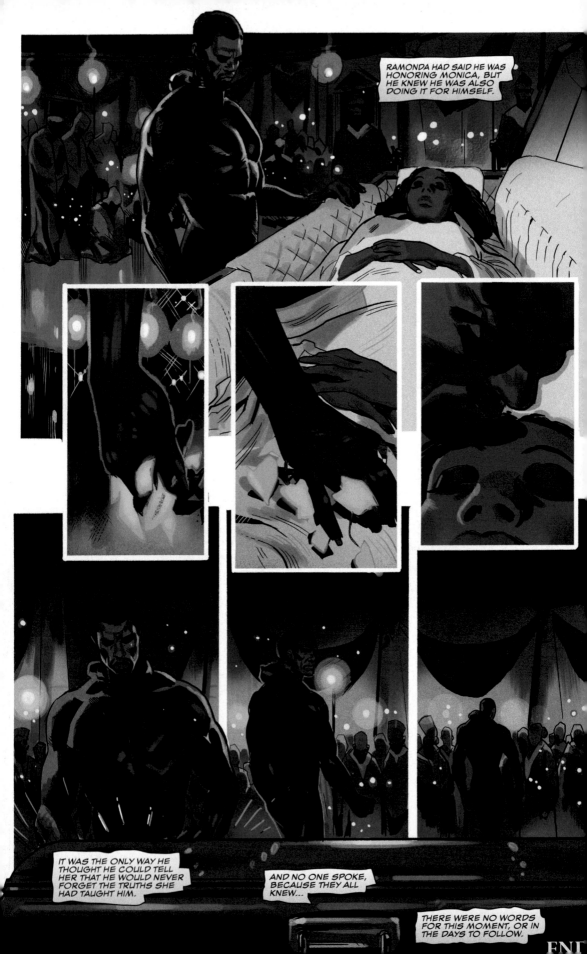

RAMONDA HAD SAID HE WAS HONORING MONICA, BUT HE KNEW HE WAS ALSO DOING IT FOR HIMSELF.

IT WAS THE ONLY WAY HE THOUGHT HE COULD TELL HER THAT HE WOULD NEVER FORGET THE TRUTHS SHE HAD TAUGHT HIM.

AND NO ONE SPOKE, BECAUSE THEY ALL KNEW....

THERE WERE NO WORDS FOR THIS MOMENT, OR IN THE DAYS TO FOLLOW.

END

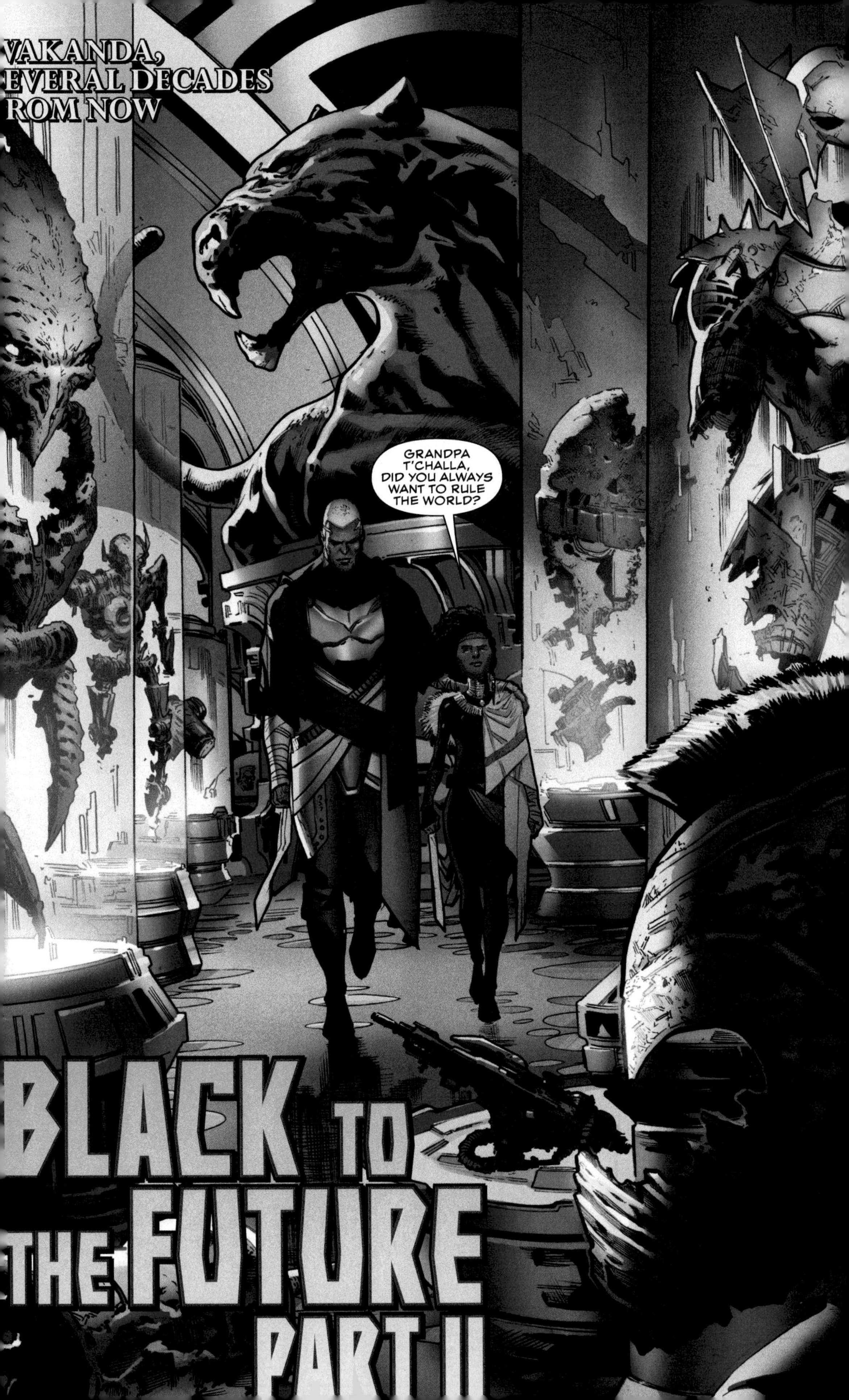
VAKANDA,
EVERAL DECADES
ROM NOW
GRANDPA T'CHALLA, DID YOU ALWAYS WANT TO RULE THE WORLD?
BLACK TO THE FUTURE PART II

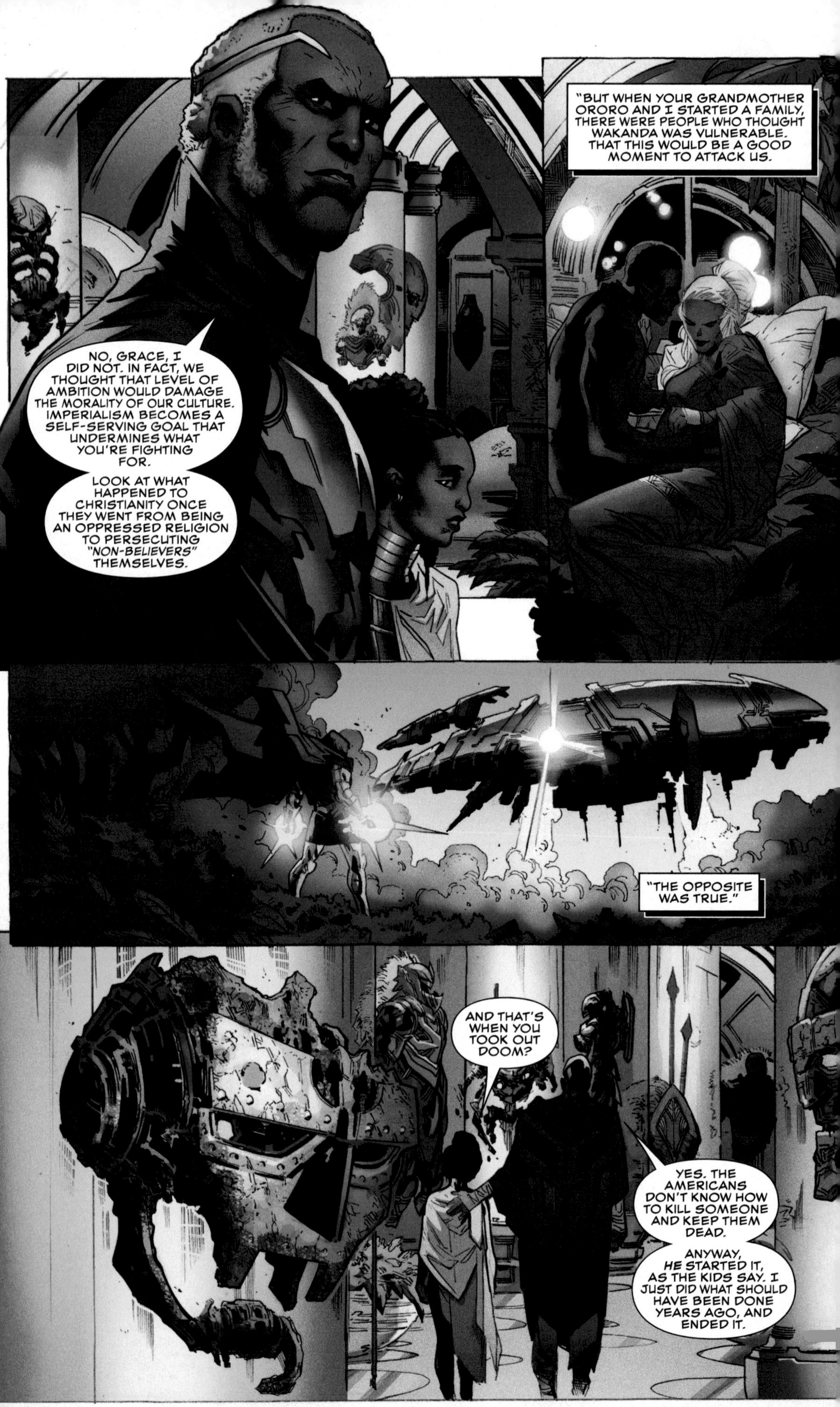

NO, GRACE, I DID NOT. IN FACT, WE THOUGHT THAT LEVEL OF AMBITION WOULD DAMAGE THE MORALITY OF OUR CULTURE. IMPERIALISM BECOMES A SELF-SERVING GOAL THAT UNDERMINES WHAT YOU'RE FIGHTING FOR.
LOOK AT WHAT HAPPENED TO CHRISTIANITY ONCE THEY WENT FROM BEING AN OPPRESSED RELIGION TO PERSECUTING *"NON-BELIEVERS"* THEMSELVES.
"BUT WHEN YOUR GRANDMOTHER ORORO AND I STARTED A FAMILY, THERE WERE PEOPLE WHO THOUGHT WAKANDA WAS VULNERABLE. THAT THIS WOULD BE A GOOD MOMENT TO ATTACK US.
"THE OPPOSITE WAS TRUE."
AND THAT'S WHEN YOU TOOK OUT DOOM?
YES. THE AMERICANS DON'T KNOW HOW TO KILL SOMEONE AND KEEP THEM DEAD.
ANYWAY, *HE* STARTED IT, AS THE KIDS SAY. I JUST DID WHAT SHOULD HAVE BEEN DONE YEARS AGO, AND ENDED IT.

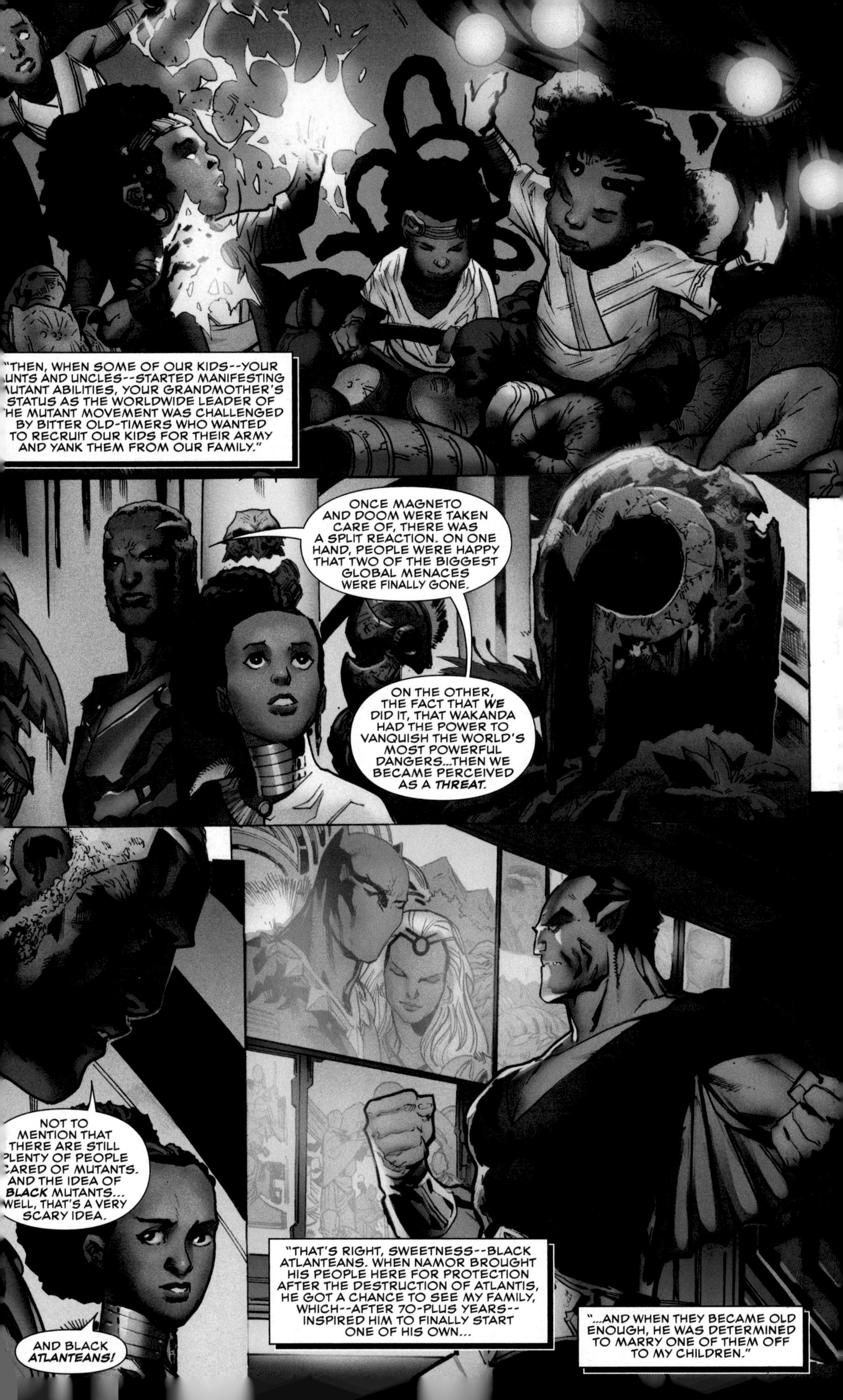
"THEN, WHEN SOME OF OUR KIDS--YOUR AUNTS AND UNCLES--STARTED MANIFESTING MUTANT ABILITIES, YOUR GRANDMOTHER'S STATUS AS THE WORLDWIDE LEADER OF THE MUTANT MOVEMENT WAS CHALLENGED BY BITTER OLD-TIMERS WHO WANTED TO RECRUIT OUR KIDS FOR THEIR ARMY AND YANK THEM FROM OUR FAMILY."
ONCE MAGNETO AND DOOM WERE TAKEN CARE OF, THERE WAS A SPLIT REACTION. ON ONE HAND, PEOPLE WERE HAPPY THAT TWO OF THE BIGGEST GLOBAL MENACES WERE FINALLY GONE.
ON THE OTHER, THE FACT THAT WE DID IT, THAT WAKANDA HAD THE POWER TO VANQUISH THE WORLD'S MOST POWERFUL DANGERS...THEN WE BECAME PERCEIVED AS A THREAT.
NOT TO MENTION THAT THERE ARE STILL PLENTY OF PEOPLE SCARED OF MUTANTS. AND THE IDEA OF BLACK MUTANTS... WELL, THAT'S A VERY SCARY IDEA.
AND BLACK ATLANTEANS!
"THAT'S RIGHT, SWEETNESS--BLACK ATLANTEANS. WHEN NAMOR BROUGHT HIS PEOPLE HERE FOR PROTECTION AFTER THE DESTRUCTION OF ATLANTIS, HE GOT A CHANCE TO SEE MY FAMILY, WHICH--AFTER 70-PLUS YEARS--INSPIRED HIM TO FINALLY START ONE OF HIS OWN...
"...AND WHEN THEY BECAME OLD ENOUGH, HE WAS DETERMINED TO MARRY ONE OF THEM OFF TO MY CHILDREN."

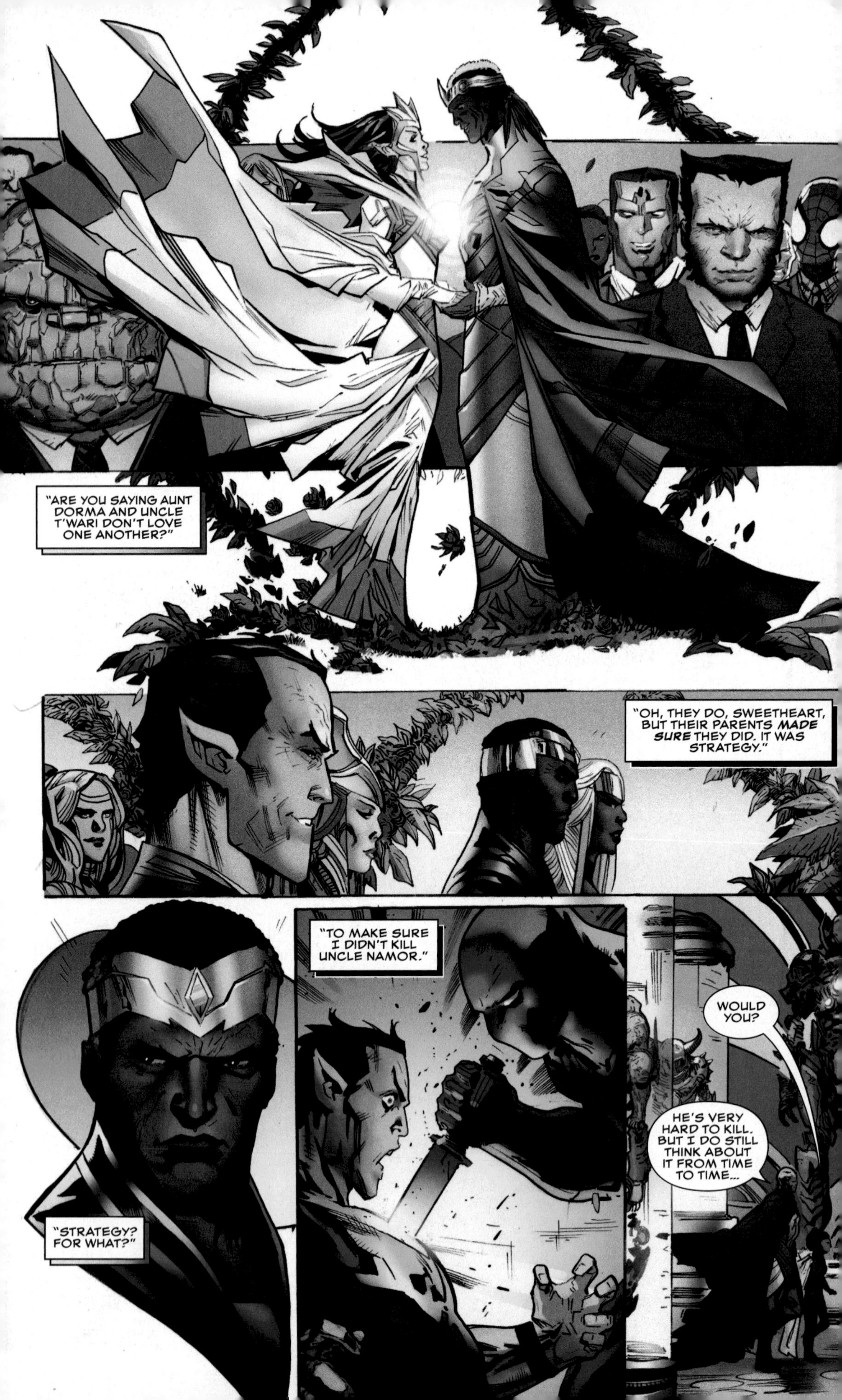
"ARE YOU SAYING AUNT DORMA AND UNCLE T'WARI DON'T LOVE ONE ANOTHER?"
"OH, THEY DO, SWEETHEART, BUT THEIR PARENTS MADE SURE THEY DID. IT WAS STRATEGY."
"STRATEGY? FOR WHAT?"
"TO MAKE SURE I DIDN'T KILL UNCLE NAMOR."
WOULD YOU?
HE'S VERY HARD TO KILL. BUT I DO STILL THINK ABOUT IT FROM TIME TO TIME...

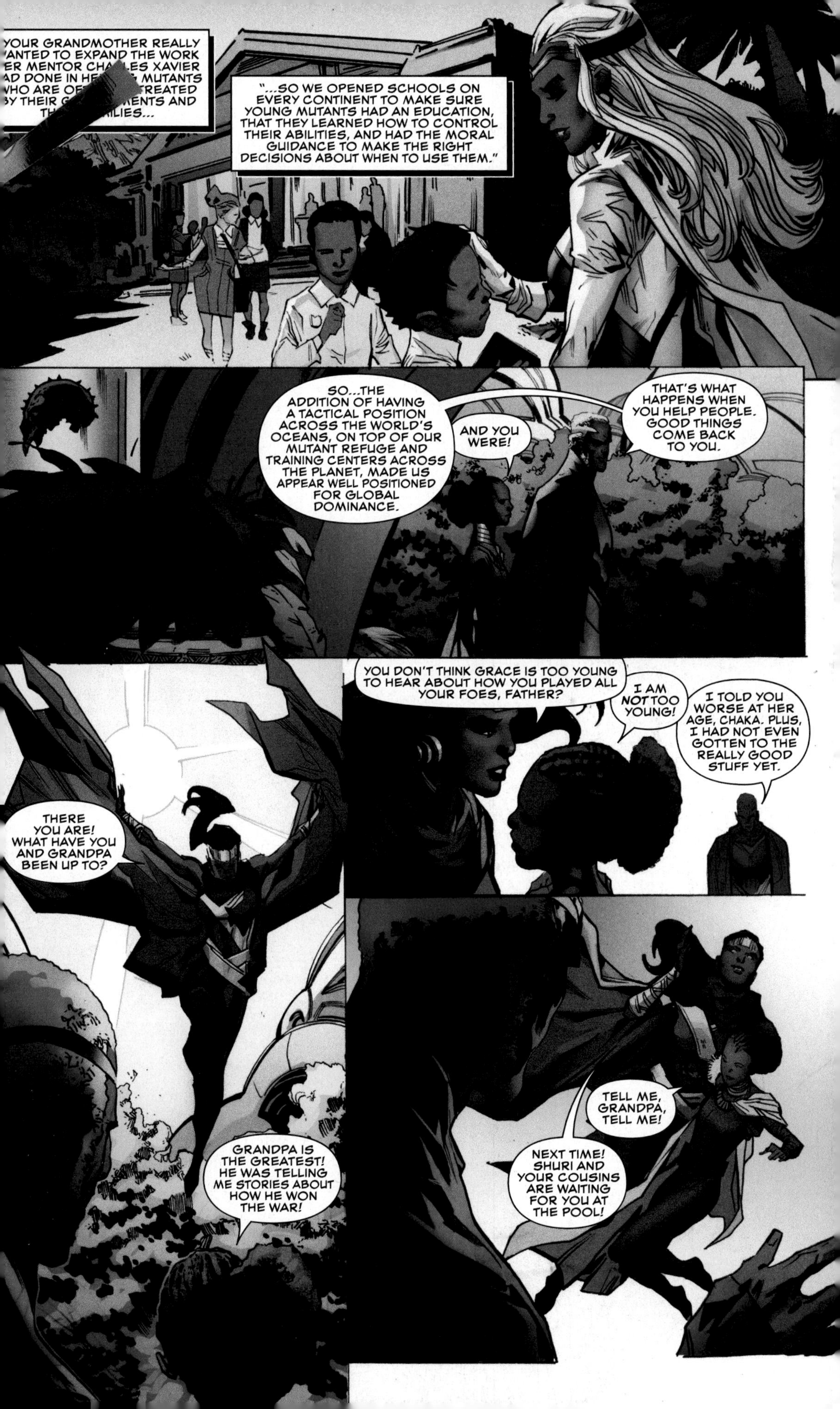

YOUR GRANDMOTHER REALLY WANTED TO EXPAND THE WORK HER MENTOR CHA LES XAVIER HAD DONE IN HE MUTANTS WHO ARE OF TREATED BY THEIR G MENTS AND TH ILIES...
"...SO WE OPENED SCHOOLS ON EVERY CONTINENT TO MAKE SURE YOUNG MUTANTS HAD AN EDUCATION, THAT THEY LEARNED HOW TO CONTROL THEIR ABILITIES, AND HAD THE MORAL GUIDANCE TO MAKE THE RIGHT DECISIONS ABOUT WHEN TO USE THEM."
SO...THE ADDITION OF HAVING A TACTICAL POSITION ACROSS THE WORLD'S OCEANS, ON TOP OF OUR MUTANT REFUGE AND TRAINING CENTERS ACROSS THE PLANET, MADE US APPEAR WELL POSITIONED FOR GLOBAL DOMINANCE.
AND YOU WERE!
THAT'S WHAT HAPPENS WHEN YOU HELP PEOPLE. GOOD THINGS COME BACK TO YOU.
THERE YOU ARE! WHAT HAVE YOU AND GRANDPA BEEN UP TO?
GRANDPA IS THE GREATEST! HE WAS TELLING ME STORIES ABOUT HOW HE WON THE WAR!
YOU DON'T THINK GRACE IS TOO YOUNG TO HEAR ABOUT HOW YOU PLAYED ALL YOUR FOES, FATHER?
I AM NOT TOO YOUNG!
I TOLD YOU WORSE AT HER AGE, CHAKA. PLUS, I HAD NOT EVEN GOTTEN TO THE REALLY GOOD STUFF YET.
TELL ME, GRANDPA, TELL ME!
NEXT TIME! SHURI AND YOUR COUSINS ARE WAITING FOR YOU AT THE POOL!

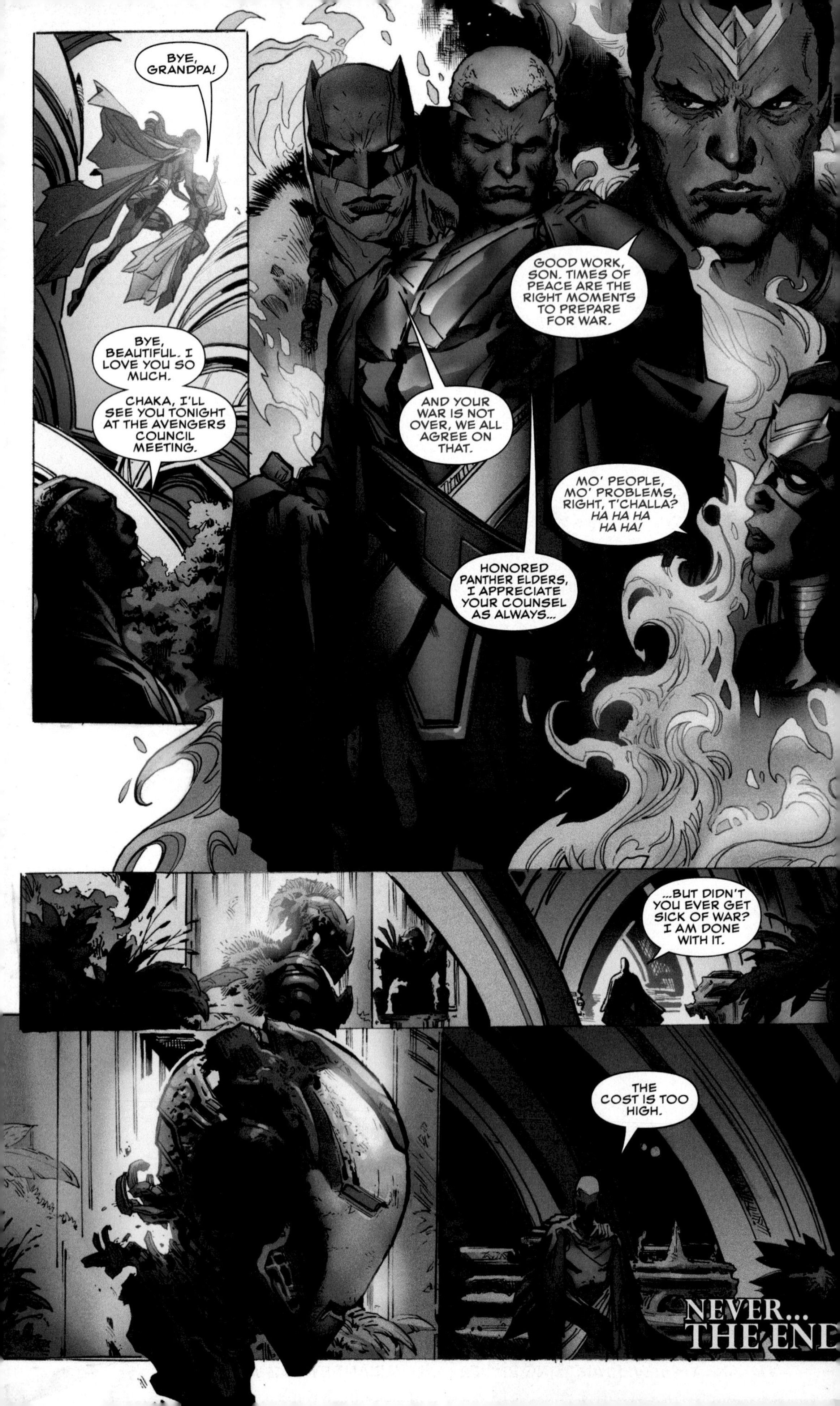
BYE, GRANDPA!
BYE, BEAUTIFUL. I LOVE YOU SO MUCH.
CHAKA, I'LL SEE YOU TONIGHT AT THE AVENGERS COUNCIL MEETING.
GOOD WORK, SON. TIMES OF PEACE ARE THE RIGHT MOMENTS TO PREPARE FOR WAR.
AND YOUR WAR IS NOT OVER, WE ALL AGREE ON THAT.
MO' PEOPLE, MO' PROBLEMS, RIGHT, T'CHALLA? HA HA HA HA HA!
HONORED PANTHER ELDERS, I APPRECIATE YOUR COUNSEL AS ALWAYS...
...BUT DIDN'T YOU EVER GET SICK OF WAR? I AM DONE WITH IT.
THE COST IS TOO HIGH.
NEVER... THE END

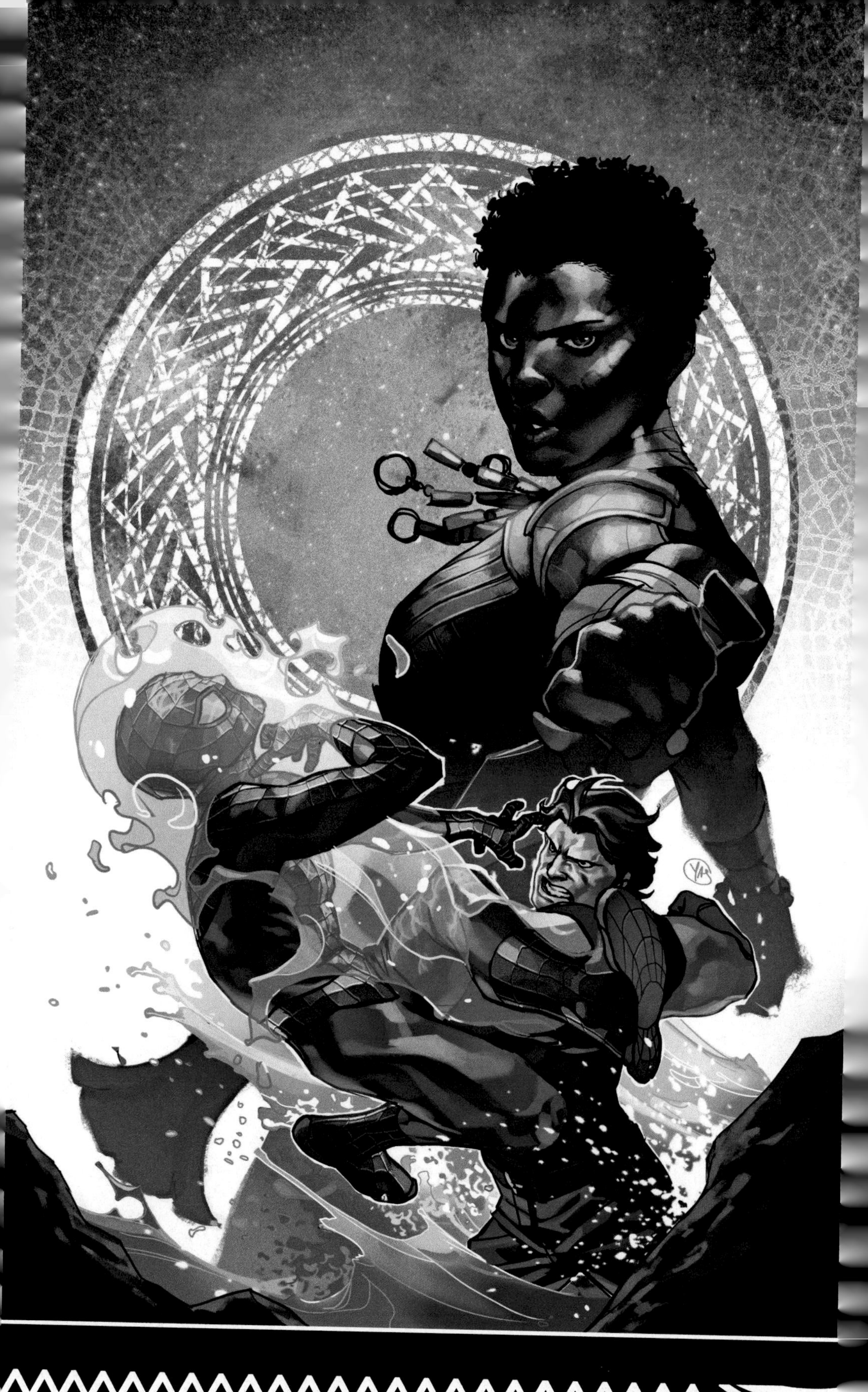

WAKANDA FOREVER: AMAZING SPIDER-MAN VARIANT BY **YASMINE PUTRI**

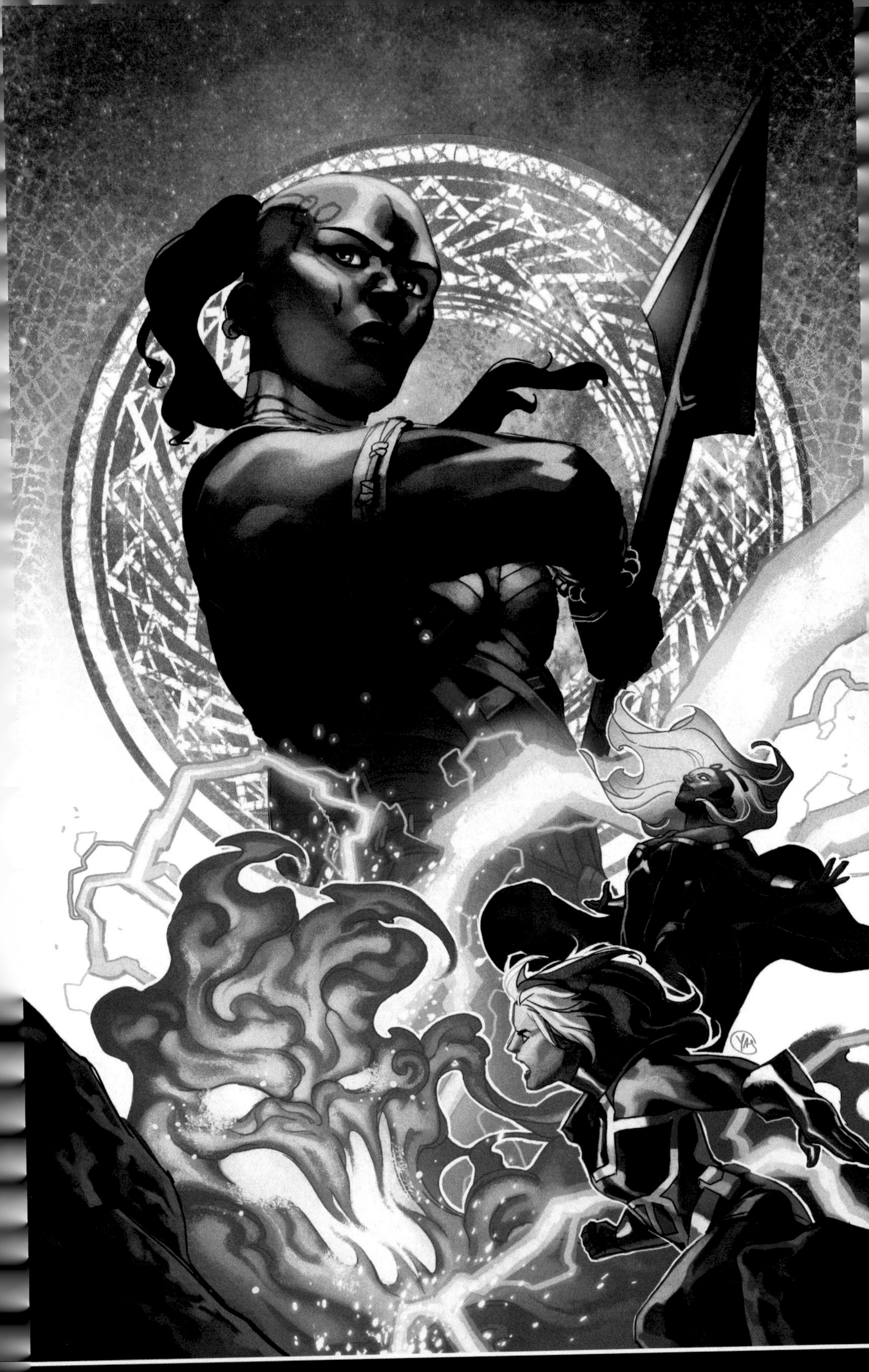

WAKANDA FOREVER: X-MEN VARIANT BY **YASMINE PUTRI**

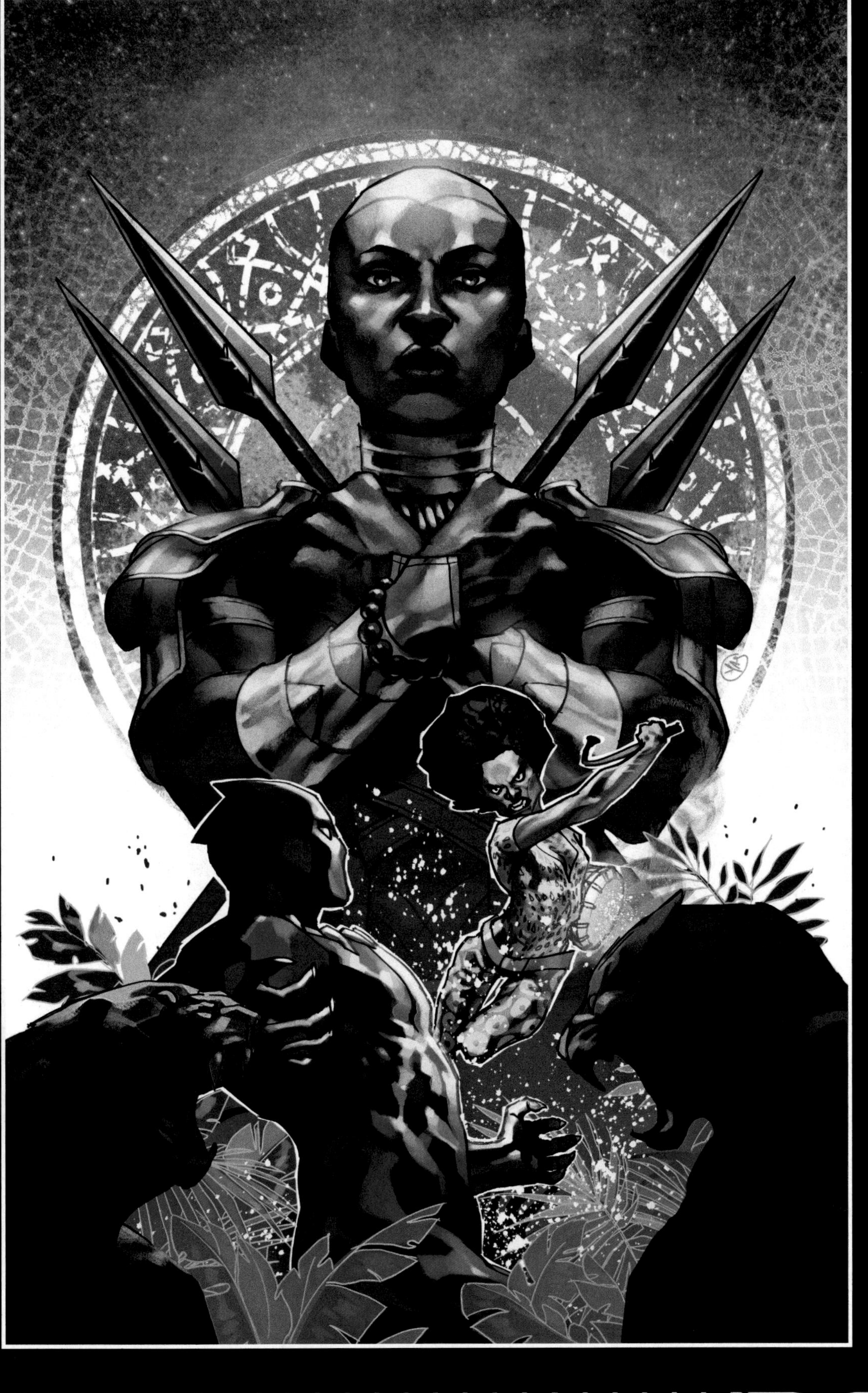

WAKANDA FOREVER: AVENGERS VARIANT BY **YASMINE PUTRI**

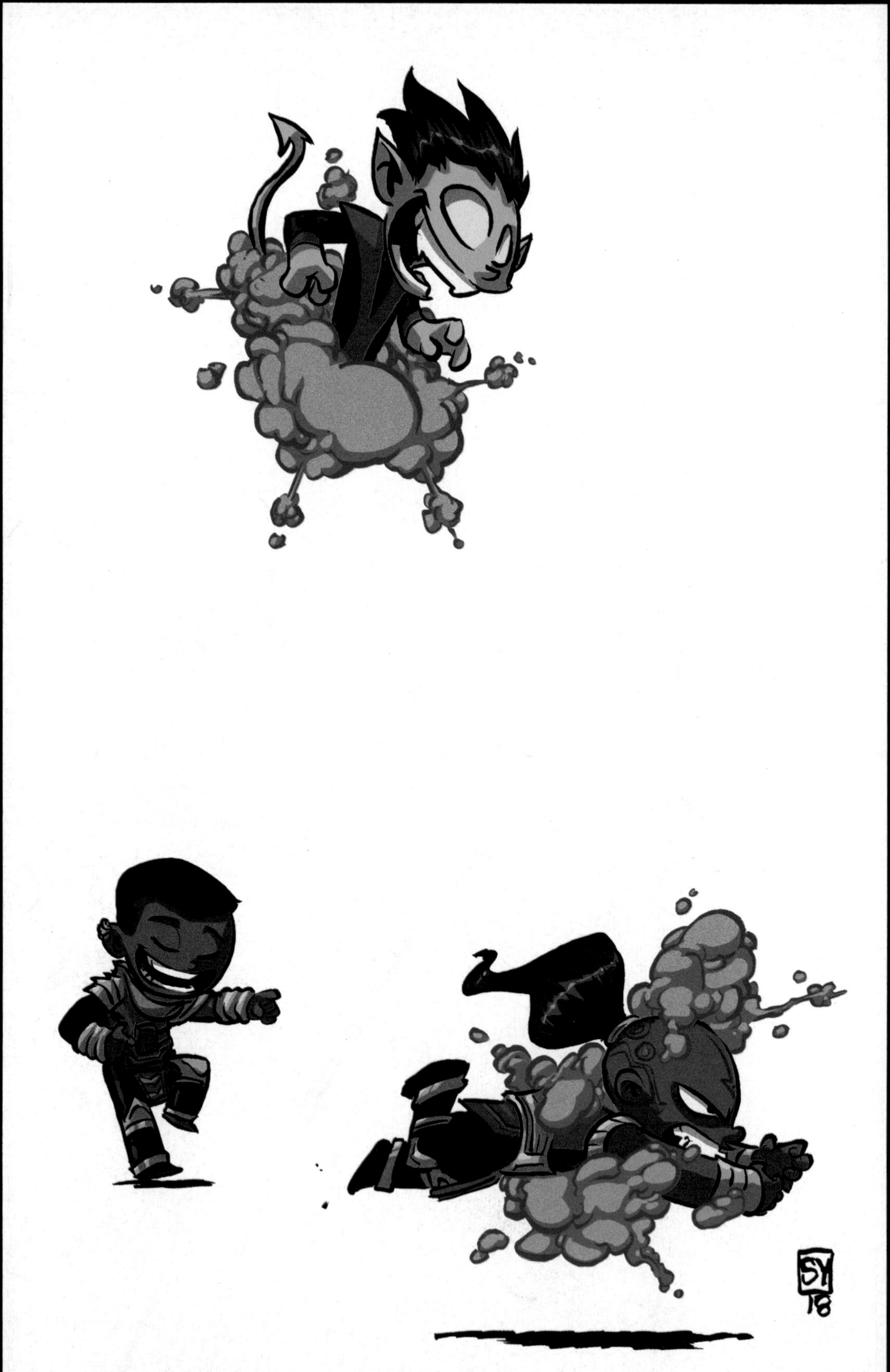

WAKANDA FOREVER: X-MEN VARIANT BY **SKOTTIE YOUNG**

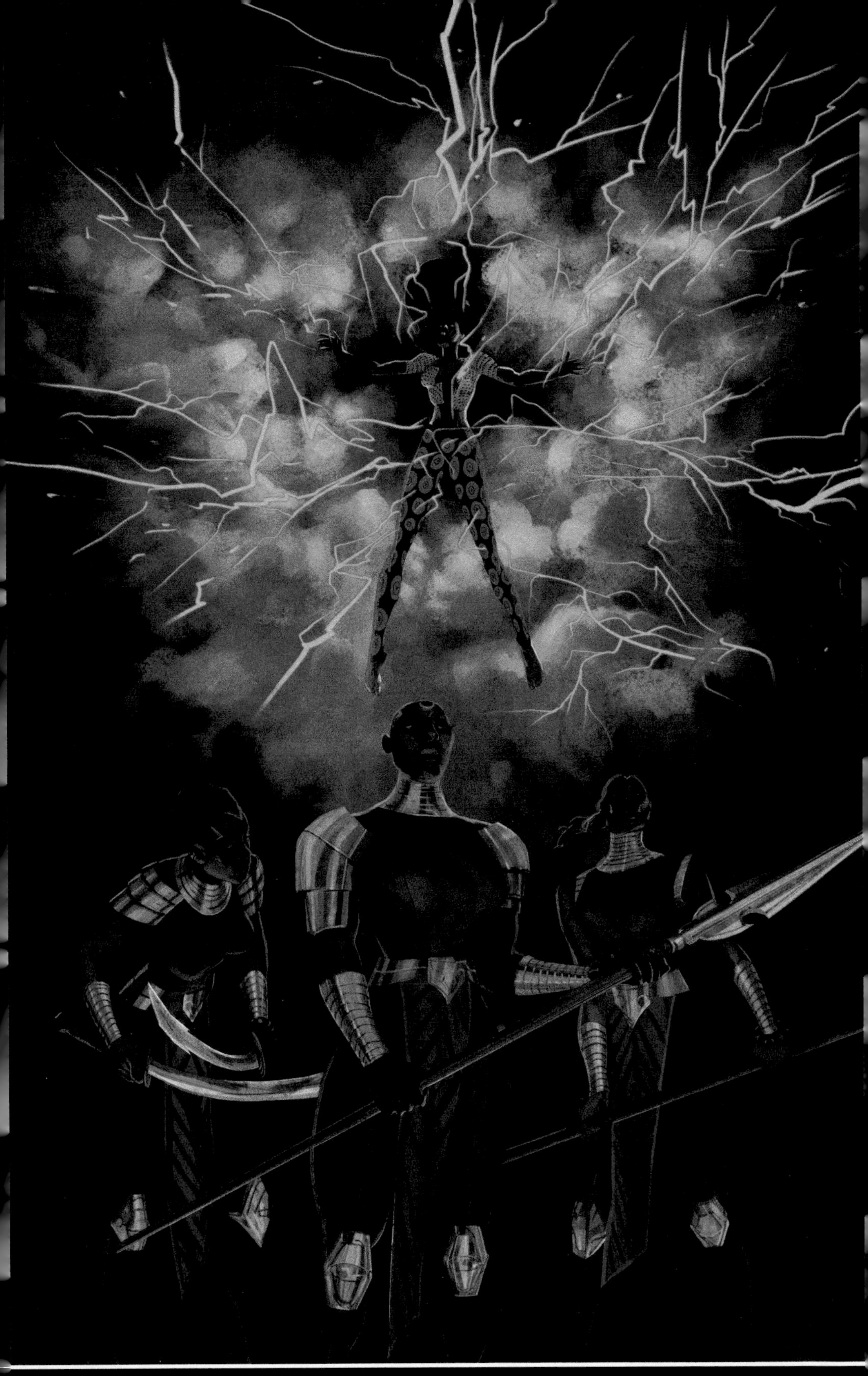

WAKANDA FOREVER: AVENGERS VARIANT BY **VANESA R. DEL REY**

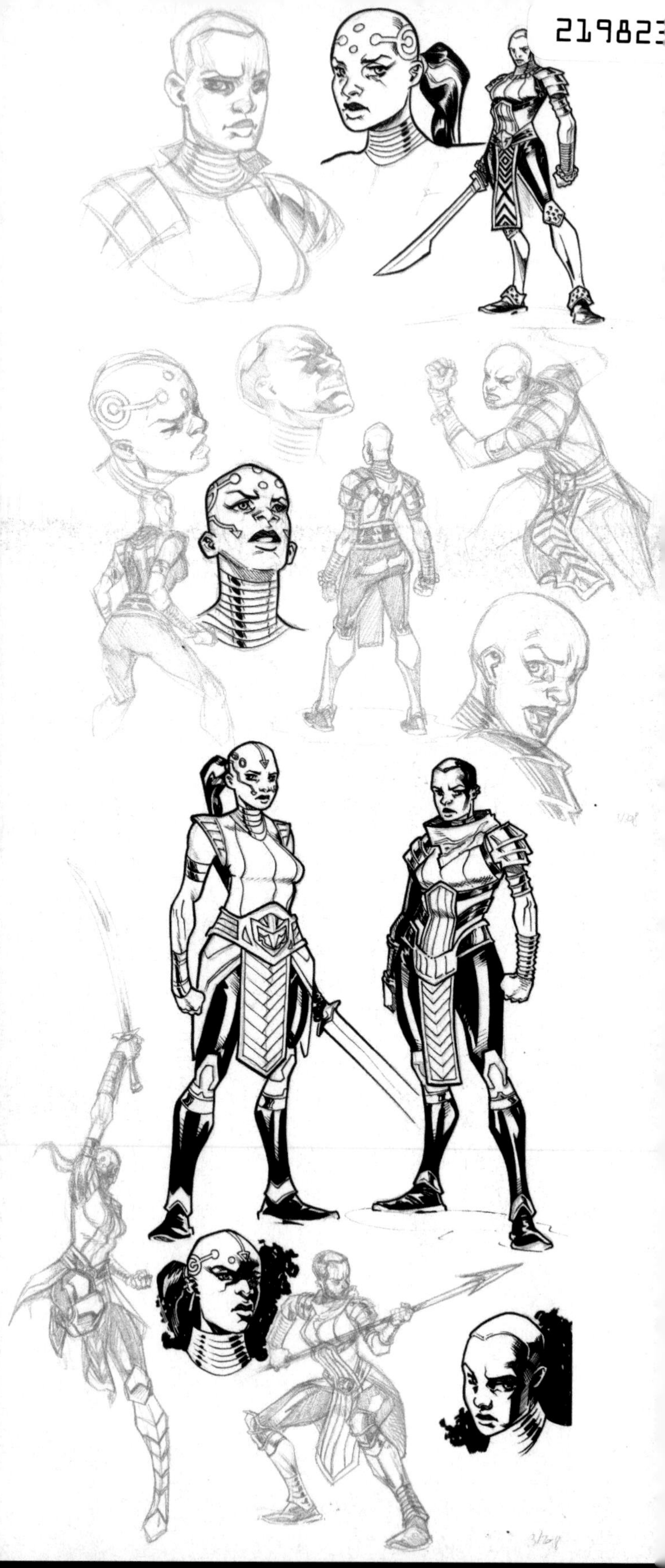

CHARACTER SKETCHES BY **ALBERTO ALBURQUERQUE**